I0759573

ANCIENT CIVILIZATIONS OF AFGHANISTAN

Ancient Civilizations of Afghanistan

From the Earliest Times to the Mongol Conquest

Warwick Ball

REAKTION BOOKS

For Jonathan Lee, in admiration

Published by
REAKTION BOOKS LTD
2–4 Sebastian Street
London EC1V 0HE, UK
www.reaktionbooks.co.uk

First published 2025

The author and publisher gratefully acknowledge
the financial support of the Aga Khan Trust for Culture

EU GPSR Authorised Representative
Logos Europe, 9 rue Nicolas Poussin, 17000, La Rochelle, France
email: contact@logoseurope.eu

Printed and bound in India by Replika Press Pvt. Ltd

A catalogue record for this book is available from the British Library

ISBN 978 1 83639 092 3

Contents

1 The Balkh plain in winter.

Introduction: Elusive Definitions

> Afghanistan is one of those places in the world in which people who know the least make the most definitive statements about it.
>
> THOMAS BARFIELD[1]

Studies of Afghanistan have often placed it within the area of 'greater Iran' or otherwise considered it as part of somewhere else. This error is a bit like claiming Scotland is part of England or (more pertinently at the time of writing) Ukraine is part of Russia. The very term 'ancient Afghanistan' has often been dismissed, even by specialists, since Afghanistan as a country did not exist before the eighteenth century. True, but neither did the United Kingdom as a country, whose ancient history has long been a subject of serious study (and Afghanistan has been the seat of four empires; the United Kingdom one). Being so often considered to be parts of 'somewhere else' and with studies of Afghanistan being peripheral to studies of 'other places', the purpose of this book is to consider Afghanistan on its own terms with a long and continuous history stretching deep into its past.

Where Is Afghanistan?

Looking for Afghanistan in a library or museum or bookshop can be a frustrating experience, as nobody is quite sure where to look. Of course, we all know *where* Afghanistan is, but it does not lend itself to easy categorization: is it Central Asia, South Asia or the Middle East?

For Afghanistan is a part of all three – and at the same time a part of none. Much of the problem lies in traditional studies – not to mention librarians, museum curators and booksellers – which have tended to view Afghanistan as peripheral to Central, Southern or Western Asia, a footnote as it were to events elsewhere.

This is reflected in the terms used in scholarly studies that include Afghanistan: part of the 'Iranicate East', the 'Persianate world', the 'Indo-Iranian borderlands', 'Turko-Persia'[2] or the 'Middle Asian interaction sphere'.[3] The former Society for South Asian Studies based at the British Academy, for example, included Afghanistan as part of 'South Asia', while the British Institute of Persian Studies, also associated with the British Academy, includes Afghanistan as part of a 'Greater Iran'. For Afghans, being viewed as a part of a greater Iran or greater India or greater somewhere else is a bit like being relegated to poor cousins. But Afghanistan is not Iranian or Indian or part of anywhere else; it was no periphery, and this book aims to place Afghanistan firmly in the centre of events in Eurasian history.[4]

It also explains the title of this book: *Civilizations* in the plural. For one cannot talk of one single 'Afghan' civilization in the same way as one can talk of, say, Persian or Chinese civilization, for Afghanistan has borne and shaped many civilizations: Central Asian, South Asian and Middle Eastern. These can either be major empires centred on Afghanistan, such as the Kushan or Ghaznavid, or components of empires centred elsewhere, such as the Persian or Abbasid.

It also means that one cannot simply stop at the present borders of Afghanistan. For all of the ancient civilizations that took place on Afghan soil extended beyond its present borders, sometimes well beyond. Of course, this can be said of any ancient civilization, but with Afghanistan it is more than most. When it was on the periphery of an empire beyond the borders, such as the ancient Persian, one cannot confine discussion just to events within Afghanistan, but must include some reference at least to how the periphery affected the centre. But when a major part of a civilization took place within its borders, one must include discussion of that civilization beyond its borders as well.

For example, one cannot write of the Oxus Civilization without reference to sites in Turkmenistan and Uzbekistan, or Gandharan art without discussing monuments and objects in Pakistan.

This is reflected in the polyglot ethnic make-up of modern Afghanistan: there is not a single ethnic group in Afghanistan that does not extend across its borders (with the possible exception of the Hazaras): Tajiks are also in Tajikistan, Pashtuns are also (mainly) in Pakistan, Uzbeks are also in Uzbekistan, Farsiwans are also (mainly) in Iran, and so forth.[5]

In discussing Afghanistan's ancient history it has often been pointed out that there was no 'Afghanistan' until the eighteenth century. However, the name 'Afghan', referring to the people who give the name to the country, first occurs in Bactrian documents as early as the fifth century AD,[6] and the anthropologist Thomas Barfield, one of the main authorities on Afghanistan, has emphasized that the area of Afghanistan has comprised four perennial 'core regions' central to its history from the Iron Age to the present day: Kabul, Balkh, Herat and Kandahar.[7] This defines a natural unit that existed long before it took formal political form in the eighteenth century. In other words, the territory of Afghanistan has an existence as a cultural and historical unit as much as any other 'centre'.

Afghanistan is also often included within the rather amorphously named region of 'Central Asia'. On one level, the term 'Central Asia' is taken to refer only to those former five republics of the Soviet Union (known in Tsarist times simply as 'Russian Turkestan') comprising Kazakhstan, Kyrgyzstan, Uzbekistan, Tajikistan and Turkmenistan. But on a broader level, 'Central Asia' is often viewed as encompassing a far greater region than mere borders laid down where Tsarist armies stopped and Soviet bureaucrats rested their pens. As well as Afghanistan, much of the eastern region of Iran known as Khurasan is often included in the definition. To the west, the Caucasus is occasionally included (or at least Azerbaijan: Georgia and Armenia, being Christian, are often defined as 'European'). To the east, Central Asia reaches well into China, including Xinjiang (called 'Chinese Turkestan' in the nineteenth century), Mongolia, Tibet and parts of western China (such as Gansu Province) and Siberia (although the term 'Inner Asia' is now often used for this vast region). Examining Afghan history in its own cultural terms against the broader background of Central, South and Western Asia is the purpose of this book.

This vast region of Central Asia might appear peripheral to the traditional centres of sedentary civilization on its rim: China, India, Persia and Russia. At the same time, it has directly affected all of these regions: the enormous effect that events in Afghanistan have had in the past decades on Pakistan, India, Iran and Russia (not to mention the United States) is merely the latest example of this age-old trend. Moreover, Central Asia has continually reinvigorated the civilizations on its rim, acting as a channel of communications that binds the great historic centres of the Eurasian continent together. Central Asia thus challenges conventional definitions of centres and peripheries. Indeed, it is true to say that no history of China, India, Iran or Russia can be fully understood without continual reference to Central Asia: it is not known as *Central* Asia for nothing. Afghanistan lies at the very heart of both the region and these questions.

Throughout history Central Asia has been characterized by mass movements of peoples and empires. The Indo-European migrations before the beginning of history and the Mongol conquests in the Middle Ages have been a part of this process. The Stalinist deportations in the middle of the twentieth century and the displacement of millions of Afghan refugees at its end show this characteristic to be a continuing one. The movement of nomads throughout history is a perennial theme of Central Asia – and Afghanistan has a higher nomadic population than most countries. To explain Afghanistan in terms of successive 'waves' of steppe conquerors – Indo-European, Scythian, Hun, Turk or Mongol – is to miss the point. Such 'invasions' (as often as not they were more peaceful migrations) reinvigorated existing cultural traditions, reaffirming international connections that already existed, with indigenous cultures reasserting their distinctive identities and eventually transforming the conquerors.

2 The central Hindu Kush in Bamiyan.

Recent research has shown Central Asia as a centre of major early sedentary civilizations of its own. Traditionally, it has been convenient to regard the development of early civilization in terms of four main centres: Egypt, Mesopotamia, the Indus Valley and China, with the Mesopotamian civilization being the earliest. While new discoveries have hardly altered this basic picture (although the picture is now far more complex and becoming more blurred at the edges), what is emerging from new discoveries is a possible fourth centre comparable to those better-known ones: Central Asia. These go back to the third millennium BC, and by the second millennium the Central Asian Bronze Age civilization already boasted an impressive urban tradition: laid-out cities, huge fortifications, religious and palatial complexes, international relations, a vibrant art, transcontinental trade. Much of the new discoveries of this civilization have been made in the former Soviet areas of Central Asia and adjacent parts of Afghanistan: an 'Oxus Civilization'.[8] The position of Afghanistan was the link between the earliest civilizations of Mesopotamia, the Indus Valley and the Oxus Civilization. More recently a new Bronze Age civilization has been proposed: the Helmand Civilization found largely within Afghanistan and extending into southeastern Iran in the third and early second millennia. The later civilizations of Kushans, Samanids, Ghaznavids, Timurids and others would have been substantially different without these cultural roots. In cultural terms, the various civilizations in Afghanistan were the culmination of traditions that have a continuity stretching back into prehistory. Out of these traditions, Buddhism became a world religion, the fusion of Hellenistic and Indian traditions produced the art of Gandhara that influenced much of Asia, and the trade routes enabled the dissemination of ideas from both East and West throughout Eurasia.

At the heart of Central Asia – between the great, classic civilizations of India, Iran and the Oxus – lie the deserts and mountain ranges of Afghanistan. Even today much still lies unexplored. In the past Afghanistan saw the rise of cities and civilizations that compared with the better known ones to the north, west and east. Much else still remains hidden where major archaeological discoveries are still being made – and are still to be made. Even much of the information that is known still lies 'hidden' in specialist academic publications, accessible only to the scholar. The region of Afghanistan holds the key to much of the movement of peoples, goods and ideas in antiquity, as well as the origins and spread of civilization in Iran, India and Central Asia.

Afghanistan also holds some of the most important, diverse and – quite simply – spectacular historical remains in Asia. On the plains of northern Afghanistan, for example, archaeologists have uncovered palatial and religious monuments at Dashli, as well as other remains elsewhere of the Bronze Age Oxus Civilization. Hints of discoveries still

3 Field patterns in the Mushkan Valley in the western Hindu Kush.

to be made of an unknown Bronze Age civilization lie in the deserts of the south, such as a possible ziggurat on the Mesopotamian model: a 'Helmand Civilization'. At Ai Khanoum in the northeast an entire Greek city was built on the banks of the Oxus by Greek colonists in the wake of Alexander in the third century BC. This initiated art and architectural styles that influenced much of Asia for a millennium and more. At Surkh Kotal, overlooking the main route connecting Central Asia with India, the Kushan emperor Kanishka (whose successors included 'Caesar' among their titles) built in the second century AD a monumental dynastic centre carved out of an entire hillside. At Begram, site of the Kushan capital further south, archaeologists discovered a treasure comprising glassware from the Roman Empire, carved ivories from India and lacquered wood from China. At Bamiyan, deep in the mountain fastness of the central Hindu Kush, one of the greatest religious complexes of the Buddhist world was built by obscure Turk kings between the sixth and eighth centuries. Along the banks of the Helmand River at Lashkari Bazar in the south the Ghaznavid dynasty of sultans in the eleventh century built one of the greatest palatial complexes of the time, whose vast ruins still tower over the surrounding plain today. At Jam, in the remote mountains of western Afghanistan, another sultan

4 The western Hindu Kush near Taiwara.

of the Ghurid dynasty built one of the greatest and most spectacular minarets in the Islamic world at the end of the eleventh century. Deep in the sands of the deserts of Seistan in the far south lie massive monuments and entire ruined cities from the Middle Ages and earlier, such as the immense circular city of Shahr-i Ghulghula. At Herat in western Afghanistan, the son of Tamerlane, Shah Rukh, moved the capital of the Timurid empire from Samarkand in the fifteenth century, turning it into one of the greatest centres of the arts and architecture in Western Asia (beyond the scope of this book). As well as these better-known monuments there are lesser-known ancient cities, temples, stupas, monasteries, cave complexes, palaces, mosques, minarets, shrines, castles and other monuments set against the breathtaking backdrop of Afghanistan's landscapes. These alone make the study of Afghanistan an important task. Taken with the broader historical and cultural issues, it is an essential one.

At different periods in its history, Afghanistan has been subject to Harappan, Greek, Persian, Indian, Central Asian, Chinese, Arab and European influences. The civilizations of Afghanistan are the syncretic fusion of these divergent traditions, the origins of which can be traced in the prehistoric, Achaemenid and Hellenistic periods. These traditions culminated in the first millennium AD in the predominantly Buddhist architecture of Gandhara, and in the second millennium in the architecture of Islam. From this extraordinarily complex background, immensely powerful architectural traditions developed that were both tenacious and diverse. These traditions both drew from and influenced many parts of Asia, with elements surviving to this day.

What Is Afghanistan?

The land itself is the natural starting point of any examination of Afghanistan.[9] To the outsider, it is what one first encounters: its great plains, its fertile valleys and its mountains are seen as a source of empire by the conqueror, a source of wealth by the merchant, a source of inspiration by the pilgrim. For the people themselves, it is the landscape that has moulded them more than any other single factor: it has inspired their genius, channelled their ideas into certain patterns, and provided a spectacular setting for the towns, villages and monuments that are a manifestation of that genius.

But in considering the land now known as Afghanistan, difficulties are immediately encountered, for its geography makes it hard to speak of Afghanistan within its modern borders. The very name 'Afghanistan' is a comparatively recent one and applies to borders that have only existed – apart from some alterations at the edges by the Russians and the British in the late nineteenth century – since about the 1860s. Its perennial 'core regions' remained largely fixed, as we have observed, but actual borders moved from east to west and north to south with the rapidity of advancing armies. A glance at a map of the region shows why. In *no place* do the modern borders of Afghanistan meet natural boundaries. Even the Oxus River forming the border to the north has always served – in the same way as the Indus or the Nile or great rivers everywhere – to *unite* regions on either side rather than divide. The absence of obvious geographical boundaries is further emphasized by Afghanistan's ethnic composition (examined below). Not only the controversial Durand Line (the present disputed border with Pakistan established by a British commission in 1893), but all borders of Afghanistan cut across geographical, cultural, historic, linguistic and ethnic units. The present borders, therefore, merely represent lines arrived at by armies in the field and bureaucrats in their offices, reflecting historical accident of the moment. Virtually all of the present borders date from a series of British boundary commissions between 1878 and 1904 that demarcated Afghanistan's borders with Russia, Iran and British India. This was largely to create a buffer zone between the rival superpowers of Russia and Britain: a creation, in other words, by international great-power rivalries.

But however we define – or fail to define – political borders, the physical area now covered by Afghanistan has always conjured up very fixed images. And it is with these perhaps intangible images of great landscapes, rather than with the unsatisfactory whims of political

5 The sands of the Rigistan Desert encroaching on the Kandahar Plain.

vicissitudes, that we must physically define Afghanistan. There is an extraordinary diversity. In the north is the almost limitless Central Asian steppe, a part of an inland sea of grassland that ranges from Hungary in the west to Mongolia in the east. In the south are the deserts of Seistan, part of the desert belt that extends into Baluchistan and Makran in Pakistan to the south and into Iranian Seistan and the deserts of central Iran to the west and northwest. In between are the mountains, a part of the world's greatest range that crosses northern India and ends near Herat. The geography, therefore, can be described in terms of three main zones from north to south.

The Steppe

The feature one soon appreciates on the immense steppes of the north is the vast canopy of the sky, unfettered by the shackles of mountains, trees or buildings. In the summer this sky sends down relentless heat – temperatures commonly reach over 40°C (more than 100°F) – made all the more remarkable by the contrasting extreme cold of the winter (illus. 1). Then one feels the true nature of the steppe: winds whip down from Siberia and at night that vast sky is lit up in the most brilliant display of stars one has ever seen, shedding their cold light onto a frozen land deep in snow.

These vast steppes mould Central Asia more than anything else. Its pastures are naturally suited to horses and nomadism, and great nomad nations have crossed its expanses for millennia.[10] Such groups occasionally erupt onto the sedentary centres on its periphery, with repercussions that can be felt right across the Eurasian continent, often due to a knock-on effect as one group of nomads displaces another. The end result can be felt thousands of miles away and years or even centuries afterwards. Groups related to the Huns evicted from the walls of China, for example, resurface at the gates of Rome, Iran, Afghanistan and India generations later. Scythians have created kingdoms in both eastern Europe and western India, while the Mongols formed the largest land empire in history. The history of Afghanistan was affected more than most by eruptions from the steppe, from the Indo-Iranian tribes of prehistory that changed the linguistic make-up of the country forever, to the descendants of Tamerlane who made Afghanistan the centre of its last great golden age.

But the steppe is no mere pastureland for transient nomads: it holds the secret to some of the most important sedentary civilizations of Central Asia as well. Its limitless horizons are regularly punctuated by the mounds – *tepes* or tells – formed by millennia of cultural accumulation, the residue of successive settlements built from the mud-brick and rammed earth of the plains. It was this region that was known to the ancient Greeks as the 'land of a thousand cities', and its main city,

6 Vine field patterns near Kandahar.

Balkh, was known to the early Arab geographers as the 'mother of all cities' – hardly descriptions of mere pastoral backwaters. Discoveries made by archaeologists on both sides of the Oxus have revealed remains going back to the Bronze Age. Important though such archaeological discoveries have been in recent decades, they are clearly only a curtain-raiser of greater ones to come.

The Mountains

It is what lies between the steppe and the desert that one remembers most about Afghanistan: its mountains. Mountstuart Elphinstone captured their flavour at the beginning of the nineteenth century:

> The stupendous heights of these mountains; the magnificence and variety of their lofty summits; the various nations by which they are seen, and who seem to be brought together by this common object; and the awful and undisturbed solitude which

7 Contrasting artificial verticals and horizontals near Kabul.

> reigns amidst their eternal snows; fill the mind with admiration and astonishment, that no language can express.[11]

These mountains, too, are but a small part of a massive chain, a chain that seems to bind Asia with gigantic, almost unbroken, fetters from China to Turkey. The largest chain of all, the Himalayas, ends at the northeastern periphery of Afghanistan at the Pamir Knot, the meeting place of six mountain ranges – the Himalayas, the Karakoram, the Kunlun, the Tian Shan, the Pamir and the Hindu Kush – thrust upwards by the Indian tectonic plate crashing into the Asian plate millions of years ago. The part lying in Afghanistan consists of the Hindu Kush range (illus. 2), beginning in the high Pamirs and ending in low foothills towards Kandahar and Herat. The central massif forms the watershed of three of Asia's great river systems: the Oxus to the north, the Helmand to the south and (with the Kabul River) the Indus to the east. Indeed, Emperor Babur in the sixteenth century comments that in a single day one can drink the waters of all three rivers. A fourth, the Herat River, rises in the mountains of central Afghanistan before disappearing in the desert of Turkmenistan. In between these great barriers are a series of lush highland valleys and rolling, hilly pasturelands, sheltering the settled communities as well as the nomads (illus. 3). Time has carved and broken these mountains into weird, sometimes moon-like, sculptures with startling arrays of colours, ranging from browns, oranges and reds to blues and even purples, contrasting with the softening contours of the snows that envelop them in the winter months.

The Desert

The desert – its two parts known as Rigistan and Dasht-i Margo, roughly translated as the 'Land of Sand' and the 'Desert of Death' – begins at the edge of the Kandahar oasis and stretches southwards and westwards. From a distance it appears as a giant, orange-coloured wave seemingly menacing the fertility of the oasis it hovers over (illus. 5). From close up the transition is completely abrupt, with no intermediate area of semi-desert: a wall of pure, lifeless sand rising up some 10 metres (33 ft) or so from the green of the oasis. On clambering up this wall of sand one looks out over a sea of dunes stretching away seemingly forever; silence seems to emanate from it almost as a tangible presence to overwhelm the familiar sounds of the oasis behind.

Desert and semi-desert cover much of southern and southwestern Afghanistan. It is increasing: in Seistan, straddling the present border with Iran in the far southwest, the dunes have claimed vast areas of land that were once flourishing agricultural settlements and even great cities (see illus. 113). Here, one can find probably the greatest concentration

8 Traditional flat-roofed architecture in Kabul.

of archaeological sites and standing monuments in the entire region of Western and Central Asia, now covered in sand or standing gaunt, lifeless and isolated, seared by the scorching *bad-o sad-o bist ruz*, the 'wind of 120 days'. The sites range in date from the Bronze Age to the medieval period. While remote desert now, the region is watered by the Helmand River, which empties into a salt marsh, the Hamun-i Seistan, on the present border. A study of the desert region by satellite imagery revealed an astonishing quantity of premodern remains under the sands, far more than hitherto thought, many of them hydrological installations, including a vast network of canals leading from the river.[12]

9 Brick patterns awaiting firing at the Kandahar brick kilns.

10 Pashtun nomad tents in western Afghanistan.

When irrigated, therefore, the region supported a substantial population in the past; when the irrigation broke down the desert claimed its own. A similar, but smaller, region of desert covers the southeastern border with Baluchistan in an area known as Shorawak. Here, maps and aerial surveys again reveal large numbers of remains now engulfed by sand – the sites of major archaeological discoveries in the future?

The landscapes are magnificent, but it is not mountains, plains and deserts alone that give the land its special quality. For the natural landscapes are still just a backdrop to the human landscapes set in them. There are the great monuments, of course, which are formed from them – quite literally so, with monuments such as Bamiyan or Surkh Kotal (illus. 65, 95) carved literally out of the landscapes on a gigantic scale. Equally spectacular are the towns, the villages, even the fields which adorn the landscapes as impressively – and as massively – as any monument or work of art (illus. 3, 6). A common motif throughout Afghanistan is the very strong division between horizontal and vertical lines. The horizontals are formed by the pronounced ridges and furrows of the field patterns, or the long mud-walled field divisions. These contrast with the verticals made by the long rows of poplar and plane trees planted for roof timbers, the effect even more pronounced when winter has both stripped the trees of their foliage and highlighted the ridges with snow (illus. 7). The same geometry of horizontals and verticals is seen in the traditional construction techniques of the villages and towns, which impart an extraordinary cuboid quality to the landscape (illus. 8). This strictly ordered, man-made geometry of the landscape is seen throughout: the boundaries and divisions of the field systems, the flat-roofed buildings of the mountain areas, the curves of the domed and vaulted buildings of the desert regions, even bricks laid out to dry (illus. 9) or the angled patterns formed by nomad tents (illus. 10). Together, this geometric landscape imposed by its people contrasts all the more with the softer, more rounded landscapes wrought by nature.

11 Traditional tea house at Zalargak between Herat and Kandahar.

The landscapes have in turn carved and shaped the character of the people they shelter: Buddhist and Muslim ascetics alike sought spiritual purity in their calm, contemplative majesty, nomads seek to escape from the harsh summers of the plains and deserts in their cool heights and the farmer makes his livelihood in the water that runs off their slopes. There are very few aspects of life in Afghanistan that are not determined, directly or indirectly, by these mountains. Except in the deserts of the far south they are never out of sight and one is constantly reminded of their splendour. Even Kabul has a range running through its centre.

The term 'crossroads of Asia' has become a cliché applied to just about every country between the Bosphorus and Hong Kong. In Afghanistan, the description is probably more apt than in most.[13] Since earliest antiquity Afghanistan's central position has meant that the great thoroughfares of history passed through it, bringing goods, peoples, ideas and conquerors. The importance of such routes in Afghanistan is paramount in any study of historical topography. Apart from the main trade routes, west–east through Herat and Balkh to China and north–south through Kabul and Kandahar to India, many minor routes existed as both variations and alternatives to the main ones. Nowadays it has become fashionable to lump the study of such routes and movements into one catch-all term, 'the Silk Road'. The term is largely a modern construct with little foundation in history or archaeology that is nonetheless now almost universally used in both popular and scholarly literature; the former is understandable, the latter inexcusable. Despite the apparent difficulty and impenetrability of the Afghan terrain these routes remained open at most times in history. Indeed, it is important to emphasize that before the advent of the large-scale wheeled transport of modern times, *anywhere* – barring unscaleable precipices – qualified as a route (and in rural areas where no roads exist, communities still use such ancient tracks). We find, therefore, signs of ancient human habitation in the remotest places, even sophisticated monuments such as the Bamiyan or the Minaret of Jam, that could only have existed with the free interaction of ideas and trade possible on international thoroughfares. But it must be stressed that such places appear remote only nowadays, dependent as we now are on the logistics of asphalt roads and internal combustion engines and all their associated paraphernalia to get from A to B. Simpler modes of transport conquered the remote mountain fastness far more easily: witness the multiplicity of routes used by the nomads through the most impenetrable terrain. It seems ironic that in such terrain, the motor car and modern technology create far more barriers than they conquer.

Today, Afghanistan lies well away from the modern routes, most of which in any case are now by sea, air or the ether. But on the roads of modern Afghanistan, a hint of the ancient days of great trade routes can still occasionally be felt. The long lines of camels still pass by and the strings of caravanserais servicing travellers of the past are mostly just ruins, but in their place have sprung up their modern successors: the ubiquitous tea houses (illus. 11). They are a lifeline for the country, welcome stopping places for the traveller wherever there is a route, however minor. And the actual roads themselves still have a glamour, whether they are wide paved highways stretching between the main cities or simply dirt tracks fighting their way across inhospitable terrain (illus. 4, 12). The feats of engineering over the Hindu Kush or through the Kabul Gorge may be as modern as the hardy four-wheel-drive vehicles competing with the camels and donkeys elsewhere, but the country they go through is old, and time still has the upper hand. Travelling these roads by whatever means still conjures up images of what has gone before, of what lies ahead, of going through places to places. Faint echoes admittedly of the great crossroads in history, but such echoes still sustain their power and excitement, even today.

Can it be said, then, that the landscapes are just tail ends of larger landscapes that begin elsewhere? After all, the Afghan deserts might boast of little when compared to, say, the wild beauty of the Wadi Rum in the Jordanian desert; the steppes are a mere shadow of the more fabled steppes of Mongolia; the mountain ranges – spectacular though they certainly are – but poor cousins of the far mightier parent ranges to the east. But Afghanistan is the *culmination*, the meeting place, of all these landscapes: while containing little of them that is unique, it is made unique by having elements of them all. Although one can find sandier deserts, wider steppes or higher mountains elsewhere, Afghanistan gives these landscapes a special quality that is all its own. In autumn – surely the loveliest time in Afghanistan – one can wake of a morning and experience this quality at its strongest: there is the first brush of snow on the hills; a new, bracing chill is felt in the air, scented by the tangy smell of woodsmoke; the soft, golden light gives everything a deeper glow after the dust and harshness of the summer; armies

12 The Soviet-built concrete road from Herat to Kandahar.

of nomads are on the move to warmer pastures. At such times, one can be nowhere else but Afghanistan; the moment is to be treasured, and not experienced in any other place.

Who Are the Afghans?

In the infinite wisdom of our government, some Afghan refugees were recently settled in the rural area of provincial Scotland where I live. It might not be so different: Afghans are, after all, used to hills and cold. But the local council felt it particularly appropriate after a previous experience of settling Syrian refugees to tap into the Arabic specialists they used then in order to communicate. One could hardly blame the local council's good intentions, for it is a common misunderstanding that all Muslims are somehow 'Arab' (Iranians in particular dislike being labelled Arab). This is particularly so in Afghanistan, which has no Arab population (apart from a tiny remnant minority in the north-west who identify as 'Arab' but have long lost their Arabic language): all languages spoken are either Indo-Iranian or (to a lesser extent) Turkish, both completely unrelated to Arabic, a Semitic language (apart from loan words). Who, therefore, are 'Afghans'?

The 'Afghans' are as difficult to define as the land they inhabit.[14] This is largely because of the very land they inhabit, its geography – mountains, deserts, rivers and other divisions – channelling different groups into different directions. Ethnically speaking an 'Afghan' is synonymous with the term 'Pashtun' or 'Pathan', the ethnonym of many of the inhabitants of Pakistan as well. When considering any of the other polyglot peoples of Afghanistan, one encounters the same problems: the Nuristanis and Brahuis are also divided between Afghanistan and Pakistan; the Baluch are similarly divided, and are found in Iran as well; the Tajiks, Turkmen, Uzbeks and Kyrgyz are but parts of larger numbers in the Tajik, Turkmen, Uzbek and Kyrgyz republics, also found (apart from the Turkmen) in parts of China; and the Farsiwans in the west linguistically have more in common with the inhabitants of Tehran than of Kandahar. It is only the Hazaras of the central highlands that

13 Pashtuns at the Kabul Gate of Kandahar.

exist wholly in Afghanistan, not crossing any international boundaries (and even the Hazaras are perhaps related to the Mongols, albeit speaking a dialect of Persian). Can one call the Hazaras, therefore, the only 'true' Afghans? Doubtless, both Hazaras and Pashtuns would disagree.

The term 'Afghan', therefore, is problematic. In the broader sense, 'Afghan' can refer to any inhabitant of Afghanistan, both the Pashtuns themselves and those non-Pashtuns who do not identify with the ethnic Afghans. However, no other national noun or adjective seems workable: the term 'Afghani' is rejected as it is the name of the national currency – a crumpled note passing from hand to hand, not a member of a nation – while 'Afghanistani' is unnecessarily clumsy (and in any case hardly exalted by usage).

The population was estimated in 2020 at about 40 million, although a census has never been carried out so this was educated guesswork. The Pashtuns (illus. 13) first emerged as a distinct ethnic and linguistic group in the fourteenth century, and soon become synonymous with 'Afghan' (although the origin of the term 'Afghan' is only definitely attested for the first time in a Bactrian document dated to about AD 460). They are, however, a more ancient group, although their exact origins are uncertain. Some have identified them with the *Paktue*, a warlike tribe of the Indian borderlands who are mentioned by Herodotus, while the Pashtuns themselves traditionally trace their descent from the ten lost tribes of Israel. The language belongs to the Iranian group of languages, so they might well have been a part of the original Indo-Iranian migrations from Central Asia in the early second millennium BC. Since the eighteenth century, different Pashtun groups have dominated Afghanistan, and today they make up anything between 30 and 50 per cent of the population, as well as some 10–15 per cent of the population of Pakistan. Many of the Pashtun tribes are nomadic (illus. 10). They are concentrated in the eastern and southeastern parts of the country, although, being the dominant ethnic group, are now found throughout the country's provinces. One major tribal subgroup of the Pashtuns, however, are the Ghilzais, who might be descended from a Turk or even a Hun group known as the Khalaj who came into Afghanistan after the seventh century AD (but have lost their language).

The next major linguistic group is the Persian-speakers (and speakers of Persian dialects), who make up about 27 per cent of Afghanistan's population, although they are not as homogeneous as the Pashtuns. They are the variously named Tajik, Farsiwan, Hazara and Chahar Aimaq groups of people, related by a common language

14 Tajiks in the Panjshir Valley.

but all distinct, with important dialect differences. In some ways the Persian-speakers figure larger than their numbers, as Persian is the lingua franca and main language of learning and administration, spoken by many Pashtuns as well. The Persian language (*Farsi* in Persian, after the province of Fars – historical Persia proper – in southern Iran) is called *Dari* in Afghanistan, which means '[language of the] court', a term coined early in the twentieth century to underline Afghan difference from Iranians. This refers to the renaissance of the Persian language at the tenth-century court of the Samanid dynasty in Bukhara, when Persian – as opposed to Arabic, at that time the administrative language of the Islamic world – was revived as a court language for the first time since the pre-Islamic period. This marked the birth of modern Persian (so in a sense *Dari* is a more correct term – even in Iran – than *Farsi*, or the 'language of Fars'). Before the arrival of Turk-speaking groups into Central Asia after the sixth century, Persian was the main language for Central Asia. The form of Persian spoken in Afghanistan today is generally more archaic than that in Iran; many view it as a purer form.

The Tajiks (or Taziks – the name given to the Persian-speaking Muslim converts of Central Asia by the Arab rulers in the eighth century) are the largest remnant group of the pre-Islamic Persian-speakers in Central Asia (illus. 14). Their homelands are the Kabul region and most of northeastern Afghanistan, as well as the present republic of Tajikistan. Bukhara and Samarkand in Uzbekistan are also mainly Tajik-speaking, and there is a small pocket in the Pamir mountain area of China. Closely related are the Farsiwan (meaning simply 'Persian-speakers') of western Afghanistan, centred around Herat.

Anomalous among the Persian-speakers are the Hazaras of central Afghanistan (illus. 15), numbering about 1.5 million or 9 per cent of the population.[15] While they speak a dialect of Persian (albeit a very distinct one), they are possibly related to the Mongols (although their supposed descent from the armies of Genghis Khan is probably a myth). Religion also sets the Hazara apart from the rest of Afghanistan: they are mainly Shiʿa, as opposed to the Sunni majority of most of the population, Pashtun, Tajik or Turk. Another anomalous Persian-speaking group are the Chahar Aimaq (a Persian–Turkish hybrid term meaning 'Four Tribes'), a group of approximately 400,000 comprising the Taimani, Firuzkuhi, Jamshidi and Taimuri tribes in western and northwestern Afghanistan. They may originally have been Turk tribes that have since become Persianized – the Firuzkuhi, for example, use the circular felt tents, or yurts, that characterize the Turk nomads of Central Asia. The Taimuri, on the other hand, might be of Arab origin.

The third major ethno-linguistic group is the Turks. In Afghanistan they comprise the Uzbeks in the north (about 9 per cent), an extension of the inhabitants of Uzbekistan across the Oxus, and the Turkmen in the northwest (about 3 per cent), again an extension of Turkmenistan. The Uzbeks are larger in number. There is also a very small Kyrgyz minority in the far northeast. The Turk language is unrelated to either Pashto or Persian (apart from loan words), both of which belong to the Indo-European language group, but belongs to the separate Altaic language group. This includes all the Turk languages from Turkey through to Xinjiang in China (Turkish, Azeri, Qashqai, Tatar, Turkmen, Uzbek, Kazakh, Kyrgyz, Uighur and so on).

There are several smaller minorities, although once again all parts of larger groups that cross international boundaries. Chief of these are the Baluch of the south, numbering some 200,000, extending into Baluchistan in both Pakistan and Iran, where they number over a million. Their language belongs to the Iranian group of Indo-European languages. An isolated survival among the Baluch is a tiny group known as the Brahui, numbering no more than 20,000 in both Afghanistan and Pakistan, whose language belongs to the Dravidian group of southern India. The Brahui are the only survival in this region of a much larger spread of Dravidian languages in early antiquity that may also have included the peoples of the Indus Valley Civilization and possibly the ancient Elamites of southwestern Iran, as well as the ancient Oxus Civilization to the north (although this remains speculative).

In the isolated mountainous eastern borderlands adjacent to northern Pakistan are the Nuristanis, numbering about 100,000, an extension of the Chitralis across the border (previously referred to as the Kalash Kafirs). The Nuristani/Chitrali languages belong to an Indo-European subgroup known as Dardic, but are quite separate from the Iranian group that comprises Persian and Pashtu. The people of Nuristan were 'pagan' until they converted to Islam in the 1890s (when it was renamed Nuristan, 'land of light', from Kafiristan, 'land of the pagans'); only the communities in Pakistan still openly retain their ancient religion.

15 Hazaras playing buzkashi in the Bamiyan Valley.

Other isolated Indo-European language groups are found in the far northeast towards the Pamir mountains: Wakhi, Shughnani, Roshani and a few others in remote mountain pockets, probably remnants of the Scythian tribes of the first millennium BC. Most are Isma'ilis, a subsect of Shi'a Islam. To the northwest are a tiny Arab minority, although they have lost their Arabic language. In the east, in the mountain areas bordering Nuristan to the north of Jalalabad, are approximately 100,000 Pasha'i, related to the Dardic language group of northern Pakistan (another isolated and very early group of Indo-Europeans).

In Kabul and Kandahar are about 30,000 Kizilbash, descendants of Turkish-speaking groups brought to the region in the eighteenth century, although they now speak Persian and are Shi'a. Also in the east are communities of Hindus and Sikhs, all urban. They are mostly traders and are probably remnants of the Hindu Shahi kingdom of the tenth century in Afghanistan. Afghanistan has been home, since early Islamic or earlier times, to a substantial number of Jews. Nearly all have now gone, although four synagogues remain in Herat and recent discoveries of Jewish documents attest to their ancient status.

A 'Greater Afghanistan'?

While it is possible, therefore, to define 'Afghan' simply as Pashto-speaking peoples of the hilly Afghan–Pakistani borderland in the east of the country, an 'Afghan' in the broader, non-ethnic sense is simply anybody who, whether by choice or chance, from immigration or invasion, has come to be included in the present-day borders of what we call Afghanistan. A clumsy definition perhaps, but the only one possible – so long as one bears the caveats in mind. So, like the geographical make-up of the country they inhabit, the people are really parts of just about every major group in Asia from every period. Like the landscapes, again, it is the culmination and combination of all these polyglot groups that give Afghanistan its marvellous uniqueness: a land in between.[16] As we shall see in the following pages, Afghanistan was central to events that affected much of Asia. It was central to the formation of the Zoroastrian religion, for example, and it was in its western borderlands that the religious movement that culminated in the foundation of the Abbasid Caliphate began. Its eastern borderlands saw the formation of a distinct Buddhist art style that influenced the subsequent art of Buddhism throughout Asia. Afghanistan has been the seat of several major empires. The region of Afghanistan was the canvas where most of Iran's great epic, the *Shahnameh* or *Book of Kings*, was both played out and first written down. In our own day, events in Afghanistan have rippled worldwide. For long Afghanistan has been viewed as a part of 'greater Iran' or otherwise as parts of somewhere else. But with history, religious ideas, art styles and peoples extending beyond – sometimes well beyond – we can view much of the adjacent regions as part of a 'greater Afghanistan': truly central to much of Eurasia.

1
Afghanistan and the Outside World

Books about Afghanistan are necessarily about the people who live there. This chapter is about foreigners. More specifically, it is about those foreigners – travellers, traders and tourists, poets and pilgrims, the conquerors and the curious, mystics, explorers and adventurers – who came to Afghanistan and revealed it to the outside world. It is how we and the wider world learnt about the country.

Afghanistan attracted travellers long before there was an 'Afghanistan' as we now understand it. It lay, of course, at the heart of Asia and astride international routes, but that is only part of the story. It has certainly always been a crossroads, and the great travellers of the past – Xuanzang from China, Marco Polo from Venice, Ibn Battuta from Morocco – all left accounts. But an outside awareness of the region can be glimpsed from much earlier accounts, from the records kept by the ancient Persian administrators in fifth-century BC Persepolis to the bureaucrats in eighth-century AD Baghdad grappling to document the eastern domains of their new Caliphate. To travellers of a later date, such as the first Mughal emperor, Babur, or the Englishman Charles Masson, Afghanistan became a fascination. Stories from the nineteenth century of fabulous monuments, lost cities and myths launched, on the one hand, a plethora of travel writing and, on the other hand, the first serious scientific interest in its cultural heritage that continues unabated. Travel in Afghanistan reached its height with the hippies and mass tourists of the 1970s, becoming in the West a fashion almost reaching cult proportions. Today, the travellers have left, but the interest remains.

The Chanceries of Babylon, Persepolis and Rome

The cuneiform tablets of ancient Mesopotamia dating from the third millennium BC and later were the first to record the lands to their east. But the only names that might relate to Afghanistan are *Meluhha*, thought to be the Indus Valley Civilization, and *Marhashi* and *Shimashki*, which might be the Oxus region, although this is far from certain. We get some impressions of Afghanistan in the ancient sacred texts of Zoroastrianism, in which broad regions such as Bactria in northern Afghanistan and Arachosia and the Helmand in the south are located.[1]

It is not until we get to the Persian royal archives of Persepolis that we find texts that can definitely be identified with places in Afghanistan. These are the tablets and other documents referring to *Harahuvastish*, Arachosia in Greek, the name of the Kandahar region, and its chief city, *Kandarash*, modern Kandahar. In fact the Arachosia documents at Persepolis are the richest in the archive, implying the considerable importance of the region. These include, for example, the names of governors, such as *Bakabadush* and *Irdatakma*, the first recorded names associated with ancient Afghanistan, and the records of rations given for royal emissaries travelling between Kandahar and Persia.[2] Otherwise, the royal proclamation by Darius I (r. 521–486 BC) of his victory in a civil war preserved in the great cliff at Bisitun in western Iran gives the names of the provinces of the Persian Empire lying within the approximate borders of Afghanistan: Aria in western Afghanistan, Bactria in the north, Drangiana in the southwest, Arachosia in the south, Sattagydia in the Kabul region and Gandhara in the borderlands of eastern Afghanistan and northern Pakistan.

Then came Greeks. That greatest of all ancient travellers, Herodotus, while never travelling anywhere near Afghanistan, had still heard enough about its inhabitants from others who did to refer to them as 'the most warlike of all the Indian tribes' (an opinion that few modern invaders would disagree with).[3] His informant might well have been a fellow Greek, for Greeks of Herodotus' time had already been travelling to Afghanistan: when Alexander of Macedon's army finally reached the plains of Bactria at the edge of the then known world in 330 BC, they encountered Greeks who had lived there for many years. There were certainly many more Greek travellers who came in the train of Alexander's invasion, although not a single one of the early accounts has survived except indirectly by later writers.

With the subsequent establishment of Greek successor kingdoms in the area there were naturally more travellers. The best-known was the Seleucid diplomat Megasthenes, who made several journeys to India between 302 and 291 BC and wrote an account – again, alas, lost (apart from fragments). One traveller to Afghanistan from Greece has been rediscovered through archaeology: Kineas. We do not know what made him set out from his home sometime in the late fourth century BC, but he eventually arrived on the remote banks of the Oxus River, becoming one of the founders of a new city there at modern Ai Khanoum. French archaeologists, excavating its ruins thousands of years later, discovered the remains of a temple dedicated by Kineas, as well as his inscription, copied from one of the maxims at Delphi:

> As children, learn good manners.
> As young men, learn to control the passions.
> In middle age, be just.
> In old age, give good advice.
> Then die, without regret.[4]

Epitaph indeed for a traveller and his people drawn by a dream to the fringes of the then known world, closer to the borders of China than to their Hellenic homeland.

During the first few centuries AD there was travel between the Kushan and Roman Empires. Several records survive of 'Bactrian' or 'Indian' visits to the Mediterranean, and the reverse have been deduced from the enormous influence of Roman art on Gandharan art, but no names or descriptions have survived. The apocryphal Acts of the Apostle St Thomas describes Thomas' journey to the court of King Gondophares, who had requested that Jesus – as a carpenter

– recommend an appropriate builder for his new palace. Although the story is apocryphal, Gondophares is a historically attested Indo-Parthian king who ruled parts of northern Pakistan and eastern Afghanistan in the first century AD, and the tradition that St Thomas was a builder gives some substance to the suggestion of Mediterranean influence on Gandharan art. A contemporaneous religious traveller from the West was the Greek mystic Apollonius of Tyana (in Anatolia) – indeed, the two traditions might be conflated. Apollonius' teachings and travels were written down in the third century by the philosopher Philostratus, and his account of eastern Afghanistan includes observations both familiar (mountains, nomads and their lines of camels) and unfamiliar (griffins, hobgoblins).[5]

The Sages of Xi'an

The adoption of Buddhism in the region and its spread eastwards was to inspire the interest of travellers from the opposite end of the world, but the interests of the first Chinese traveller was political rather than religious. The Chinese diplomat of the late second century BC General Zhang Qian (Chang Ch'ien) travelled as far as northern Bactria between 138 and 126 BC but never went south of the Oxus – a pity, as his observations are among the most perceptive of early travellers' (and his adventures perhaps the most astonishing). But he does report on the regions beyond his travels and his description of Bactria is revealing. He describes Bactria as a country of 'walled cities and regular houses' which

> have no great king or chief, but everywhere the cities and towns have their own petty chiefs. While the people are shrewd traders, their soldiers are weak and afraid to fight, so that when the Yuezhi [Kushans] migrated westward, they made war on the Bactrians, who became subject to them. The population of Bactria may amount to more than a million.[6]

This gives a reasonably accurate picture of Bactria after the collapse of the Greek kingdom: politically fragmented but still populous and wealthy, living off the surviving infrastructure and with a sedentary lifestyle.

The greatest of all Chinese travellers was Xuanzang (Hiuen Tsiang). Born in AD 602, at the age of 27 he set out from Xi'an on a journey right across Central Asia, down through Afghanistan and into northern India on a mission to bring back the sacred Buddhist texts to China. In addition to a prodigious memory that could recall entire books, Xuanzang was also endowed with both inexhaustible curiosity and accurate observation, which enabled him to leave to posterity one of the most valuable ancient source books for ancient Central and South Asia ever written. We are indebted to Xuanzang for contemporary descriptions of the monuments of Balkh, the Kabul Valley, the Jalalabad area and – most of all – Bamiyan and its colossal statues. Indeed, his detailed first-hand account of Bamiyan is the only one that has survived that describes it at the height of its prosperity:

> The people inhabit towns either in the mountains or the valleys, according to circumstances. The capital leans on a steep hill, bordering a valley six or seven *li* in length. On the north it is backed by high precipices . . . To the northeast of the royal city there is a mountain, on the declivity of which is placed a stone figure of Buddha, erect, in height 140 or 150 feet. Its golden hues sparkle on every side, and its precious ornaments dazzle the eyes by their brightness. To the east of this spot there is a convent, which was built by a former king of the country. To the east of the convent there is a standing figure of Sakya Buddha, made of metallic stone, in height 100 feet.

Today, Xuanzang's journeys still retain almost legendary status in China.[7]

A more unusual visit by a Chinese monk to Afghanistan was that by Changchun (Ch'ang-ch'un) in the thirteenth century. His story is astonishing not only for the journey but for his extraordinary encounter in Afghanistan with that greatest and most terrible of conquerors, Genghis Khan. Changchun was a Taoist monk and ascetic born in 1148. By 1220 he had become one of the elder philosophers of China, having achieved considerable renown for his wisdom. Hearing of this, Genghis Khan wrote to him while on campaign in Afghanistan, inviting him to his war camp to learn more of his wisdom. The elderly Changchun – he was by now in his seventies – set out for the west accompanied by his disciple. He crossed the Oxus in 1222 while Genghis Khan was still engaged in his conquests in Afghanistan, finally catching up with him at his camp at Parwan, north of Kabul. The great warlord was deeply flattered that such a renowned sage had journeyed all the way from China to meet him (even though an 'invitation' from Genghis Khan doubtless was the same as a command) and many conversations were held between the monk and the conqueror: Genghis Khan was particularly interested in the question of immortality. After a stay of several months Changchun departed on the return journey with a personal escort provided by the great khan. They passed by the utterly devastated and deserted city of Balkh, silent apart from the barking of dogs, which Genghis Khan had wiped out shortly before. Perhaps it was the horrifying stench from the Mongol slaughter at Balkh, formerly one of the great cities of Asia, that prompted Changchun to advise Genghis Khan against the taking of life – probably the only person ever to have given such advice to one known to some as the greatest mass-murderer in history.

Exotic Imagery and the First Muslims

The next group of travellers to leave us their records of Afghanistan came in the wake of the Arab conquests. Whereas the Chinese came as pilgrims the Arabs came as traders and administrators; both were marked by a curiosity for the places they travelled through. For the first time we have a huge body of accurate information and commentary on almost all aspects of the country. That such travellers existed we know from the ninth-century works of the geographer Ibn Khurradadhbih, the historians al-Baladhuri and al-Tabari, and many others. The former may well have visited Afghanistan in his position as Postmaster General for the Caliphate – and he was, in any case, a native of the region. Soon these were supplemented by many more geographic and historic works that drew upon either the earlier ones or more recent travellers' accounts, as well as on official archives. Many of these accounts were gathered together in the writings of al-Idrisi, a Moroccan who settled in Sicily at the beginning of the twelfth century and wrote detailed descriptions of the cities and routes of Afghanistan and other parts of the east.[8]

In the fourteenth century the most famous of the Arab explorers, Ibn Battuta, another Moroccan, passed through Afghanistan and left us with a description of what was left of Ghazna after Genghis Khan had destroyed it: 'The greater part of the town is in ruins, with nothing but a fraction of it still standing, although it was [formerly] a great city.'[9] A testament indeed to the ferociousness of the Mongol sack of one of the greatest cities and courts of Asia (which we will be looking at in the final chapter).

If the Persian and Arab travellers left us with accurate but prosaic images of Afghanistan, far more romantic images were left by the poets, whose imagery came surprisingly close to some modern romanticized impressions of Afghanistan. For the Persian poets, Afghanistan and its people became a stock image for barbaric beauty and the exotic, anticipating Western nineteenth-century romantic images of the noble savage. This sense is conveyed in a passage by Farrukhi Sistani, a Persian poet who died in 1037:

> Your dwelling through its beautiful people is like paradise
> And your palace like Kandahar in respect of its beauties.

It is evoked even more strongly by another Persian poet in the eleventh century, Manuchehri: 'O mighty prince consume with sugar as long as desired the lips of the beauty which is from Kandahar.' In the end, the country became a poetic image for exotica and distance in much the same way as later Samarkand would for Flecker or Xanadu for Coleridge.[10]

In the Wake of Marco Polo

It was not until the travels of Marco Polo, who in the late thirteenth century journeyed across what is now northern Afghanistan and up through Badakhshan on his way to China, that European interest in Afghanistan and Central Asia was awakened. As the poet John Masefield, in his introduction to the Everyman edition of Marco Polo's travels, writes, 'When Marco Polo went to the East, the whole of Central Asia, so full of splendour and magnificence, so noisy with nations and kings, was like a dream in men's minds.'[11]

Marco Polo was to change that – and to reaffirm it. For the first time he brought back to Europe descriptions of the lands of Central Asia that he travelled through, narrative that at last laid to rest some of the myths. Like Changchun and Ibn Battuta he writes of the horrors of the Mongol devastation when he passed through Balkh. He writes also of Balkh melons, famous still today, and of the lions around Balkh, now extinct. And he describes lyrically the 'lofty' mountains of Badakhshan with its 'large streams of the purest water . . . [with] trout and many other delicate sorts of fish. On the summits of the mountains the air is so pure and so salubrious.'[12] At the same time Marco Polo was creating a new myth: the myth of the mystique, idyllic pictures that dreams are made of, a mystique and a vision of 'the mysterious East' that remains. Before his travels, Europeans had only the vaguest notions of the East, compounded partly of myth and the wildest of fancies, and partly of the few titbits of distorted fact that managed to drift to the Mediterranean. Now the European public were presented with an accurate description of the countries of the East, and its publication caused a furore. Not wishing to have their traditional fancies of the East shattered, many denounced it as pure invention.[13]

Other travellers followed. Many left famous accounts of famous journeys by famous people. But equally, there were obscure travellers whose very memories are long lost. In 1832 in Kabul, for instance, Charles Masson (of whom more below) noted a mysterious gravestone bearing the following inscription in Roman letters: 'HERE LYES THE BODY OF JOSEPH HICKS THE SON OF THOMAS HICKS AND ELDRETH WHO DEPARTED THIS LYFE THE ELEVENTH OF OCTOBER 1666.'[14] Was he the first Englishman to visit Afghanistan? What an Englishman was doing in Kabul at this time one can only conjecture.

Soldiers, Charlatans and Scholars

In the first half of the nineteenth century there was an immense upsurge in European interest in Afghanistan. Even before any of the military adventures or major explorations there made Afghanistan a household name, a new wave of Europeans came to the region. These were drawn to the court of Ranjit Singh, the Sikh king of the Panjab who was carving out a new Sikh kingdom in northwestern India. Ranjit Singh wanted his army trained on the European model and was prepared to pay well for it. It could hardly have come at a better time: Europe was flooded with unemployed officers following the end of the Napoleonic Wars, and soldiers, medical officers, horse trainers, adventurers and scoundrels all answered Ranjit Singh's call. This ragtag officer corps included French, Swiss, Italians, English, Scots and Americans. Many were highly talented and well intentioned; some were just charlatans. For Afghanistan it marked a new era of exploration.

Perhaps the most extraordinary of these adventurers was the Scot Alexander Gardner. Such was the fascination and mystique exerted by Afghanistan by this time that travels through there even had to be invented in order to satisfy a curious public: Gardner fabricated an extraordinary series of quite exotic – and fictitious – adventures in Afghanistan, a credit to his imagination, if not his integrity. Gardner's supposed adventures in Afghanistan, however, inspired Kipling's famous story 'The Man Who Would Be King'. Long after the adventures of his more worthy peers had been relegated to out-of-print books gathering dust in specialist libraries, Alexander Gardner's apocryphal adventures in Afghanistan were being screened in a film starring Sean Connery and Michael Caine.[15]

Probably the most remarkable – and harrowing – of these accounts is that by the former Napoleonic general J. P. Ferrier, who in the end was unable to reach the Panjab and had to turn back after many months criss-crossing Afghanistan. But apart from the better-known explorers there must have been numerous other lesser-known travellers who, for money, adventure or just curiosity, were attracted to Afghanistan, but never left any records of their wanderings. In the 1840s for instance, Ferrier, while a prisoner in Kandahar, was introduced to a young man, a lone, aimless, ragged German wanderer with few possessions and fewer words – a sight that would surely not have been out of place in Kandahar in the 1960s or 1970s. Perhaps this man was the first ever hippie traveller?

The one nineteenth-century explorer of Afghanistan who stands head and shoulders above all others was Charles Masson, deemed by one modern major scholar of the region, Gérard Fussman, to be 'one of the best archaeologists having ever worked in Afghanistan'.[16] Between 1827 and 1838, motivated by a spirit of adventure and a fascination for Afghanistan – not to mention a need to escape punishment for deserting the East India Company army in 1827 – he roamed back and forth over much of eastern Afghanistan. He was often alone enduring immense privations; at other times he was the honoured guest of Afghan nobility. His three-volume *Narrative of Various Journeys*, published in 1842, is a delight to read, full of a gentle humour and warm understanding of the Afghan character that is rarely found elsewhere. Masson's greatest achievement was as one of the earliest pioneer archaeologists. He was the first European to bring to light the immensely wealthy archaeological heritage of Afghanistan and he himself surveyed and excavated at the now famous sites of Bamiyan, Begram, Hadda and elsewhere. As well as recording many Buddhist religious monuments (many no longer extant), Masson's pioneering work resulted in the recovery of vast numbers of coins (some 30,000 in all), which still form the basis of Afghan numismatics today, as well as other objects, prompting increased scholarly interest in Afghanistan and its past.

Masson disapproved strongly of the British policies that led to the First Afghan War (1838–42) and after the suspicion and mistrust these policies wrought in Afghanistan was unable to return as he had hoped. Although ranking with other giants of nineteenth-century exploration such as Alexander Burnes (see later) or David Livingstone, he was never lionized or achieved popular fame as they did. He was never forgiven for predicting that British policies would lead to the disasters of the First Afghan War and he eventually died in England, embittered and in obscurity. Masson's contribution to the archaeology of Afghanistan, at least, finally received its due recognition 150 years after his death with the British Museum exhibition 'Discovering Ancient Afghanistan: The Masson Collection' in 2002.[17]

Players in the Great Game

With the establishment of a British imperial presence in India and a Russian one in Central Asia, first-hand information about Afghanistan came to be of primary strategic importance for the two great powers. The three British–Afghan wars and the related British–Russian cold war that lasted throughout the nineteenth century and into the twentieth – the 'Great Game' – are beyond the scope of this book. But the travel accounts and archaeological discoveries that were a by-product are not. And there were a great many who came. Most were from Britain, but they were also from Germany, India and Russia; they crossed and re-crossed Afghanistan and wrote valuable accounts on what they saw. Most were distinguished by inexhaustible energy and perceptive powers of observation. Many were sent on official business by their governments, but others simply came in search of adventure.

The glamorous Alexander Burnes was one who achieved instant popular fame from his travels, being dubbed 'Bokhara Burnes' after his return from Afghanistan and Central Asia. His travels were colourful from the start, as his initial mission was to sail on a raft up the

Indus bearing a gift of massive shire horses to Ranjit Singh from the East India Company. From there he continued into Afghanistan and on to Bukhara, before returning home to lionization and a knighthood. He returned to Afghanistan as a British political agent during the First Afghan War, where his short-sighted policies (not to mention his reported philandering with Afghan women) led to disagreement with Masson and his eventually being torn apart by a mob in Kabul, one of the events that sparked off the notorious retreat of the British army from Kabul in 1842. Burnes wrote copiously on his impressions of Afghanistan, but in some ways of more interest was the travel memoir written by his Indian secretary, Mohan Lal, whose book provides a balance and a different perspective to Burnes's. Mohan Lal also brought considerable common sense to the disasters of the First Afghan War, something in short supply with his employer.[18]

The peak of nineteenth-century exploration of Afghanistan came towards the end, with the despatch by British India of several boundary commissions between 1883 and 1905 to the southeast, west and north of the country, with the main purpose of drawing a line – literally – between Afghanistan and the Russian Empire. This resulted in a massive amount of new information being recorded. Although the work of the boundary commissions was ostensibly to demarcate international borders, it was also an opportunity to secure geographical and military intelligence by mapping and exploring much of the rest of the country. Rarely had more able a body of geographers and surveyors been gathered for a single project. The voluminous records of the many British and Indian officers involved made it the most thorough and comprehensive information-gathering exercise ever undertaken in Afghanistan, with a wealth of information on archaeological sites and historical monuments not known from other sources. Their results still form perhaps the most important single source for the topography, geography and antiquities of Afghanistan generally. These records are particularly important for the archaeologically rich regions of Herat and Seistan, as well as the still little-explored region of central and northwestern Afghanistan.[19]

Looking for Alexander

In the latter half of the nineteenth century, archaeological research received a stimulus from another quarter: ancient Greece and Rome. In an expanding British Empire, Rome was the ultimate and the natural model: as empires go, this was the big one, and Europe ever since antiquity has never tired of reinventing itself in various Roman guises. This was manifest in an explosion of Neoclassical architecture and other public art in the eighteenth and nineteenth centuries throughout Europe. But by the later nineteenth century, Britain's classicizing changed subtly as it found another model, an empire to which even ancient Rome looked back as its ultimate ideal. This was the empire of Alexander the Great. For by the middle of the nineteenth century, the British Empire for the first time overlapped with that of Alexander's. Britain extended its empire into the area where the great conqueror had trodden before when it expanded into northwestern India, particularly after the Sikh Wars of 1845–9 which culminated in the annexation of the Panjab and the extension of British India to the Northwest Frontier. For the first time British regiments fought on the same territory as Alexander's phalanxes had fought millennia before. The identification of the British Empire with that of Alexander's was in effect explicitly stated by a former senior British soldier and diplomat of the Government of India, Sir Kerr Fraser-Tytler, when he referred to the time 'when over 2,000 years ago the Greeks crossed the Hindu Kush to found the *first* European Empire of India'.[20] Hence the British in their incursions into the Northwest Frontier and the adjacent parts of Afghanistan in the nineteenth and early twentieth centuries chose to see signs of Alexander everywhere. Jonathan Lee points out that, to this day, Classical geographical names in the region remain in European common usage rather than current indigenous ones: Oxus, Jaxartes, Indus and Bactria, for example, as opposed to Amu Darya, Syr Darya, Mehran and Badakhshan.[21]

The tacit identification of the British Empire with that of Alexander was reinforced by the discovery of the astonishing art of Gandhara in this region, evidently derived from ancient Classical art. This has, of course, been demonstrated to be later and quite separate from Alexander's conquests, but nonetheless it served to reinforce in the Victorian mind the idea that the British Empire really was stepping into the shadow of Alexander's epic conquests – or at least bathing in his reflected glory. This prompted a frenzy of scholarly ventures 'looking for Alexander' throughout the nineteenth century that continued into the late twentieth. It began with Masson's archaeological explorations in the 1830s when he accumulated huge collections of Graeco-Bactrian coins and other antiquities, and continued nearly a century and a half later with the British excavations at Kandahar whose specific question was whether the site was 'the Hellenistic city of Alexandria'.[22] The Buddhist remains of the Northwest Frontier and adjacent parts of Afghanistan where 'Grecian art' was most evident in the sculptural reliefs were, if not exactly ransacked, stripped for the treasures they revealed to fill museums in British India and elsewhere in the world, often with no record of the original context or location. Such a lack of context has plagued the study of the art ever since, but it did stimulate more serious studies of both the art and the history.

Furthermore, by the late nineteenth century there circulated rumours that can only be described as electrifying: hidden within the mountain fastness of the Northwest Frontier and adjacent parts of Afghanistan were actual living descendants of Alexander's army! Such astonishing rumours even at the time were suspected to be the fiction that they are, but they fed into an imperial imagination all too ready to identify with the Classical past – and the Classical past's most heroic figure at that. This was the discovery of peoples in the Hindu Kush who, in contrast to the peoples of India, were blond and blue-eyed. This 'lost tribe of Greeks' was associated with various peoples of the region. Olaf Caroe, one of the last of the soldier-administrators of British India, wrote in 1958, for example,

> It is often said now upon the Frontier that such-and-such a tribe, or even family, claims Grecian or Macedonian blood inherited

> from Alexander or his soldiers. The Afridis, for instance, have their tradition of an admixture of Greek blood. They point to their Grecian features, and indeed many a young Afridi might stand as a model for Apollo, while the Afridi elder can display the gravity of Zeus. There are young Pathan warriors, not only among the Afridis, whose strong classical profile and eagle eye recall the features of Alexander himself. It is said that Alexander's army in its passage through this country left behind deserters who mingled their blood with that of the people of Tirah and the Khaibar.[23]

Caroe further emphasizes the point by comparing a photograph of a Pathan tribesman with an image of Alexander the Great.

The purported Alexandrine descent was applied most of all to the so-called 'Kalash Kafirs' of the Hindu Kush, found on either side of the British Indian–Afghan border, numbering approximately 100,000 in present-day Chitral in Pakistan and Nuristan in Afghanistan. They are a distinct ethnic group, having maintained their distinction due to their extreme isolation in their mountain fastness until recent times. Many aspects of their culture and ways of life were also distinct, but most of all it was their physical appearance, which was viewed as 'European-looking' and occasionally of blond colouring, that gave rise to the stories of their Macedonian descent (the Macedonians, it must be pointed out, were in any case dark-haired).

Today, the idea that the Kalash are descendants of Alexander's army has become if not exactly established fact then at least accepted wisdom that is related unquestioningly in numerous travel accounts and websites. The BBC television series *In the Footsteps of Alexander the Great*, for example, which was first broadcast in 1997, featured presenter Michael Wood having a fireside chat with 'the descendants of the last survivors of the Macedonian army which had burst across Asia like a meteor'.[24] So widespread is this belief that Hellenic Aid, a Greek NGO that is Greece's official overseas-development assistance programme, established a Development Education Centre in the main Kalash community in Pakistan to encourage the Greek language and civilization and to finance young Kalash to travel to the 'Greek homeland' for education. Needless to say linguistic, ethnological and DNA studies have shown not a trace of connection to Greeks: the Kalash speak a distant Iranian-related language and are probably descendants of the early Indo-Aryan tribes who entered through the Karakoram passes in the second millennium BC. A fabricated descent is the result of a British desire to walk in the great conqueror's shadow; they *wanted* to see Alexander, so they created one in their own image: a 'British Alexander'.[25] In the Buddhist remains of Afghanistan it was felt that he had been found – and looking for traces of Alexander still remains a primary aim of archaeological research. But descendants of Alexander's army still living in Afghanistan is as fictional as the Kipling story and John Huston's film adaptation of it. The essential hollowness of the image of Alexander is explored in Chapter Four.

The Tourist Invasion

For the first half of the twentieth century, Afghanistan still remained largely closed to tourism apart from the occasional hardy traveller such as Robert Byron. After the Second World War, however, the gates opened wide, so that by the mid-1960s Afghanistan became most definitely 'fashionable'. All of a sudden, the fabulous Golden Road was in reach from anyone's suburban street, as it were. But whether travel to Afghanistan became real adventure or crude self-gratification, it did reflect – as well as inspire – a very real upsurge of interest in all things Afghan. Books on every conceivable aspect were churned out. Some were immense learned tracts on the sort of minutiae that delight specialists; others were travelogues for the mass market.

So, bolstered by an image of the land of remote inaccessibility pictured in the books and films, foreigners flooded in. They arrived by plane, by Land Rover, by bus or by the ubiquitous VW Kombi; the more adventurous – or perhaps the more affected? – even travelled on horseback or bicycle. Not all of this steady stream were tourists in the traditional sense. Many were sent by foreign governments to implement grandiose, showpiece aid projects, as big-power rivalry for influence in neutral Afghanistan caused the great powers to vie with each other: sophisticated agricultural machinery that the Afghan peasant could never use, vast cotton mills for more cotton than the country could grow, irrigation systems designed to flow uphill, or simply voluminous 'feasibility studies' on ambitious projects that Afghanistan could not possibly implement, consigned to gathering dust in files later forgotten. There were also 'expeditions', many appealing more by their good intentions than their professionalism. Well-meaning though such expeditions were, their inevitably harmful effect on the Afghans was summed up by Wilfred Thesiger, probably the most renowned traveller of the mid-twentieth century, when writing of Nuristan in 1965:

> Kamdesh had recently been made accessible from Kabul by road, and it was now fashionable in the Embassies to visit Nuristan by driving as far as Kamdesh. The results were predictable. The Nuristanis had retained their individuality as a race even after conversion to Islam. Now they would be visited by an ever-increasing number of expeditions seeking adventures in wild places. This would disrupt a society utterly unprepared. Each expedition by its very presence would help to destroy what it had come to find.[26]

Writers such as Wilfred Thesiger and Robert Byron are among the best-known travellers of the twentieth century, and Afghanistan seemed to – and still does – attract that twentieth-century (and mainly English-speaking) literary phenomenon, the travel writer, like no other country. Indeed, Afghanistan almost became a qualification for the successful travel writer, with such well-known names as Freya Stark, Peter Levi, Bruce Chatwin, Dervla Murphy, Ella Maillart, Eric Newby, Nick Danziger, Rory Stewart, Christina Lamb, William Dalrymple and many others associated with Afghanistan at some point – often a crucial point – in their writing careers. The volumes that are the collective result belie the image of remoteness and inaccessibility that they write about. Ultimately, most are read for the insight they shed on the authors rather than on Afghanistan.

One of the more extraordinary social phenomena in the West in the 1960s and '70s was the hippies. This phenomenon had no less an impact on Afghanistan: the traditional mystique that this land held became, for the hippies, almost enshrined as a sacred goal. It offered everything: a colourful people seemingly untouched by the smear of 'Western materialism' that they were trying to escape from, and the mystical beauty of the landscapes that had inspired the Buddhist ascetics whom some wished to emulate. And, sadly, it also offered cheap opium and hashish, both of which were grown in abundance and inexpensively and readily available on the streets of Kabul or Herat. On the long road to Kathmandu – that twentieth-century mockery of Flecker's golden road to Samarkand – Kabul became a high point of the hippies' quixotic pilgrimage. The products of Afghanistan became high fashion in a public conscious of 'Afghan-mania' back home, and nomad dresses and embroidered sheepskin coats featured in boutiques in London, Milan and New York. At the beginning of the twenty-first century, with a reawakening of interest in Afghanistan following the war that toppled the Taliban, it came as little surprise to observe a revival of sheepskin coats in Western fashion (albeit mainly made from artificial sheepskin in the Far East – twenty-first-century animal rights and political correctness did nothing for the Afghan peasant).

There were, of course, many other types of traveller without the beards, beads and image of the hippie who also felt inspired to take the great overland route across Asia. But taken as a whole this era of travel was marred by a lack of understanding of the people and places they encountered. Many resented any hint of Westernization or modernization, as though places ought to be deliberately kept primitive and backward ('picturesque'!) for their own curiosity and snapshots. Just one popular travel book forms a very typical example:

> The light here [Kandahar] goes out every ten or fifteen minutes, which is very right and proper; it would be too boring to travel all the way to Central Asia and then have an infallible electricity supply . . . [Afghanistan's] simplicity, its courtesy and its leisureliness and with its underlying *sanity* of an area *fortunate enough* to remain very backward indeed . . . what one might describe as the poverty of Afghanistan but what I prefer to call its simplicity.[27]

As well as gross misunderstanding, such attitudes were thinly disguised Western arrogance. The above was written some fifty years ago, but the book is still in print today and such sentiments still current. In a *Times* travel article of June 2003, for example, the author extols Afghanistan as 'a world unspoilt by modernity'.[28] To an Afghan, the very suggestion that they are not modern but 'backward' and ought to be kept so is insulting; that their poverty is 'fortunate' is merely preposterous. The myth of inaccessibility, too, shows no sign of abating: a 2004 *Daily Telegraph* review of an Afghan travelogue, for example, contains the extravagant nonsense of how the reviewed author's '500-mile route through the Ghor mountains had been completed in living memory by only one Westerner, a French explorer, in 1957'. I recall when making the same journey myself in 1977 that I encountered an average of five parties of Western tourists a day travelling this route.[29]

The image of the non-materialistic, colourful Afghan became merely a euphemism for their poverty; the extreme cheapness of travel branded so many of these travellers with the very materialism that they imagined they were escaping. Overdoses of drugs and underestimations born of ignorance of Afghan ways resulted in many of them coming to grief: a visit in the 1970s to any of the Western consulates in Kabul would show sad but long lists of names of those believed missing, while a visit to the Christian cemetery – laid out originally for that earlier generation of ill-informed foreigners of the Second Afghan War (1878–81) – would show sadder records of those who were eventually found (as well as, even more sadly, those who could not be identified: many sold their passports for drugs).

I recall wandering around the streets of Kabul in 1981 under the Soviet occupation recording the rather forlorn and fading signs of a passing era to the sound of Soviet helicopter gunships overhead. Hotels still had names such as 'Peace Baba Hotel' or 'Flower Power' or 'Place with No Name' (with a rather sad 'HOTEL FOR SALE, PLACE WITH NO NAME' scrawled in clumsy biro in English and Persian on a sheet of A4 pinned to its closed door). Their signs claimed such delights as 'Pleasure Room, Open Late' or 'Good clean and cheap breakfast' or 'Old and New Things Shop'. A sign on the road to the airport read bluntly 'Welcome to the USSR'.

Afghanistan closed to tourism after 1979, and the gates have effectively remained closed ever since. But ironically this led to Afghanistan becoming better known to a worldwide public than ever before as major events continued to be enacted on its soils – and carried across the world by television and media more powerful and far-reaching than ever. The Afghan resistance to the Soviets brought a steady stream across the borders: journalists, adventurers, advisers, writers, medical practitioners and the merely curious. The Afghan resistance movement became the romantic image of the heroic Mujahedin – until their accelerated infighting after the Soviets withdrew clouded this image, and the Taliban's fanaticism subsequently destroyed it utterly. The blowing up of the great Buddhas of Bamiyan by the Taliban in the year 2000 was deliberately televised to shock an entire world audience. This and the terrorist attacks on America brought in the U.S.-led invasion of 2001 which toppled the Taliban. The subsequent twenty-year war to bring stability to Afghanistan – the longest war ever fought by the United States – resulted in a virtual avalanche of television and media reporting, books and even films to mass audiences until the chaotic withdrawal in 2021 and re-establishment of Taliban rule. Never had Afghanistan – nor few other countries – been so under the spotlight.

Perhaps because it was so under the spotlight that travellers still continued to come throughout this time. Some of this new breed of traveller were eminent television journalists in search of accurate news; others came in search of adventure. Others still were more quixotic, such as an ethnologist who came in search of an embroidery motif, or a former British soldier (and future politician) who decided to walk in winter across Afghanistan immediately after the fall of the Taliban. Another, although spending only two months in Afghanistan during the Soviet occupation, pursued the Afghan ideal in Beijing by attempting to officially lobby the Chinese government on behalf of the Mujahedin (Chinese officials must have been *utterly* baffled!) and on the completion of his journey when disembarking ship at Southampton still wore his Afghan clothing as a badge as if to say 'look where I've been'. Many of these travellers seemed to be in a tearing hurry, many were surprisingly ignorant of the places they travelled through – as often as not the reader cannot even trace their routes accurately on a map (could the writer?) – and many of the occasional bits of information that are dropped turn out to be erroneous (such as one writer who imagined the Khyber Pass to be in Afghanistan).[30] More regrettably, with many one senses a voyeurism, albeit often unwitting: the fortunate watching a people in their agony, the rich observing the poor. To the Afghans, such travellers and the hospitality that is instinctively offered to them must have been at best an inconvenience, at worst a distraction from the struggle simply to survive. But it was not all bad. On the contrary, our Chinese lobbyist later started a charity for Afghan orphans, one prominent journalist became a major supporter of Afghan charities, while our former soldier on foot founded another charity that encourages the revival of traditional Afghan handicrafts (and went on to enjoy a political career). But they were manifestations of a popular mystique nonetheless.[31]

Unearthing the Past

The nineteenth century had put Afghanistan's cultural heritage firmly onto the map of European awareness, and the twentieth consolidated this. The work of the nineteenth-century explorers had shown that an extraordinary wealth of archaeological material existed in Afghanistan. Indeed, out of the approximately 2,000 archaeological sites recorded in the *Archaeological Gazetteer of Afghanistan*, nearly 40 per cent of them were recorded before the establishment of scholarly research in the twentieth century.[32] This includes many of the twentieth century's more spectacular 'discoveries', such as Surkh Kotal, Ai Khanoum and the Minaret of Jam, which we will be reviewing in the following chapters.

Formal archaeological research began in 1922 when an official agreement between the French and Afghan governments established the Délégation archéologique française en Afghanistan (DAFA) on a permanent basis in Kabul (apart from a gap between 1982 and 2002). The agreement gave the French a monopoly on Afghan archaeology until after the Second World War. Over the years the French archaeologists shed considerable light on Afghanistan's past and the DAFA's monopoly was not wasted, for the results are truly impressive. Ultimately, all subsequent archaeological research in Afghanistan is indebted to the DAFA's pioneering work. The first director of the DAFA, Alfred Foucher, surveyed the ancient route between Balkh, Bamiyan, Begram and Jalalabad between 1922 and 1926, one of his primary aims being to search for traces of Alexander the Great. This survey culminated in excavations at Hadda (1923–30), Begram (1924–46) and Balkh (1924–5). Smaller-scale excavations were also carried out shortly after elsewhere in the country, as far as Seistan in the southwest, but most were focused in the east. Many of these excavations concerned the documentation and archaeological context of the Gandharan art style of the first few centuries AD and its antecedents. After the Second World War, the work of the DAFA became more diversified. Excavations were at first resumed at Balkh (1947–9), but in 1949 French efforts moved to the monumental early Islamic palatial city of Lashkari Bazar on the Helmand River, where large-scale excavations continued until 1952. The major prehistoric site of Mundigak in Kandahar Province was excavated between 1951 and 1958, work that still stands as one of the key excavations for the entire Indo-Iranian borderlands region and the newly named 'Helmand Civilization'. In 1954 the spectacular Kushan dynastic capital at Surkh Kotal shifted the DAFA's attentions back to the north once more, and excavations continued there until 1963. The even more spectacular discovery of the Greek site of Ai Khanoum in 1963 ensured that the attentions of the DAFA remained both in the north and in the Hellenistic period, with excavations beginning in 1964. Also groundbreaking was the discovery and excavation of the Harappan site of Shortughai, near Ai Khanoum, between 1976 and 1979, a discovery that first pushed the frontiers of the Indus Civilization of the Bronze Age beyond the Indian subcontinent. The DAFA also devoted considerable energies to large-scale survey work, with surveys carried out around Bamiyan and northern Afghanistan, culminating in a major series of surveys in eastern Bactria between 1974 and 1977.[33]

After the Second World War, the DAFA's exclusive right to work in Afghanistan ended as the government sought cultural relations with other nations. An increasing number of foreign missions became involved and the establishment of the Afghan Institute of Archaeology initiated major research by the Afghans themselves. The Americans were the first outsiders after the French, just before the war, when the American Institute of Iranian Studies surveyed monuments in and around Herat. A longer-term American presence, together with a major commitment to prehistoric research, was established in 1949, with surveys around Kandahar and Seistan by Walter A. Fairservis of the American Museum of Natural History. Seistan and the Helmand Valley remained a major focus of U.S. archaeology with the surveys and excavations there by a Smithsonian team between 1972 and 1978, resulting in this being one of the most thoroughly documented regions of Afghanistan. In 1950 Louis Dupree, also of the American Museum of Natural History and a student of Fairservis, began a long-term presence in the country. Apart from some excavations by the University Museum of Pennsylvania at Balkh in 1953, subsequent American work remained mostly in the field of prehistory.

Despite the British dominating both nineteenth-century exploration and the archaeology of the entire adjacent subcontinent, they were slow to resume contact in the twentieth century until 1972, when the British Institute of Afghan Studies was established in Kabul as a permanent base – the first such base in Afghanistan since the DAFA. This resulted in excavations at Kandahar between 1974 and 1978, one of its aims being to establish whether the city was an 'Alexandria' founded by Alexander the Great. Another project initiated by the British Institute was the first attempt to catalogue an accurate sites and monuments record for Afghanistan. This started off as a simple card catalogue in the premises of the institute, but its potential was soon recognized by the French archaeologists as a way of publishing material in the archives of both the DAFA and the National Museum and it was greatly expanded under French auspices and published in Paris as the *Archaeological Gazetteer of Afghanistan* in 1982. It has since become the standard reference work for the archaeological sites and monuments of Afghanistan and appeared in a new and expanded edition in 2019.[34]

German investigations were instigated by Klaus Fischer of the University of Bonn, who carried out a series of major surveys, mainly in Seistan. Italian work began in 1956 with excavations at the Islamic site of Ghazni and subsequently at the nearby Buddhist monastery of Tepe Sardar by the Italian Institute for the Middle and Far East (ISMEO). In 1960 the University of Kyoto in Japan began several important surveys, mainly of Buddhist sites, followed by excavations at a number of sites in eastern Afghanistan. The university in addition carried out the first systematic record of the Buddhist caves at Bamiyan between 1974 and 1978, resuming work there from 2003 to 2007. In 1967 an Afghan–Soviet Archaeological Mission was established, beginning with surveys of Islamic monuments around Herat. Large-scale excavations began in 1969 at several sites in the Balkh area and surveys along the left bank of the Oxus. Of these, Dashli was the most important Bronze Age excavation after Mundigak, and Tillya Tepe produced one of the most spectacular gold treasures of late twentieth-century archaeology.

Afghan archaeologists also began to make substantial contributions: Ahmad Ali Kohzad carried out a series of archaeological explorations in west central Afghanistan in the 1940s, then from 1965 until activities were interrupted by the Soviet invasion Afghan archaeologists carried out major excavations at Hadda. The Afghan archaeologist Zemaryalai Tarzi was the first to resume archaeological work at

Bamiyan after the year 2000, and since then Afghan archaeologists have been at the fore, excavating Buddhist remains in and around Kabul and revealing it to be one of the most important centres of Buddhism until well into the Islamic period.

From War Archaeology to Space Archaeology

The Soviet invasion of 1979 and subsequent occupation followed by civil war brought fieldwork to a halt. Major excavations such as the French at Ai Khanoum, the British at Kandahar and even the Soviets' own work in northern Afghanistan remained unfinished. Of course, history has taken its course and there has been great destruction of cultural heritage in Afghanistan – most notoriously the National Museum and the Bamiyan Buddhas – and this has been well enough publicized not to require reiterating here. In the light of this, it is all the more encouraging to look back at what was achieved in that bleak period. Important works of synthesis and discussion continued to appear on archaeology, art, architecture, numismatics, religion, prehistory, Graeco-Bactria, the Kushans and historical studies generally, to list just some of the main areas.

In addition to the very solid publication achievements mentioned above, there were important new archaeological discoveries as well. Several accidental discoveries of documents also radically changed our interpretation of Afghanistan's past. The discovery of the Rabatak inscription of Kanishka in the 1990s considerably enhanced our understanding of Kushan history. A major discovery in the 1990s was of documents in the Bactrian language written mainly on leather and parchment. Dating from about the third to the seventh century AD, they not only increase the number of known Bactrian texts from just a handful of inscriptions to several hundred, they rewrite much of the history of the Sasanians, Huns and first Muslims in Afghanistan.[35] More recently, a hoard of some fifty Aramaic Achaemenid documents, probably from Balkh, came to light written on leather and wooden strips documenting the last years of Achaemenid rule in Bactria, part of it being the correspondence of the Persian satrap of Bactria.[36] Further documents continue to appear: new discoveries of Jewish documents from Bamiyan and Ghur from the early Islamic period are currently being assessed at the time of writing (early 2024). These discoveries foreshadow greater ones still to come.

There was a brief revival of fieldwork in the early 2000s. The Afghan excavations in Bamiyan and Kabul referred to above began during that period. That flurry also saw the DAFA reopen in 2002. To the southeast of Kabul a vast Buddhist monastic 'city' was excavated at Mes Aynak. New work by French archaeologists at Balkh revealed for the first time evidence of Graeco-Bactrian monumental architecture, backed up by the recording of a complex system of canals on the Balkh plain. In the mountains to the south of Balkh a newly discovered Achaemenid city was recorded at Chasma-i Shafa. Between 2004 and 2012 a German team from the State Museum of Berlin carried out a survey programme in the Herat area and excavations in Herat city, the latter in collaboration with the DAFA, revealing for the first time remains of the pre-Islamic city. In 2004 a Sasanian rock relief was discovered at Rag-i Bibi not far from the main north–south road near Baghlan in eastern Afghanistan. Deep in the mountains of Ghur east of Herat the Ghurid capital, Firuzkuh, associated with the Minaret of Jam, was recorded. Large-scale programmes of conservation and preservation work on Afghanistan's built heritage, from major monuments such as the Herat citadel and Buddhist stupas to traditional forms of handicrafts, were initiated, much of it by the Agha Khan Trust for Culture, and are still ongoing. Afghanistan's cultural treasures were also brought to worldwide attention with a touring exhibition of the spectacular treasures of the National Museum between 2007 and 2014 that attracted huge public attention. A brief archaeological survey of the Helmand was even carried out by the U.S. Marines in 2011.

A new, updated and expanded edition of the *Archaeological Gazetteer of Afghanistan* appeared in 2019. The first edition claimed with some confidence that the bibliography was comprehensive; in the more than thirty years since, such a claim was no longer possible, such is the huge flood of information that has appeared and is still appearing even in a relatively small subject such as Afghan archaeology.

Just the years 2016 and 2017, for example, saw at least ten international conferences, workshops and other scholarly activities either focusing directly on Afghanistan or relating to it. A new scholarly journal, *Afghanistan*, the journal of the American Institute of Afghanistan Studies, appeared in 2018 and a new academic book series, Ancient and Medieval Afghanistan, was launched in 2024.[37] In Switzerland, the independent Bibliotheca Afghanica, originally started in the 1970s to gather together all publications related to Afghanistan, became an unofficial 'museum in exile' for Afghan cultural treasures. These were returned to the National Museum of Afghanistan in 2007 and at the time of writing its unrivalled library is being transferred to the University of Basel. The Balkh Art and Cultural Heritage Project initiated in Oxford in 2011, the Oriental Institute–National Museum Partnership Project initiated in Kabul and Chicago in 2014, and the European Society for Afghan Studies initiated in St Petersburg in 2017 are a small sample of the many, and increasing number of, such initiatives.

At the time of writing, Afghanistan seems to have closed its doors once more. However, some programmes of excavation and preservation continue, even on the pre-Islamic past: the preservation of the spectacular Buddhist stupas at Topdarra and Shewaki, for example, was completed after the return of the Taliban.[38] Moreover, the interest in the outside world shows no signs of abating. The initiatives mentioned above still continue, while more projects open up. A major new project, for example, is 'Invisible East' at the University of Oxford, a research programme to study, transcribe and translate documents and texts of the Islamic period from Afghanistan and the surrounding region.

A new tool that is now increasingly used in archaeology is satellite imagery. An ambitious new project was initiated in 2015 at the Oriental Institute (now the Institute for the Study of Ancient Cultures), University of Chicago: the Afghan Heritage Mapping Partnership. Using formerly classified U.S. high-resolution satellite imagery, the project is mapping the entire archaeological sites and monuments of Afghanistan visible from space, increasing by many times the number of recorded sites. By comparing the images with older satellite images going back to the 1960s, the project is also able to record the amount of damage, illicit digging, urban encroachment and other relevant details affecting Afghanistan's heritage and pass the information on to the Afghan authorities. The resolution of such new satellite images is astounding: as well as details of illicit digging one can see sheep walking over the sites. Space archaeology indeed!

A Poor Man's Moon?

Few countries have held the fascination for foreigners that Afghanistan has. For travellers of every description Afghanistan has exerted an almost magnetic appeal. The great travellers of early times – Xuanzang, Marco Polo, Ibn Battuta – left vivid accounts of the country. To travellers of a later date this attraction became a fascination. This fascination became in European fashion a mystique almost reaching cult proportions.

In trying to explain and analyse Afghanistan's mystique, however, one runs into continual difficulties, as the more one looks, the more elusive the attraction. True, the country is stunningly beautiful. But so too are Turkey, Iran, Pakistan and other countries in the region. The people have a reputation that is a byword for bravery, independence and pride – qualities, however, that are flawed by elements of cruelty, venality and apathy. It boasts some of the great historic monuments of Asia, but as many and as great are found in Iran, India and Central Asia. Its traditions for remoteness, too, are largely myth.

So exactly what is this attraction? Perhaps, as an American Peace Corps volunteer in Kabul once put it to me, 'Afghanistan is kinda like a poor man's moon: if you can't afford to go to the moon, you go to Afghanistan.' Perhaps it is like trying to explain the obsessive fascination for blue jeans. Or perhaps Afghanistan is simply 'the places in between.'[39] Whatever it is, I hope that in evoking Afghanistan's extraordinary heritage and its breathtaking setting, I can indicate just some of the answers.

16 The main Bronze Age sites in western Asia.

2

A Land of Two Rivers: The Oxus and Helmand Civilizations of the Bronze Age

What is civilization – or, more pertinently, *a* civilization? We all know what it is and use the word without thinking: Greek, Egyptian, Mayan, Islamic or whatever. But Kenneth Clark in his classic 1969 television series of that name was famously unable to define it.[1] For a long while the very term fell out of fashion among many archaeologists as it implied that many cultures who were *not* a part of our conventional 'civilizations' – many in, say, Africa, Australasia or Oceania – were not, by implication, 'civilized'. 'Complex societies' was often used instead, although even that term came with its own baggage. Hence, when a new civilization was identified in Central Asia in the 1970s, for example, it was rather cautiously (and wordily) named the 'Bactro-Margiana Archaeological Complex' (of which more below). When Felipe Fernández-Armesto wrote his own book on the subject in the year 2000 it was named (with a nod to Clark) *Civilizations* in the plural, with all societies from Palaeolithic hunter-gatherers to modern nomads a 'civilization'.[2]

This book is not in the business of definitions, but however we define it – or not – no civilization sprang into existence like Athena, fully armed, and so it is here. Before we discuss the first civilizations that took place in the modern boundaries of Afghanistan therefore – the Oxus and Helmand Civilizations of the Bronze Age – we must examine, however briefly, what came before.

Palaeolithic and Neolithic Background

Research into the Palaeolithic and Neolithic in Afghanistan – the Stone Age – remains in its infancy, a reflection mainly of the state of research which only began in the 1950s and, of course, which never progressed after the upheavals of the 1970s. Surface scatters of stone tools that appear to be Lower Palaeolithic, perhaps some 50,000 to 40,000 years old, have been recorded south of the Hindu Kush at the edges of the Dasht-i Nawur,[3] a seasonal brackish lake west of Ghazni, with more evidence for the Middle and Upper Palaeolithic (roughly 30,000 to 10,000 years ago) north of the Hindu Kush. A number of excavated caves and rock shelters of the later Palaeolithic, as well as the major open-air site of Aq Kupruk,[4] south of Mazar-i Sharif, represent transient seasonal settlements by hunter-gatherer groups – evidence for the hunting of sheep, goat and gazelle were found, and simple grinding tools suggest that wild barley was harvested – but finds so far have been too sporadic for any definite patterns to emerge. One of the main investigators of the Palaeolithic sums up by stating that 'practically no one who has actually looked for Palaeolithic sites in Afghanistan has failed to find them, but with no exception has there been anything other than preliminary survey and excavation'.[5]

While the herds of game found in the grasslands far to the north in Inner Asia were adequate to support Palaeolithic ('Old Stone Age') hunter-gatherer communities, the settlements of the Neolithic period ('New Stone Age', roughly 8000–5000 BC) required more reliable water and arable land for agriculture and pastoral herding, so we find their traces more towards the band of hills and water run-off north of the Hindu Kush. The transition from hunter-gatherer to settled communities represents such a radical change that archaeologists referred to it as the 'Neolithic Revolution', not only here but elsewhere in Western and Southern Asia at about the same time (although many now view the changes as more gradual and complex).

Knowledge of the Neolithic of the sixth and fifth millennia BC in Afghanistan is equally sparse, known only from a few excavated sites and some surveys in northern Afghanistan, mainly in the Balkh area.[6] Based upon these excavations, as well as comparative material north of the Oxus – mainly the Jeitun (or Djeitun) Culture in southern Turkmenistan – we can say that agriculture consisted of domesticated wheat and barley (flint sickle blades for harvesting have been found), and gazelle, wild goat and boar were hunted (this based upon butchered bones found at early settlements). There is also some evidence for animal domestication and temporary settlement (post holes, for example). There are simple anthropomorphic and zoomorphic clay figurines, as well as simple jewellery. This adds up to a society of mobile pastoralists with some sedentary agriculturists.

In the Chalcolithic period (the term refers to the transition to metalworking, mainly copper, but with the continuation of stone tools), approximately 5000–2900 BC, hunting and gathering gave way increasingly to cattle raising and permanent settlements relying on agriculture. Barley was widely grown, wheat less so, aided by increasing understanding of irrigation techniques, itself demanding cooperation between communities and specialization of skills. There was also gold and silver jewellery production, as well as the working of precious stones. Lapis lazuli, whose only source in the ancient world was northeastern Afghanistan, was mined and traded over a wide area, and turquoise and carnelian were also mined, worked and traded. New technology, such as spinning wool, brick making, copper working and wheel-made pottery, were introduced in the Chalcolithic period. We see the first copper and bronze weapons as well as figurines of animals and 'mother goddesses', showing an increased mastery of both art and abstract thought.

Southern Afghanistan emerges more into the picture towards the end of the fourth millennium BC when we see the beginnings of a long period of settlement at Mundigak in the Kandahar region.[7] Connections have been traced through the artefacts with southwestern Iran and Mesopotamia to the west, Turkmenistan and the Oxus region to the north, and southeastern Iran, the Quetta region and the Indus Valley to the south and east. This is connected to an increasing trade in copper and other raw materials. The international connections of this period over an astonishing area of Asia were to be a characteristic feature of Central Asian civilization in all subsequent periods. This forms the background to the emergence of the first civilizations in the region.

The Civilization of the Oxus

With the advent of the Bronze Age in the third millennium we come to the beginnings of civilization in Afghanistan and Central Asia, a civilization contemporary with the better-known ones of the Indus Valley, Iran and Mesopotamia. All affected Afghanistan in direct ways; at the same time Afghanistan affected all by acting as the link that connected them.[8]

The civilization of the Oxus has only relatively recently been identified as a distinctive 'civilization' in its own right, mainly since excavations in southern Turkmenistan and northern Afghanistan revealed hitherto unrealized levels of development and sophistication. Although identified mainly in those parts of Central Asia to the north and northwest of the Hindu Kush, its orbit extended to major sites further south as well, such as Mundigak in southern Afghanistan and Shahr-i Sokhta in southeastern Iran (now forming a part of a distinctive civilization of its own, as we shall see below). Further afield, the civilizations of both Elam in southwestern Iran and the Indus Valley also came within the greater orbit.

Some uncertainty occurred over what to call this 'civilization'. It was first identified in 1974 by the Soviet archaeologist Viktor Sarianidi, who excavated its key sites, Gonur Depe in Turkmenistan and Dashli in Afghanistan. Sarianidi coined the cautious – and perhaps clumsy – term 'Bactro-Margiana Archaeological Complex' (or 'Culture', as it was also known), which, being somewhat of a mouthful, was quickly abbreviated to 'BMAC'. Following the excavations of the Indus Valley-related site of Shortughai on the banks of the Oxus in northeastern Afghanistan, its excavator, the French archaeologist Henri-Paul Francfort, in 1984 suggested the broader term 'Oxus Civilization', by analogy with the other great riverine civilizations of the Nile, the Tigris–Euphrates and the Indus. More recently, archaeologists working in northeastern Iran have proposed 'Greater Khurasan Civilization' after the early Islamic province of Khurasan that covered much of those parts of Central Asia and Afghanistan where the civilization was centred, and not just the modern province of Khurasan in Iran. None of the terms have been entirely accepted by archaeologists: much of it (the Merv Oasis, its core area in Turkmenistan, for example) was not actually located on the Oxus; 'Greater Khurasan' has had reservations, particularly among Afghan and Central Asian archaeologists, because of its implications of Iranian origins.

There is also lack of agreement over whether these cultures constitute a 'civilization': uncertainty, for example, as to whether its settlements could be defined as true 'cities' (one of the main generally accepted criteria). There is also a complete absence of writing, one of the most important constituents in the conventional definition of a civilization. Of course, a lack of writing or even of cities rivalling Ur in Mesopotamia or Memphis in Egypt has never stopped the ancient Andean, Central American or Bronze Age European cultures being conventionally regarded as 'civilizations'. And the existence of many fine upstanding Indus sites away from the Indus River (Shortughai, for example, cited above), or Mesopotamian monuments not washed by the waters of Babylon, has not made them any less a part of the Indus or Mesopotamian civilizations respectively. Francfort's term 'Oxus Civilization', therefore, seems appropriate and has gained wide acceptance, but it must be emphasized that many scholars still prefer Sarianidi's more cautious (and more limited) 'BMAC'.

Large numbers of Bronze Age sites have been recorded right across northern Afghanistan, mainly by Soviet–Afghan teams in the 1970s north and northwest of Balkh and by a French survey of the late 1970s in eastern Bactria (illus. 16).[9] In the Herat region, formerly a blank on the Bronze Age map, an Oxus-period site was recorded northwest of Herat in the early 2000s. Excavations of Bronze Age sites reveal a long history of simple mud and mud-brick domestic buildings that

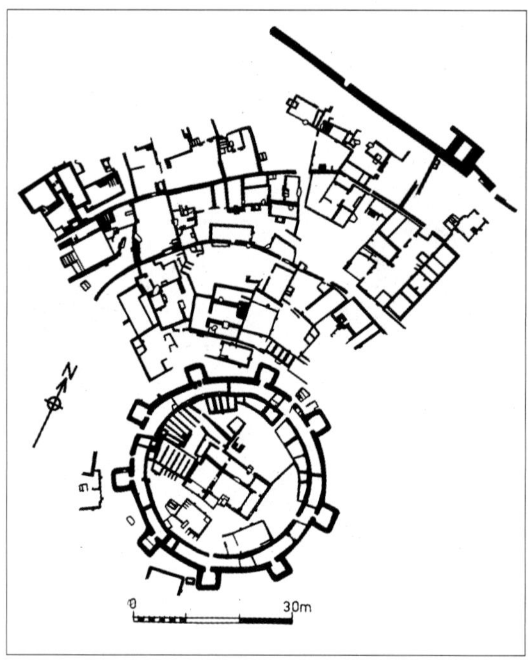

17 Plan of the 'temple' at Dashli 3.

culminate in monumental forms in the later third millennium BC. The monumental forms that developed in this early period would be both persistent and far-reaching. The first half of the third millennium in the Oxus region can be called 'proto-urban'. It was a vital and energetic period: there is the earliest evidence for large towns and fortifications, monumental architecture suggests cults and social stratification, and there is abundant evidence for long-distance trade. The period corresponds to the Sumerian Early Dynastic in Mesopotamia and Early Harappan in the Indus Valley. Monumental architecture is viewed as evidence for early state formation, as it implies the existence of an elite, of collective work and of social stratification, all requirements for a state. Monumental buildings are usually in the centre of settlements and are constructed of mud-brick. Massive monumental public buildings also make their first appearance, notably at Dashli in northern Afghanistan.

The Bronze Age also saw the introduction of increasingly sophisticated agricultural techniques in the oases. Complex irrigation systems have been recorded in particular detail in the Balkh oasis and in eastern Bactria, which included long-distance irrigation canals up to 3 kilometres (nearly 2 mi.) long, supported by artificial reservoirs.[10] These required organization and cooperation over large areas, together with the control of massive resources of manpower. These canals remained in use and increasingly expanded in all subsequent periods to the end of antiquity. That such sophistication and command of resources began in the Bronze Age also suggests some form at least of state formation to provide the organizational infrastructure for planning, constructing and perpetually maintaining these major public works.

Dashli, one of the main sites that defines the Oxus Civilization, in fact applies to a number of sites, mainly of the Bronze Age, scattered over the Dashli Oasis south of the Oxus River northwest of Balkh. It was the focus of investigations by the Afghan–Soviet Archaeological Mission between 1969 and 1973.[11] The main site, Dashli 3, comprises a hill with massive Late Bronze Age and Iron Age defences and a lower settlement. In the lower settlement a large, circular building was excavated, possibly a temple with associated living quarters and storage areas (illus. 17). Next to it is another monumental building, probably a palace, with the exterior decorated with pilasters, an enduring Central Asian architectural tradition (illus. 18). At nearby Dashli 1 a large square fort was also excavated.

The figurines and pottery decoration show increasingly rich artistic expression and refinement, a sign that there were ample resources to employ a class of professional artists. Another feature of civilization that expanded greatly in the Bronze Age was international communications, which became increasingly more sophisticated, developed and tightly knit. This is seen most dramatically at another important site of the Bronze Age, Shortughai on the Oxus River in Afghanistan. It seems to have been a trading colony of the Indus Valley Civilization, located more than 1,000 kilometres (620 mi.) to the southeast.[12] Excavations by Henri-Paul Francfort between 1976 and 1979 revealed a series of mud-brick domestic structures, with ceramics imported from the Indus. It was also a major centre

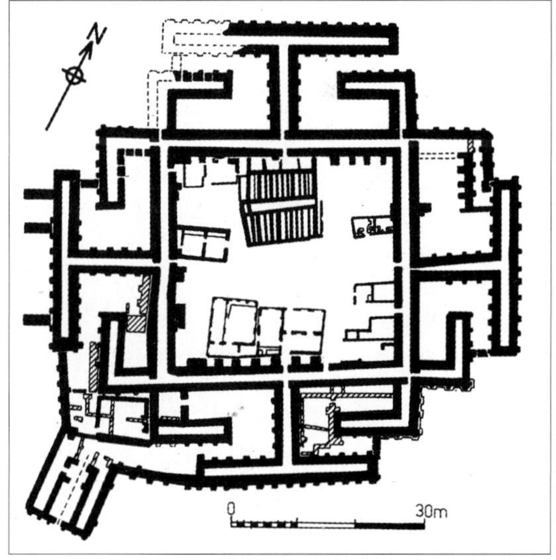

18 Plan of the 'palace' at Dashli 3.

for the trans-shipment of lapis lazuli throughout the greater region, for Shortughai had access to the lapis mines of Sar-i Sang in Badakhshan to the northeast (illus. 19).

Another key site of the Oxus Civilization (even though it is some way from the river) was Gonur Tepe, one of a number of oases on the northern fringes of the Merv oasis in Turkmenistan, where important excavations of Bronze Age settlements have been carried out since the 1970s. Although now in the desert, Gonur was originally a fertile part of the greater Merv oasis, watered by the Merv River delta, which emptied into the Kara Kum desert further north. It has since become swallowed by the desert through retraction of the river and the drawing of irrigation water from it further upstream. The site was extensively excavated by Sarianidi, who suggested that Gonur was the capital of a Bronze Age kingdom of Margiana between about 2400 and 1600 BC. Gonur consists of two parts: north and south. The older northern part is a settlement dominated by a citadel where a large palace surrounded by strong walls was excavated. An audience hall, throne chamber and residential area have been identified, as well as two rooms for possible religious use containing 'altars'. A fire temple complex was constructed

19 The excavations of Shortughai.

20 Bronze seals of the Oxus Civilization (not to scale).

alongside the citadel to the east, undergoing various modifications over a long period of time. Both temple and palace have been compared to similar buildings of the same period in ancient Anatolia and Syria. At a later period of the Late Bronze Age in the second millennium BC a sacred religious precinct was built at the southern end of Gonur, consisting of inner and outer precincts.

The art of the Oxus Civilization was one of the most highly distinctive of all the Bronze Age. Sadly, many of the objects have come from illicit excavations and so are without secure context, 'evidence of just how knowledge of this civilization has been lost in recent years'.[13] But the excavations at both Gonur Depe and Dashli recovered a large number of bronze stamp seals (albeit with even larger numbers from unknown sources in museums and private collections worldwide). These are usually circular, but floral, cruciform, lozenge-shaped and other forms also occur (illus. 20). Most have geometric or abstract designs, but many too are anthropomorphic, zoomorphic or floral. They are presumably personal tokens denoting ownership when impressed onto clay; when found in burials they are worn around the neck by women and at the waist by men. It has been suggested that some of the circular and cruciform shapes reflect the distinctive plans of the buildings at Dashli (compare, for example, illus. 20, second row from top, with illus. 18). The necessity of marking ownership of goods beyond the immediate crops and herds maintained by villagers, and the social inequalities it might suggest, is evidence of the complexity of the civilization that grew up along the Oxus River.

Even more distinctive are the composite statuettes from the Oxus Civilization, where statuettes of human figures are made from

21 Oxus Civilization figurines (not to scale).

combined calcite, steatite and other materials, including lapis lazuli. Typical of the female statuettes are the 'Oxus Lady' type, and of the male the 'Monstrous Standing Man' type (illus. 21), both presumably deities. When found in excavations – again, mainly at Gonur – they are in funerary contexts, but so many examples found in museums and private collections worldwide are from illicit excavations that have been smuggled abroad, so whether they were used in other contexts remains uncertain.

A particularly fine example of Oxus metalwork is an elaborate bronze ritual shafted axe head in the Metropolitan Museum in New York (illus. 22). It is partly gilded and depicts a boar on one side and a twin bird-headed hero battling a dragon on the other, a masterpiece of the metalworker's art. Regrettably, it too is unprovenanced apart from the Oxus region generally, but is of a style of ritual axe heads that are found elsewhere in the broader region, mainly in southeastern Iran, such as the axe head from Khurab near Bampur. Of better provenance, albeit not from controlled excavation, was an accidental discovery in 1966 from Khush Tepe in northeastern Afghanistan of an important treasure consisting of gold and silver vessels (known as the Fullol Hoard). The objects are both plain and decorated with motifs such as the bearded bull, the serpent and the vulture, reminiscent of contacts in Mesopotamia and Baluchistan. Subsequent excavations by the National Museum of Afghanistan revealed that they probably came from a burial.

There is considerable hesitation in defining the exact geographical limits of this Central Asian civilization. There is also doubt as to whether the emergence of the various earlier 'cultures' of Central Asia into something more homogeneous and sophisticated in the Bronze Age can really be called a true 'civilization'. On the one hand it bears all the hallmarks of a 'civilization': monumental architecture; sophisticated irrigation; agriculture and engineering; a complex, stratified society; structured organization; international communications; and many of the other characteristics that define a 'civilization'. On the other hand there is no writing and there is no consensus among

22 Oxus Civilization ritual bronze axe head.

specialists as to whether any of its large-scale settlements can be called true 'cities'.

The Helmand Civilization

Even more recently identified – or at least named – than the Oxus Civilization is that centred on the Helmand River in southern Afghanistan, a 'Helmand Civilization', a term first coined by Italian archaeologists working in southeastern Iran.[14] The term has found particular favour among Afghan archaeologists because it is almost wholly within Afghanistan, without the modern political implications of Iran that, for example, the term 'Greater Khurasan' implies. Other more imprecise terms to incorporate this civilization have been 'Trans-Elam' and the even clumsier 'Middle Asian Interaction Sphere'. Its core area is the Kandahar region of southern Afghanistan, particularly the key site of Mundigak northwest of Kandahar. Further sites extend southwestwards down the Helmand River to the major Bronze Age site of Shahr-i Sokhta just across the border in Iran. Bronze Age material recorded near Farah, as well as Gardan Rig and Dam in the far south-western corner of Afghanistan, hint at major discoveries still to be made in Afghan Seistan. In fact, the sites in this area (as well as across the border in Pakistani Baluchistan) are covered with remains of ancient copper production over a vast area of the desert, making it potentially one of the most important Bronze Age sites in Afghanistan.[15]

Mundigak was excavated by French archaeologists in the 1950s.[16] Period IV in the later third millennium BC (a date contemporary with the urban phase of the Harappan Civilization at Mohenjodaro and Harappa) was one of large-scale building activity. Monumental town walls were constructed, and two buildings, tentatively identified as a palace and a temple, had massive exterior walls and buttresses built of fired brick with surface coatings of plaster. The palace, located on the highest part of the site, had a facade on the northwest side that, when excavated, was still standing some 35 metres (115 ft) in length and nearly 3 metres (10 ft) in height. The line of semicircular buttresses fronting this facade was capped by a frieze of stepped merlons (illus. 23, 24). This type of structure appears to have been a favourite form of architectural adornment, as even the ramparts at Mundigak are distinguished by more closely spaced, square buttresses than would normally be required for either structural or defensive reasons. The interior plan, in contrast to the regularity and solidity of the exterior, appeared haphazard and comprised small rooms of flimsy mud-brick construction around a central courtyard. Much, however, had been lost through erosion, particularly since the building was first excavated in the 1950s.[17] The temple was more regular in plan, with a facade of decorative triangular buttresses traceable on three sides, although erosion had reduced the height of the building almost to foundation level (illus. 25).

Shahr-i Sokhta, just on the Iranian side of the Afghan border, was another important urban site and covered a huge area in the third millennium. It was extensively excavated by Italian archaeologists in the 1970s and by Iranian archaeologists more recently. There was evidence of literacy, as clay tablets in the still little-known pictographic

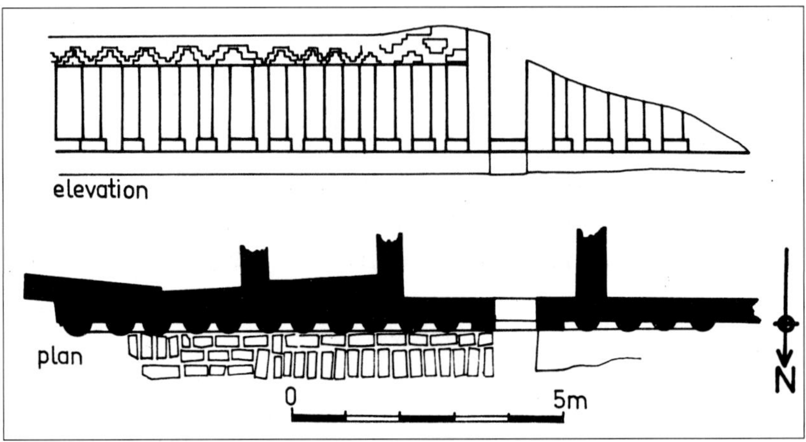

23 Plan and elevation of the monumental building at Mundigak.
24 The monumental building at Mundigak.

proto-Elamite script were found. It was also a major production and trans-shipment centre for lapis lazuli objects. If a lack of literacy casts doubt on whether the Oxus Civilization can be defined as a 'civilization', the proto-Elamite tablets from Shahr-i Sokhta confirm the Helmand Civilization to be firmly within the conventional definition.

Another site that has more recently been identified as belonging to the Helmand Civilization is Nad-i Ali in Afghan Seistan.[18] This is a vast multi-period urban site with remains of all periods from the Bronze

Age to early Islamic. Of particular interest in the present context is a massive mud-brick structure that was partially excavated in the 1930s and again in the 1960s. A re-examination of the excavation records in the 1990s identified the mound as a possible Bronze Age ziggurat or pyramid on the Mesopotamian model. Such a pyramid would have stood at least 40 metres (131 ft) high and some 50 metres (164 ft) at its base. If so, the platform at Nad-i Ali extends the spread of this building type by some 1,300 kilometres (810 mi.) further east of Chogha Zanbil in southwestern Iran, which was previously the easternmost known ziggurat. The more recent excavation and possible identification of the monumental platform at Konar Sandal at Jiroft in southeastern Iran as another ziggurat supports the supposition. Jiroft is a newly discovered 'Halil Rud' or 'Jiroft' Civilization that had close connections to the Helmand Civilization or may have been a part of it.

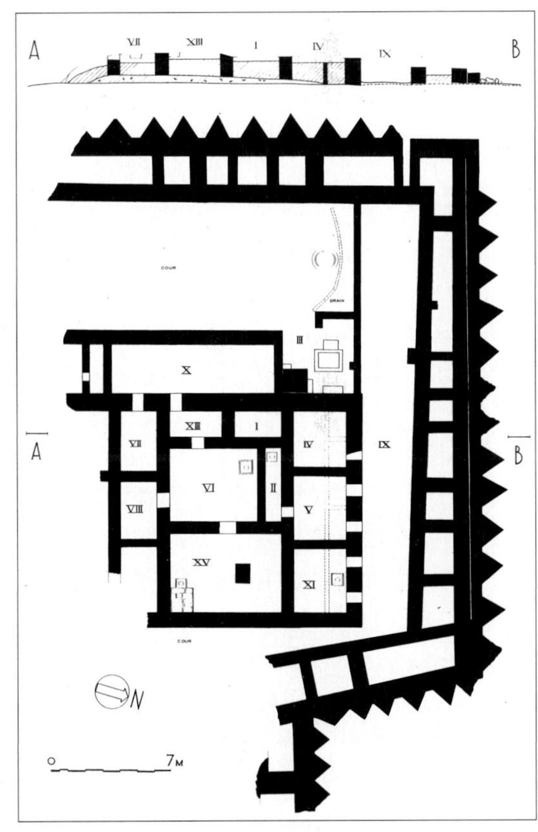

25 Plan of the 'temple' at Mundigak.

A re-examination of sites along the Helmand River that were first surveyed in the 1960s has revealed further Bronze Age material. Excavations at Sa'id Qal'a Tepe and Deh Morasi Ghundai in the Kandahar region, as well as Bronze Age material in a secondary context at Kandahar and surveys elsewhere in the 1950s and '60s, have further documented the spread of the Helmand Civilization. Excavations at Lat Qal'a in Afghan Seistan in 1975 by the Smithsonian Helmand–Sistan Project, together with further discoveries on the Iranian side of the border, now show an extensive network of Helmand Civilization remains.[19]

The art of the Helmand does not appear to be as sophisticated as that of the Oxus, consisting mainly of large numbers of simple terracotta figurines, found mainly at Mundigak. However, the nearby and closely connected Jiroft Civilization in Iran has produced vast numbers of highly sophisticated and decorated chlorite vessels and other objects, albeit mainly looted from graves, and these must also have found their way into the Helmand. We can now stand back, therefore, and look at the broader picture and contextualize both the Helmand and the Oxus Civilizations.

The Broader Picture

While the Oxus and Helmand Civilizations developed in and around Afghanistan during the Bronze Age, they were very much influenced by, and in turn influenced, the other cultures – both advanced and more unstructured – in the broader region.

To the north, the cultures of the Oxus merge imperceptibly into those of the inner Asian steppe. The cultures there were mainly semi-nomadic pastoralists in the period in question, but there were important sedentary cultures and developments as well, such as the so-called 'Country of Towns' in the southern Urals between about 2000 and 1700 BC which saw the development of the world's first chariots. It also saw extensive copper mining on a large scale, at least some of which would have been traded with the Oxus region. But the main culture contemporary with the Oxus Civilization was the Andronovo Culture from the beginning to the middle of the second millennium, spread over a vast area from the Urals to the Altai of southern Siberia, with some evidence traced as far south as northern Afghanistan. It is characterized by livestock breeding (mainly cattle), with semi-permanent settlements in semi-subterranean houses. There is evidence for extensive metalworking, with a high tin content producing harder bronzes: it is estimated that between 30,000 and 50,000 tons of copper ore were mined at the Kenkazgan mine in central Kazakhstan alone, for example. Some aspects of the funerary remains bearing similarities to later

Zoroastrian practices suggest an element of proto-Zoroastrianism. The Andronovo Culture is generally believed to be Indo-Iranian, perhaps proto-Scythian.[20]

The main Bronze Age civilization affecting the Helmand was that of the Indus Valley. The Indus Civilization (sometimes called the Harappan Civilization, after the site of Harappa in the Panjab where it was first discovered) shares with the other great riverine civilizations in Mesopotamia and Egypt the distinction of being among the world's first (although the Indus Civilization is slightly younger than the other two), but the Indus Civilization was the most widespread, with Indus sites being discovered as far away as the Oxus River to the north, Oman to the west and Gujarat to the south, a gigantic area by any standards. This has led some scholars to speculate that the Indus was the world's first empire. What makes it more surprising is that this astonishing civilization was entirely unsuspected until its spectacular rediscovery by archaeologists, first at Harappa, only in the early twentieth century, in contrast to Mesopotamia and Egypt, which have been known since antiquity through Greek and biblical lenses.[21]

The Indus Civilization is indigenous, although it probably received some stimulus from Mesopotamia, with which it remained in contact throughout its history. It very roughly spanned the years 3200 to 1800 BC. The origins are rooted deep in the prehistory of the Afghan–Pakistan borderlands centred in the hill country of Baluchistan to the west of the Indus Valley, with various stages of hunting and gathering and early agricultural societies over many thousands of years slowly evolving into the complex, urban society of the Indus Civilization. Its decline was brought about by a combination of circumstances, not all of which are yet fully understood. There may have been several factors that caused this upset, such as massive flooding of the Indus River (which can still occur today). In early scholarship, the collapse of the Indus Civilization was considered the result of the arrival of the Indo-Aryans (discussed in the next chapter), as described in the early Hindu sacred texts, but this theory is now widely discounted.

The other culture related to the Helmand Civilization is the least known and most intriguing – indeed, it is still in the early processes of rediscovery. This is known broadly as the 'proto-Elamite' culture, which covered most of Iran from about 3300 to 1800 BC. It is distinguished by the use of the proto-Elamite script, a writing system that is still largely undeciphered. The cultural area revolved around two main centres: Elam in the southwest and the Kerman–Seistan region in the southeast, extending southwards to the shores of the Gulf of Oman. The main excavated sites are Shahdad, Tepe Yahya and (most recently discovered) Jiroft. This brilliant civilization – the terms 'Halil-Rud Civilization', 'Jiroft Civilization' and 'Trans-Elam' have been proposed – may correspond to 'Marhashi' and 'Shimashki' in the cuneiform texts of Mesopotamia. But all of these references are surrounded with considerable uncertainty.

Whatever the label, this culture produced extraordinary art. Many outstanding painted terracotta sculptures have been excavated at Shahdad, exquisitely carved steatite objects have been found at Tepe Yahya and Jiroft, and elaborately wrought bronze axe heads and other metalwork has also been discovered elsewhere in southeastern Iran. Manufacturing and trade figured highly: Shahdad had highly advanced copper smelting and working; Tepe Yahya was a production centre for high-quality vessels made from the steatite found locally and exported all over Western Asia from Tepe Yahya. There are many connections with Central Asia, which may have been the origin of this culture. What is certain is that early civilization developed in southeastern Iran, and it was to be a constant reference point for the later history of Iran, Afghanistan and the region as a whole.

Of course, with the lack of any written evidence we have no indigenous name for any of these civilizations. Even though both the Trans-Elam and Indus Civilizations had writing, they remain undeciphered, while no writing has yet been discovered for the Oxus. Hence, we do not know who the people were who formed them, what languages they spoke or the names of their kings, heroes and gods. How, then, can we characterize these civilizations?

At Mundigak major monuments – fortifications, a palace, a temple – suggest that it may have formed a part of a larger state. Comparisons can be drawn with the emergence of monuments elsewhere, for example at Shahr-i Sokhta in southeastern Iran, Altyn Depe in southern Turkmenistan and Tureng Tepe in northeastern Iran. Metallurgy becomes more sophisticated with increased experimentation in casting and alloys. Pottery is almost entirely wheel-made and the decoration shows a uniformity between the southern Afghanistan sites such as Mundigak and Deh Morasi Ghundai near Kandahar and sites in both Turkmenistan to the northwest and the Quetta Valley to the southeast. Professional potters worked in specialized parts of settlements using sophisticated kilns.

Already by 2600 BC a distinctive architectural style emerges. It is seen in the two buildings tentatively identified as the palace and temple at Mundigak, and consists of lines of semicircular and triangular buttresses forming facades, capped (at the palace at least) by a frieze of stepped merlons. The palace at Dashli 3 in northern Afghanistan is similarly decorated with regular lines of square buttresses, on both the interior and exterior facades. The form recalls late fourth-millennium monumental architecture at Uruk in Mesopotamia, where semicircular, triangular and square buttressing were all used to decorate exterior facades. The semicircular buttresses of the palace at Mundigak seem to particularly resemble the 'Pillar Hall' at Uruk. The merlons also perhaps recall Mesopotamian prototypes. This type of structure appears to have been a favourite form of architectural adornment: later ramparts in Seistan and Central Asia are often distinguished by more closely spaced buttresses than otherwise seems necessary. The form was to have a long and venerable later history. Similar forms of decoration were used for the facades of the third-century AD city walls of Bishapur in southern Iran, the possible eighth–ninth century AD *kushks* or 'mansions' at Merv in Turkmenistan, the tenth-century caravanserai of Rabat-i Malik between Bukhara and Samarkand and the eleventh-century forts at Chehel Burj in Afghan Seistan, discussed in Chapter Eight.

Another important early characteristic was the development of a distinctive urban form, the circular walled town. At the Dashli 3 temple we see a fully developed circular plan, part of a Central Asian tradition of circular town and city plans that was to have a very wide influence. It probably began in the fourth-millennium BC settlements in the Geoksur Oasis in Turkmenistan, which were already characterized by circular walled ramparts. Later Central Asian town layouts of the Achaemenid and Hellenistic periods in Afghanistan and Merv in Turkmenistan adhere to this circular plan. The Iranians brought this plan with them from their Central Asian homeland and it later achieved considerable popularity in Parthian and Sasanian town plans. This culminated in the foundation by al-Mansur of the Early Islamic round city of Baghdad. It is notable that Plato's 'ideal city' was circular.

These architectural forms are found throughout the Indo-Iranian and Central Asian borderlands centred on Afghanistan roughly at the same time, between 2600 and 2000 BC. The question posed, therefore, is whether all of this region formed a part of a single state. Indeed, there has been speculation that the contemporary civilizations of the Oxus, the Indus Valley and Elam in southwestern Iran were all parts of the one single civilization speaking a Dravidian language. Only Elam and the Indus Valley had forms of writing (albeit differing), and proto-Elamite tablets are now found throughout Iran as far east as Seistan. But since neither script has yet been deciphered we do not know the language, although there is evidence that the Indus Valley language may have belonged to the Dravidian group of languages. These are now only spoken by the Tamil, Malayalam and other related peoples in southern India and by a small pocket, the Brahuis, in – significantly – southern Afghanistan and Pakistani Baluchistan. Until the decipherment of proto-Elamite and Harappan, we will not know for certain. An alternative theory suggests that the language of the Oxus Civilization at least belonged to the Indo-European group (discussed in the next chapter), so may have been 'proto-Iranian'. The Oxus Civilization is certainly crucial in any discussion of the origins and dispersion of the Iranian peoples.

There was a decline in these civilizations by about 1700 BC, with general depopulation recorded throughout, in the Indus Valley and northeastern Iran as well as in Afghanistan and southern Turkmenistan. The more complex and sophisticated aspects of Bronze Age culture at Mohenjodaro and Harappa in Pakistan, Hisar and Tureng Tepe in Iran, Namazga and Altyn Depe in the Oxus Civilization, and Mundigak and Shahr-i Sokhta in the Helmand Civilization all appear to decline. Some are abandoned forever, others are reoccupied with much simpler cultural forms. It is possibly related to the arrival of new nomadic groups on the steppes – perhaps the first Indo-Iranians? This decline at the end of the Bronze Age in Central Asia is marked by many movements and the arrivals of new peoples, mingling with the older sedentary populations. But there is no evidence for destruction or violence – no 'Indo-Iranian' invasions. The decline is more likely due to increasing salinization and exhaustion of the soils.

Seistan in the Bronze Age was one of the most formative regions for the later history of both Afghanistan and Iran. It was the homeland of the legendary Rustam, for example, hero of the great Iranian epic the *Shahnameh*, written at the Ghaznavid court in Afghanistan in the eleventh century. It was in Afghan Seistan that some of the largest urban areas in the historical periods developed, such as Nad-i Ali in the Iron Age and Sar-o-Tar in the Parthian and Sasanian periods. It was Seistan that saw the first revival of Iran after the Arab invasions with the rise of the Saffarid dynasty. The Helmand Civilization was, therefore, one of the more formative periods for subsequent developments in both Afghanistan and Iran. We will be returning to these subjects in the ensuing chapters.

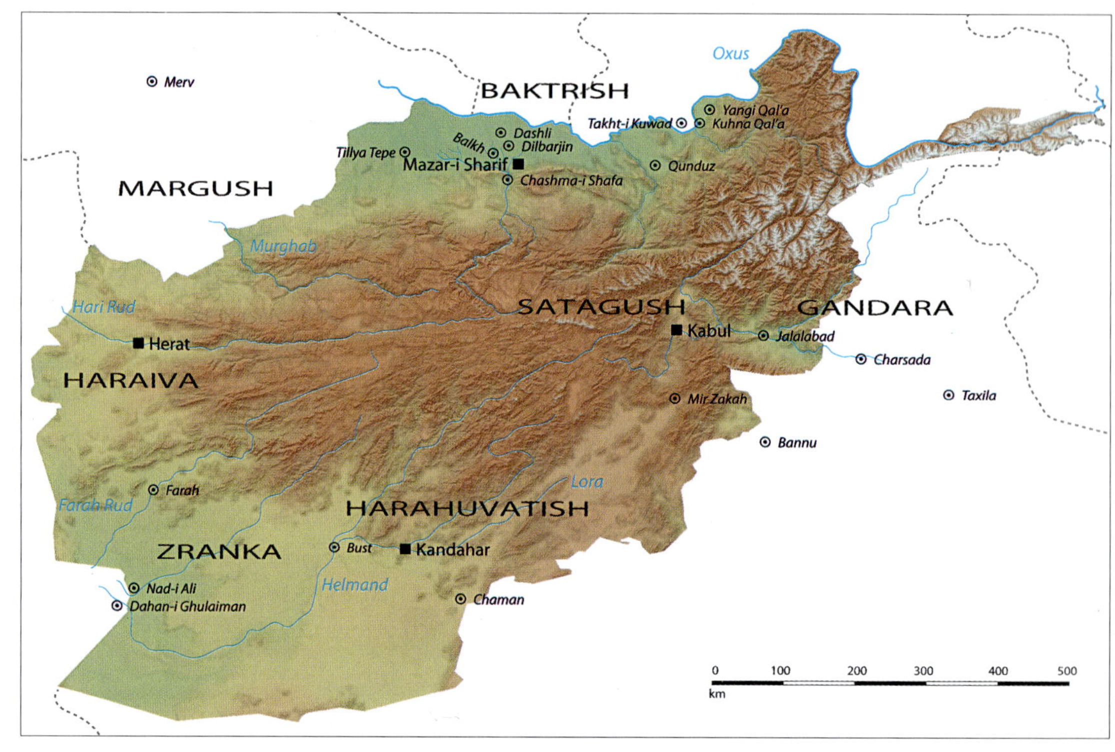

26 Afghanistan in the Achaemenid period.

3

Iron Age Changes: Indo-Iranian Languages and the Rise of the Persian Empire

The Iron Age in the early first millennium generally marks a break from the Bronze Age. Few sites have been recorded that continue from the Bronze Age into the Iron Age and subsequent historic periods. Many of the great historic urban centres of Afghanistan and elsewhere in Central and South Asia have their beginnings in the Iron Age rather than the Bronze. However, surveys in eastern Bactria at least have shown that this is not as consistent a pattern as was once thought, particularly in view of the continuity of the canal systems recorded there. These had their origin in the Bronze Age and remained more or less in constant use through the Iron Age and into the Hellenistic period. Part of the problem lies in the nature of Iron Age sites. Many are large urban areas that were continuously occupied in subsequent centuries (Kandahar, for example), so that any early development – and with it, continuity from the Bronze Age – is lost underneath metres of urban overlay representing millennia of later occupation.

The Iron Age in Afghanistan and Central Asia was one of expansion. Settlements expanded massively, such as the major Iron Age city of Kandahar (see illus. 30). There is more extensive irrigation, such as the sophisticated irrigation systems that have been mapped in eastern Bactria. The material remains show increased sophistication, and iron-working replaces copper. New urban centres appear in the middle of large oases, usually dominated by citadels, often monumental and sitting on large artificial platforms that were usually the rulers' residences. By the end of this period many of the great historical urban centres of

Central Asia had emerged: Merv, Balkh, Samarkand, Kandahar and possibly Herat became major cities, culminating in their establishment as provincial capitals of the Achaemenid Persian Empire in the sixth to fourth centuries BC (illus. 26). They remained major urban centres for the regions during the ensuing thousand years or more. The Iron Age and Achaemenid period was, therefore, a key watershed, laying the foundations of subsequent cultural and urban development.

What Is the 'Iron Age'?

'Iron Age' is not as easy to define as one might suppose. The term was first coined to define the appearance of ironworking to replace that of bronze, but there was no sudden change (such as might characterize an invasion) – the changes were more gradual. Its beginnings in Afghanistan and adjacent regions are usually put somewhere between 1500 and 1200 BC: the very imprecision of that 'date' is itself evidence of how difficult it is to define it – as well as the paucity of our evidence. It also implies a gap from the end of the Bronze Age, but this reflects more a gap in our knowledge about Afghanistan in the mid-second millennium.

Pinpointing its end is also problematic, at least in Afghanistan. In Near Eastern archaeology, for which the term was first coined, the end of the Iron Age is conventionally dated to about 550 BC, the beginning of the Achaemenid Persian Empire. However, the Achaemenid Empire is considered here together with the Iron Age. This is partly because the material remains show continuity from the Iron Age (indeed, archaeologists cannot always distinguish between the material remains of the Iron Age and that of the Achaemenid period in Afghanistan). Moreover, the event marking the end of the Achaemenid period – the invasion of Alexander of Macedon – does mark a substantial cultural break, both historically and materially, and so is considered separately.

There is another reason for considering the Persian Empire and the Iron Age together. The gap between the end of the Bronze Age and the beginning of the Iron Age – a 'dark age' – is generally regarded as marking the arrival of new peoples, not only in Afghanistan but in the adjacent regions of Iran and South Asia as well. Whether this movement was an invasion remains disputed, but it is generally acknowledged that these new peoples were the Indo-Iranians (or Indo-Aryans), who permanently changed the linguistic make-up of both India and Iran as well as Afghanistan and whose languages are still being spoken in the region today. Afghanistan played a crucial role in these movements. As well as new languages, the movement brought new religious ideas, notably Zoroastrianism, which many believe originated in Afghanistan. The entire period, therefore, might be considered an 'Iranian' or perhaps 'Iranic' age (without the modern political overtones that the term 'Iranian' might imply). In many ways Afghanistan is at least as important in the formation of Iran as Iran itself is. It is appropriate, therefore, to begin with a summary of Indo-Iranian origins and the movement of Indo-European languages, crucial to the history of Afghanistan.

Philosopher's Stone and Can of Worms: The Indo-European Languages

At a famous lecture in 1786 to the Asiatic Society of Bengal, the philologist Sir William Jones – at that time chief justice of India – was the first to articulate the theory that the ancient languages of India and Europe were not only connected but must have had a common origin (at least in linguistic terms). The implications are enormous: it suggests that peoples as widely separated as Bengalis at one end of Eurasia and Irish at the other were, at some point in their ancestry, connected. It includes many branches in Europe, such as Celtic, Slavic and Germanic. In Asia the main branch is Indo-Iranian, which includes Persian, Kurdish, Baluch, Pashto and some ancient Central Asian languages such as Sogdian, Scythian and Bactrian. It also includes Panjabi, Urdu, Bengali and many other languages of South Asia (often categorized as Indo-Aryan, distinct from the Dravidian languages of southern India such as Tamil and Malayalam). The search for an Indo-European 'homeland' has been described as both a 'philosopher's stone and can of worms', subject on one hand to some of the most magnificent scholarly detective work of the past century or so, and on the other to extravagant claims, political jockeying and myth-making.[1] The common linguistic root implies a common geographical origin, and places as diverse as the Baltic, the Balkans, Anatolia, southeastern Russia and western Siberia have been posited as an Indo-European 'homeland'. Without entering the discussions and the minefield of controversies, the general consensus among scholars has located this Indo-European 'homeland' very broadly in the region either side of the Urals in Russia. This region corresponds in the archaeological record with the Afanasievo Culture of the Bronze Age, which flourished a few centuries either side of 3000 BC. The Yamnaya Culture further west, roughly contemporary with and connected to the Afanasievo of the third millennium to early second millennium BC, has been associated with the movement of Indo-European speakers westwards. In a series of migrations between approximately 4500 and 2500 BC the original Indo-European group migrated from its homeland to points in Europe and Asia, splitting into its various branches in the process.[2]

The 'Country of Towns' in the Urals mentioned in Chapter Two was a development of the Afanasievo–Yamnaya Culture. This, as well as similarities between it and ancient Iranian and Indian cultures, has led to the suggestion that the area was the homeland of the Indo-Aryan language group, one of the first languages to break away from proto-Indo-European. The Iranian peoples are a sub-branch of the Indo-Iranians and are relative newcomers to the country they gave their name to: Iran (ancient Eranshahr, deriving from 'Aryan'). In addition to the name 'Iran', the name survives in the city Herat, ancient Haraiva, in western Afghanistan, another derivative of 'Aryan'. Eranshahr, Haraiva and even the name 'Ireland/Eire' go back to the same root: Vedic Sanscrit *aryaman*, Avestan Persian *airyaman* and Irish *Eremón* (the legendary first king of Ireland) from the proto-Indo-European *aryo-men* meaning 'trusty, honourable, worthy' – hence 'Aryan'. The Iranians came into Iran in a series of migrations that might have begun as early as the late third millennium BC before the end of the Bronze Age and only ended in the first century BC with the arrival of the last Iranian tribe from Central Asia, the Parthians.

With the first Iranian tribes known in the historical period – the Medes and Persians – being centred on western and southern Iran, it was previously thought that they had arrived in Iran via the Caucasus to the west of the Caspian. The centre of earlier Indo-European peoples known in Anatolia further west, such as the Hittites, seemed to support this view. It is now more generally recognized, however, that the Iranians arrived via Turkmenistan and the region southeast of the Caspian beginning in the early second millennium BC. An alternative theory is that there may have been an earlier Indo-Iranian migration into the Iran–Afghan borderland region of Seistan before they split, with one group migrating westwards to become the Iranians and the other eastwards to become the Aryan overlay in South Asian society. The arrival of the Aryans in the Indian subcontinent was one of the most important events in its history. It established the Rigveda texts as the primal source of Indian civilization and the earliest holy books of Hinduism.

Remnant pockets of early Indo-European groups are still to be found today in the remoter valleys of the far northeast of Afghanistan and north of Pakistan. These groups speak languages distinct from the major Indo-Iranian languages of India and Afghanistan, but form part of the Dardic language group, a much earlier branch of Indo-European. It was once thought that these represent evidence of the Indo-Iranian route into India, coming from their original homelands in Central Asia sometime in the second millennium BC and filtering down through the Karakoram passes into India. It is now thought, however, that the main Indo-Iranian movement into India was through the lower mountain passes of Afghanistan and Baluchistan to the west of India, and that the Dardic language–speakers are remnants of an earlier and separate Indo-European incursion that probably did not advance much further into the Indian subcontinent beyond the mountain passes, remaining there until today. Archaeologists excavating in Swat in northern

Pakistan have found remains – mainly in graves – which they have tentatively identified with this earlier population movement.

But whatever the truth – and there is still a great deal more archaeological investigation to be carried out – the whole question of Indo-Iranian movements was probably a more complex one than it first appears. There was probably no sudden invasion, such as the Mongols in later history, or even mass migrations of large bodies of people, but more likely a series of slow and largely peaceful migrations and gradual assimilation along a number of different routes over a thousand or more years. Above all, it must be emphasized that these movements are only really referring to *language groups* and not races. Despite the political implications of the term 'Aryan' in modern times, linking racial types with language groups has no scholarly legitimacy.

Afghanistan, Homeland of Zoroastrianism?

Perhaps the single most important cultural element that the Iranian tribes brought with them from Central Asia was an idea that had a profound effect upon subsequent history. This was the Zoroastrian religion. The historian of Zoroastrianism Mary Boyce has written that 'Zoroastrianism is the oldest of the revealed credal religions, and it has probably had more influence on mankind, directly and indirectly, than any other single faith.'[3] Zoroastrianism was first transmitted orally but later written down in the *Avesta*, revered by Zoroastrians as a sacred text. Zoroastrianism was the first religion with a concept of a hopeful hereafter offering a day of judgement, salvation, resurrection and paradise. It was the first to articulate the idea of an ascent to a form of heavenly existence after death. It was the first religion to introduce an abstract notion of deity representing the concept of purity and goodness, of the universal single god, of god the creator. Women as well as men, slave as well as master, poor as well as rich, may all enter Paradise.

The religion was first articulated by Zoroaster, whose message is essentially dualist: the concept of good and evil, light and darkness, the truth and the lie. The two concepts are known as *Ahura Mazda* and

Angra Mainyu (or *Ahriman* in its better-known Middle Persian form). These two concepts are entirely distinct, unrelated and uncreated, unlike the Christian concept of good and evil where they are ultimately related (the idea of a fallen angel). The conflict between good and evil was not indefinite, for it was believed that right worship and good actions would ultimately usher in the 'third time', aided by the *Saoshyant* – literally 'one who will bring benefit', in other words 'saviour' or 'redeemer' – who would ultimately appear and overthrow the forces of darkness, thus beginning a new era of rule by the forces of light, with the forces of light represented by fire (leading to the religion being misrepresented as 'fire worship'). The Saoshyant, moreover, was to be born of a virgin from the family of Vishtaspa, the prophet Zoroaster's own family and the name of a mythical king of Bactria.

Central Asia broadly is now generally accepted as Zoroaster's homeland. Much of the discussion has centred on Bactria (southern Uzbekistan and northern Afghanistan). Chorasmia in the region of the lower Oxus near the Aral Sea (modern Karakalpakstan) has also gained wide currency, although one recent study places his homeland in Margiana in southern Turkmenistan, and another in the Pamirs on the upper Oxus. Others have placed Zoroaster as far north as southern Kazakhstan or even the southern Urals, prior to the migration of the Indo-Iranian tribes southwards in the Bronze Age. Whatever the exact location, a Central Asian origin of Zoroastrianism – the original homeland of the Iranian peoples themselves – is not seriously in doubt. The increasing number of fire temples of the Parthian and Sasanian periods coming to light in the general Turkmenistan–Iran–Afghanistan borderlands region – five in Afghan Seistan alone (discussed in Chapter Five) – supports an overall picture of the eastern roots of Zoroastrianism.

The date when Zoroaster lived (if he was a historical person) and proclaimed his message is similarly widely divergent. The main dating evidence is the language of the sacred texts themselves, the *Avesta*. The texts were transmitted orally (still an important tradition in Iran) and only written down for the first time in about the ninth (or perhaps as early as the sixth) century AD; the earliest surviving manuscript fragments are from the thirteenth century. However, the form of the language used in the *Avesta* was a much more archaic form of Persian. The language of the oldest portions of the *Avesta* (the *Gathas*, which is the only part that may be ascribed to Zoroaster himself) appears closest to the sacred Vedic texts of Brahmanism, and is possibly even older. The nineteenth-century philologist Max Müller's dating of the Vedic texts to about 1400 BC is still generally accepted. Hence this suggests that Zoroaster may have lived before the Indo-Aryan migrations into Iran and India. However, these portions contain no geographical indicators. The only portions that do are later portions of the *Avesta* written in a language closer to the Old Persian of the Achaemenid inscriptions, almost a thousand years later than Müller's date for the Vedic texts. These contain specific references to locations that can be identified with places in Central Asia and the Afghan–Iranian borderlands. Hence some studies have put the date of Zoroaster as late as the sixth century BC and others as early as about 2000 BC. Mary Boyce, probably our main modern authority on Zoroastrianism, dates Zoroaster somewhere between about 1700 and 1500 BC, although this might be an extreme view. Most modern scholarship now regards Zoroaster as having lived in the early Iron Age, about 1000–900 BC, but there is no consensus.[4]

In support of an early date for the birth of Zoroastrianism has been the excavation of some (assumed) Zoroastrian fire temples dating to the early first millennium BC. The most significant is that at Tepe Nushijan near Hamadan in western Iran, dated to the Median period of the eighth to seventh century BC. Another, probably earlier, fire temple has been excavated at Gonur Depe in Turkmenistan, belonging within a tradition of similar Central Asian temples going back to the Bronze Age. However, while the identification of these buildings as fire temples is established, there may have been a form of fire cult not necessarily associated with Zoroaster and the religion he proclaimed.[5] Suffice it to say that the Central Asian origins and very early date for Zoroaster are not seriously in doubt.

The Zoroastrian religion was administered by a priestly caste, the Magi. The institution of a priestly hierarchy is one of the most fundamental of Iranian traditions. Its exact origins are hazy: the Magi may pre-date Zoroaster, going back to early Iranian origins in Central Asia prior to their migrations. When Indo-Iranian tribes migrated to India in the second millennium BC the idea of a hereditary high priesthood was taken with them and became the Brahmans, the Indo-Iranian overlay on Indian Hinduism. The institution of the Magi followed Iranian migrations to the Iranian plateau too, becoming a specific religious caste. The idea of a priesthood became a central part of Zoroastrianism and has remained an integral part of Iranian society to this day. Many important Iranian dynasties, such as the Sasanians of Persia, the Barmakids (a dynasty of viziers at Abbasid Baghdad who originated from Balkh), the Samanids of Bukhara and the Safavids of Persia, began as hereditary priestly families: Zoroastrian, Buddhist and Sufi respectively. Today, Iran is the only country in the Islamic world that has a structured governing priestly hierarchy, the mullahs and ayatollahs.

Afghanistan's 'Core Regions'

It was in the early Iron Age that the map of Afghanistan that we roughly know today began to take shape. The anthropologist and historian Thomas Barfield sees what he calls the four perennial 'core regions' of Afghanistan first appearing in the Iron Age, regions that have been central to Afghanistan to the present day. These core regions are Balkh, Kandahar, Herat and Kabul.[6] One might also add Seistan as a fifth. We may now examine these regions.

Balkh

The site of Balkh is historically and archaeologically one of the most important in Central Asia, with a history spanning several thousand years from at least the early first millennium BC to its abandonment

27 The ramparts of Balkh.

in the eighteenth century.[7] According to many sources it may have been the home of Zoroaster in about 900 BC, and it formed the capital of a posited early Iron Age kingdom of Bactria as well as the capital of both the Achaemenid satrapy of the same name (examined below) and the subsequent Graeco-Bactrian kingdom. Balkh is a vast urban site covering an area of 11 square kilometres (4 sq. mi.). It is surrounded by high mud and mud-brick ramparts in the form of an irregular polyhedron defended by towers with a secondary fortified area, the Bala Hisar, to the north (illus. 27). The Bala Hisar is in the form of an immense circle a kilometre across, part of an ancient Central Asian tradition of circular walled towns. Pre-Achaemenid and Achaemenid ceramics have long been known at Balkh, but following recent research there, a more substantial presence is now recognized.[8]

The most significant recent discoveries for the Achaemenid period in Bactria have been the results of French excavations at Chashma-i Shafa to the south of Balkh. Here a substantial city of the Achaemenid period (sixth to fourth century BC) has been recorded on a plain between the Balkh River and the mountains. It has been identified as the possible site of ancient Zariaspa, the ancient capital of Bactria instead of Balkh. Remains include a monumental fire temple that included a large limestone fire altar in the form of an inverted 'step pyramid'. This is one of the oldest fire temples recorded and has implications for the development of Zoroastrianism.[9]

Altin 1 and Altin Dilyar Tepe northwest of Balkh are both Achaemenid fortified towns consisting of high citadels surrounded by a town and massive outer defensive walls. This type of urban layout was to characterize Central Asian town planning for several millennia: the classic *ark* ('citadel') and *shahristan* ('lower town'). The circular plan

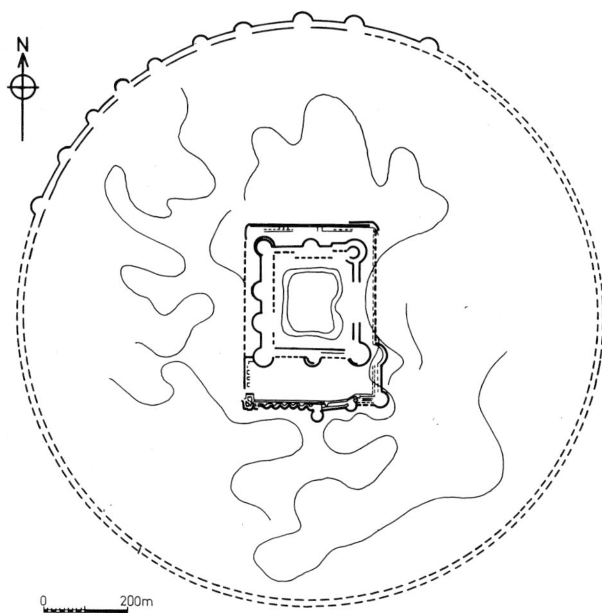

28 Plan of the circular city of Altin Dilyar on the Balkh plain.

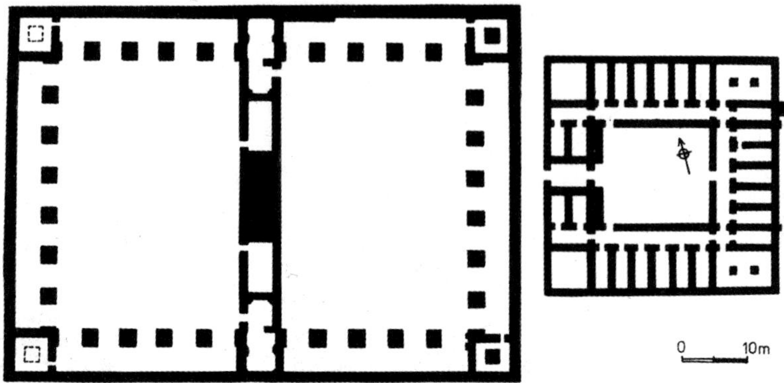

29 Plan of the excavated 'palaces' at Altin 10.

was popular: Altin Dilyar is circular (illus. 28); the Achaemenid citadel at Dilberjin is also circular (although the surrounding town is largely later), as is an Achaemenid building at Kutlug Tepe, tentatively identified as a temple, that comprises three massive concentric mud walls pierced by embrasures. Both sites are in the Balkh plain. Altin 1 was probably the administrative centre for a group of settlements. The most significant settlement in this group was Altin 10, which contained two buildings, probably palaces (illus. 29).[10]

Kandahar

The most important site for the Iron Age in southern Afghanistan is Kandahar, a large urban area at the foot of a precipitous ridge, one of the key locations for the historical periods for the whole Indo-Iranian borderlands region (illus. 30).[11] Excavations there revealed the existence of a major city with continuous occupation from the early Iron Age through to the eighteenth century. There was an indeterminate but small settlement in the Bronze Age, but the real foundation of Kandahar was in the early Iron Age, when it was laid out as a large, fortified city surrounded by earthwork ramparts and a moat more than 14 metres (46 ft) wide, a scale hitherto not seen in the region. Interior secondary walls divide the site into nine quarters. Kandahar's Iron Age expansion might be explained by the regional centre moving there from Bronze

30 The Buddhist stupa overlooking the site of Kandahar. The ancient ramparts and internal walls are clearly visible below; the modern city is in the distance.

Age Mundigak, a plausible explanation considering the decline of Mundigak in this period. Kandahar appears older than any other Iron Age city at present known in South Asia, thus marking the beginning of a tradition of large fortified urban areas that subsequently spread through the region during the first millennium BC. Accordingly, it has been speculated that it might have been the capital of a kingdom of Arachosia in this period. Not only does Kandahar have all major periods represented from the Iron Age in the first millennium BC to the Islamic conquest, but the size and nature of the site are that of a city of major military and strategic significance – that is, of more than purely local importance. There is evidence that the overall city layout was planned from the beginning, either in the Iron Age when the ramparts were first built or in the Achaemenid period, when it was a provincial capital. Evidence of occupation is found up to 8 metres (26 ft) deep, but the site is heavily eroded and robbed in most places.

Throughout the Iron Age and into the Achaemenid period the ancient province of Arachosia has been rightly emphasized as being of key importance in the interaction between Iran and India. The laying out of an ambitious new planned city and system of fortifications at

31 The east face of the massive citadel at Kandahar.

Kandahar might in fact mark the arrival of a new people to the region and the establishment of a possible kingdom. It has been emphasized that the Indo-Iranian borderland region played a key role in the Indo-Aryan migrations from Central Asia.[12] The occurrence of the large-scale fortified city of Kandahar – still not accurately dated within the broad time span of the Iron Age – on a possible Indo-Iranian migration route into India is one of the most important developments of the period for Afghanistan and for South Asia as a whole. That Kandahar might be evidence for these migrations can neither be substantiated nor ignored.

Kandahar was considerably rebuilt and enlarged in the Achaemenid period, when the massive citadel some 30 metres (98 ft) high (illus. 31), as well as several inner lines of ramparts dividing the city into quarters, was probably constructed. Excavations uncovered some fragmentary Elamite accounting tablets that are nearly identical to corresponding tablets from the Achaemenid capital at Persepolis, also written in Elamite – indeed, the tablets and other documents referring to Arachosia are the richest in the Persepolis archive. Although fragmentary, the Kandahar tablets almost certainly formed part of an imperial archive there and confirm the identity of Kandahar as the Achaemenid provincial capital, Harahuvatish, a supposition supported by the substantial programme of rebuilding and enlargement.[13] An underlying overall urban plan dating from the Achaemenid period that determined the orientation of subsequent building has also been discerned.[14]

It is significant that in Alexander's subsequent conquest he chose to divert to Kandahar rather than go directly to Bactria from north-eastern Iran in his pursuit of Bessus, as discussed in the next chapter. One authority emphasizes the importance of Arachosia and its satrap in the Persian Empire, implying that the lands to the east of it – India – were ruled from Arachosia rather than directly from Persia.[15] Perhaps Arachosia – and with it Seistan – was an important separate kingdom before the Persian conquest, rather as we speculate Bactria may have been (discussed below). The accession of Darius in 522 BC brought about a major change in the Afghan satrapies. It was marked by revolts in the east and subsequent campaigns to crush them, the first major Achaemenid campaigns in the region that we read about. This probably brought about an end to the semi-autonomy that the Arachosian and Bactrian 'kingdoms' had enjoyed up until then, resulting in their being absorbed directly into the Persian Empire. Thus Darius's reign was probably a greater watershed for the east in the Iron Age than Cyrus's initial conquests had been.

Seistan

Seistan at first sight might not appear a 'core region' (and was not included as such by Barfield, who initially designated these regions) as today it is an arid desert region largely devoid of major settlement. This is exacerbated by the notorious *bad-o sad-o bist ruz*, the 'wind of 120 days', which relentlessly scores the land for much of the year, making life almost unbearable and covering much of the region in sand. But its sands hide one of the highest concentrations of ancient remains in Asia. Surveys and excavations in Seistan by a U.S. team from the Smithsonian in the 1970s revealed a hitherto high level of sophistication in the Iron Age.[16] Up until then, Iron Age remains were mainly documented at the vast site of Nad-i Ali, the main early historic urban site in Afghan Seistan, but the Smithsonian surveys documented a complex system of irrigation canals drawing water from the Helmand River that was initiated in the Iron Age. This appears similar to parallel developments in Bactria. Such a system could only have been carried out by a centralized authority calling on large resources of manpower. The canals are associated with the appearance of structures built on large packed-earth platforms, resembling similar 'platform architecture' elsewhere in Afghanistan, Central Asia and northwest Iran. Over a dozen sites of this type were identified, found mainly in the Sar-o-Tar region of Seistan, a basin east of the Helmand River that is now complete desert but which in the Iron Age had been intensively irrigated with managed agriculture. Radiocarbon dates are between the twelfth and seventh centuries BC.

In the Achaemenid period Seistan was known as Zranka in Persian and Drangiana in Greek, although most of the monuments known so far have been discovered in Iranian Seistan. The most significant there was Dahan-i Ghulaman, where Italian excavations in the 1960s, supplemented by further Iranian investigations in the 2000s, recorded important Achaemenid monumental remains, all dated to the sixth to fifth century BC. The excavators suggest that this site was the capital of the satrapy in Achaemenid times, a suggestion that has much merit, given the size and complexity of the site.[17]

Herat and Kabul

The remaining 'core regions', Herat and Kabul, show less evidence for the Iron Age. Joint German and French excavations in the early 2000s at Herat revealed for the first time definite evidence for Iron Age and Achaemenid settlement there, confirmed by a series of radiocarbon dates ranging from the ninth to the fifth century BC. Although excavations were limited, it probably represents the Achaemenid satrapal capital, Haraiva, consisting of a fortress on the citadel mound with a separate settlement, the two perhaps linked by a circular rampart.[18] At Kabul the discovery of some Achaemenid silver – one with a cuneiform inscription – shows evidence of some form of settlement there, but much is obscured by modern building.

Early Iron Age Kingdoms

For the first time we can give names to the regions of Afghanistan in the Iron Age, recorded both in Zoroastrian sacred texts and in the administrative documents of the Persian Empire. These are Baktrish (Bactria in Greek) on either side of the upper Oxus, Margush (Margiana) for the region around Merv extending into northwestern Afghanistan, Haraiva (Ariana) in western Afghanistan around Herat, Zranka (Drangiana) in Seistan, Harahuvatish (Arachosia) in southeastern Afghanistan around Kandahar, Satagush around Kabul, and Gandara

32 Bactrians depicted on the Persepolis reliefs.

straddling the Afghan–Pakistani borderlands (illus. 26). Many of the peoples from these regions were depicted on the Persepolis reliefs (illus. 32). With the absence of pre-Achaemenid documents in the area it cannot be certain whether these regions were actually kingdoms in the early Iron Age before being absorbed into the Persian Empire. But there is increasing indirect evidence that Bactria and Arachosia at least were kingdoms, with their capital cities at Balkh and Kandahar, both represented by substantial urban remains in the early first millennium BC.

When the Persian Empire expanded into Afghanistan in the sixth century, what state structures, if any, did they find? There has long been speculation on the existence of a pre-Achaemenid kingdom of Bactria.[19] This rests largely on the account in the *Avesta* of Vishtaspa, the supposed king of Bactria and patron of Zoroaster, who might have ruled in about 1000 BC (although, as observed above, Vishtaspa's 'kingdom' and the homeland of Zoroaster may not have been Bactria). Classical accounts also describe how Cyrus the Great's conquest of Bactria met with stiff resistance, implying the existence of an organized state. Furthermore, Bactria – as well as Arachosia in the Kandahar region – seems to have been of high importance to the Achaemenids: Bactria alone supplied a cavalry force of 30,000 to the Achaemenid army; it paid

300 talents annually into the treasury, the highest of any single province in the empire; and it formed the stiffest resistance to Alexander's later invasion.

Archaeology has lent weight to the suggestion of pre-Achaemenid states in Afghanistan. The evidence reviewed in the last chapter suggests a highly developed civilization in Afghanistan in the Bronze Age – the Oxus Civilization in Bactria and the Helmand Civilization in Arachosia and Seistan – that raises the possibility of states developing in the Iron Age. Cities were often surrounded by massive ramparts: excavations at Kandahar at least have confirmed that the first construction of the massive urban fortifications date from the pre-Achaemenid period, earlier than any other fortified city in early South Asia, also suggesting more than just a city state or trade emporium in Arachosia. A pre-Achaemenid fortified settlement was excavated at Tillya Tepe in Bactria (a site more known for its first-century AD burials, discussed in the next chapter). The early settlement of Tillya Tepe is a mud-brick fortress with circular corner towers still preserved up to a height of some 4 metres (13 ft) when first excavated.[20] Thus archaeological evidence points to centralized rule and the need for large-scale defence, larger than would be posed by the nomadic threats of the Bronze Age. In other words, such ramparts were built to repulse armies. This, together with the large urban centres, suggests the existence of some form of state. In addition, archaeological surveys have recorded sophisticated systems of irrigation canals in eastern Bactria, the Balkh oasis and Seistan dating from the Iron Age that can only have been built by large-scale cooperation and a centralized organization, implying a state system.[21] These systems are characterized by marked continuity into the Achaemenid and Hellenistic periods.

Trade was established over a wide area into adjacent regions. Lapis lazuli, whose only source in the ancient world was in Bactria, was traded as early as the Bronze Age as far as Egypt, but precious stones, metals and other commodities were also traded widely in the Iron Age: tin from Bactria, for example, has been identified in a wreck off the Aegean coast of Turkey, and the foundation tablets of Darius at Susa refer to gold and precious stones coming from the region. Whatever existed in either Bactria, Arachosia or Seistan, it is clear that when the Achaemenid Persians conquered them the elements of urbanism and sophisticated state structures were already in place.

The Persian Empire

To a large extent, the history of the Persian Empire has been skewed by being viewed almost solely through European lenses. This is mainly because of the sources, which are almost wholly Greek – notably Herodotus – but also because the Greek victories against the Persian Empire are conventionally viewed as one of the most formative events in European history.[22] That it was ultimately overthrown by the West's greatest superhero, Alexander of Macedon, has also contributed to this bias, although many historians now give a more balanced view. The Persians' own view of their empire, however, would have been radically different. To begin with, the Persian Wars with Greece were probably viewed as merely a sideshow: in the longer term they could be viewed as ultimately a Persian victory when the Greeks tore themselves to pieces in the Peloponnesian War, as Persian money paid off one side against the other. It is also often glossed over that more Greeks fought on the side of Persia than on the side of Athens. More important, the Persians themselves looked towards their own ultimate hinterland and origins: the east. The region of Afghanistan and Central Asia was crucial for the Persian Empire. The expansion there and into Central Asia was one of the first priorities of Cyrus, the founder of the empire, and there is no reason to doubt that 'the challenges presented by the Central Asians to the Persian king and the surrounding ruling class were no less significant than those brought by the Greeks'.[23] The wealth of Bactria supplied the highest amount of any satrapy into the Persian treasury. Darius' campaigns there and further east were of more importance than his campaigns in the west, and more successful. New interpretations of the Persian royal archives indicate that Bactria, Arachosia and the eastern provinces generally were among the most important and were 'tightly woven into the tapestry of empire', while archaeological investigations in Bactria have confirmed that both the road network and the settlement pattern were well integrated into the imperial system.[24]

Afghanistan, and with it the ancient Iron Age 'kingdoms', were incorporated into the Persian Empire by its founder, Cyrus the Great, who became King of Kings in 559 BC. It has been suggested, however, that Cyrus and his immediate successor, Cambyses, were not Persians but Elamites, that his rise was a reassertion of older Elamite power against the Iranian newcomers and that the empire he founded did not become 'Persian' until Darius, the third emperor. The suggestion is a very controversial one, but at the very least the new empire incorporated many older Elamite cultural elements (such as the language for administration).[25] Be that as it may, Cyrus soon extended the borders northwards as far as the Jaxartes (Syr Darya) River and eastwards as far as the Indus, the former 'kingdoms' becoming satrapies of the new empire. By 500 BC the Persian Empire was the largest the world had seen. It has been argued that there was a major Central Asian element in the Achaemenid Empire from the beginning. One authority has recognized a pervasive Scythian substratum in Achaemenid society and power.[26] Or there is the possibility that Cyrus had already formed an alliance with a major Central Asian power – a hypothetical Bactrian empire? – that was absorbed into the Persian Empire.

Archaeological investigations in the Balkh oasis identified an Achaemenid-period irrigation network flowing northwards from Balkh that included a 4-metre-wide (13 ft) aqueduct stretching for several kilometres north of Altin Dilyar Tepe.[27] More significant were the detailed eastern Bactria surveys between 1974 and 1978 which recorded a dense pattern of settlement in the Achaemenid period. The most important feature recorded was a sophisticated canal-fed irrigation system comprising eighteen 'irrigation zones' dating from the Bronze Age but maintained to full operational capacity through the Achaemenid period, suggesting a high level of administrative control. This is amplified by the high number of fortified sites recorded. Many of these were

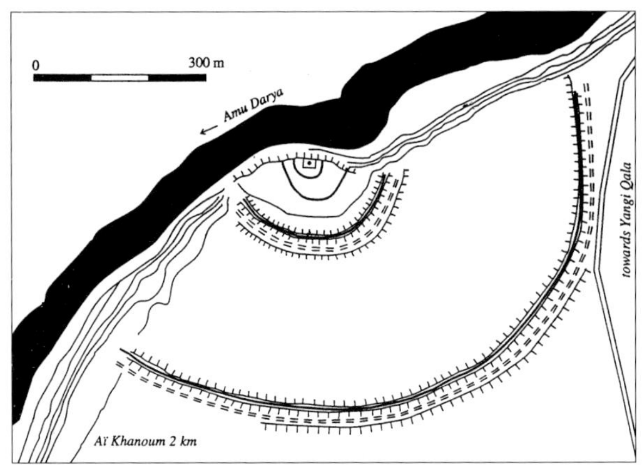

33 Plan of the circular city of Kuhna Qal'a cut by the Oxus River.

substantial settlements with impressive ramparts that can be described as urban, or at least proto-urban. Notable are Kuhna Qal'a, a huge circular settlement with inner and outer ramparts 900 metres (2,950 ft) across on (and cut by) the Oxus River just upstream from the later Greek city of Ai Khanoum (illus. 33) and probably forming its urban precursor, and Khwaja Hafiz further upstream consisting of a lower and an upper city on a promontory.[28] Clearly, Achaemenid Bactria was urban, prosperous and highly organized.[29]

The Persians ruled from four capitals, all in the west of the empire: Pasargadae, Hamadan, Susa and Babylon. However, the eastern provinces of the empire in Central Asia – Bactria in particular – remained a constant source of invigoration, a power base for the Persians. It was, after all, towards this area that the last Achaemenid king, Darius III, fled when Alexander pursued him across Asia. He fled towards Bactria not merely because his pursuer came from the west, but because this place was a source of potential support for the Iranians to draw from in order to face Alexander's invasion. Indeed, even after Darius' death, the next claimant to the throne, Bessus, was able to rely on considerable support and even raise another army to oppose Alexander in Bactria, drawing Alexander further and deeper into Central Asia.

Probably the most spectacular discovery of Achaemenid gold and silver treasure was the so-called Oxus Treasure.[30] Although from just a few kilometres beyond the present borders of Afghanistan on the right bank of the Oxus River in what is now Tajikistan, the nature of the treasure is directly relevant to the Achaemenid period in Afghanistan. The Oxus Treasure comprised a magnificent hoard of Achaemenid gold and silver workmanship: the model gold chariot drawn by three gold horses is the object most illustrated, but it also included a gold scabbard, massive gold armlets, silver statuettes and many other objects, as well as some two hundred gold and silver coins. It was excavated by looters probably sometime in the 1870s at or near the Temple of the Oxus at Takht-i Sangin, just across the Afghan border from Badakhshan. It was then sold to merchants in Bukhara, who decided to take it down through Afghanistan to be sold in the markets of British India, but (to cut a long story short) the merchants were waylaid and killed by robbers. British officials learnt of the treasure and were able to seize the bulk of it, recovering more from the markets, and eventually deposited it in the British Museum.

General Themes

The Bronze Age tradition of constructing monumental buildings on platforms developed further in the Iron Age. Massive structures, usually on immense brick platforms, include Nad-i Ali in Seistan, the citadels at Maiwand and Kandahar in the southeast,[31] and many fortifications in Bactria in the north. The same monumentality is also found in Iron Age and Achaemenid buildings of Pakistan and Iran, culminating in the immense palace platform of Persepolis.

A particular urban feature of Iron Age Bactria is that many settlements were planned circular towns. These included many major settlements such as Altin Dilyar, Kuhna Qal'a (illus. 28, 33) and the Balkh Bala Hisar.[32] To the southwest of Balkh the site of a major Achaemenid fortified site has recently been identified at Barkah. This is in the form of an immense perfect circle more than 600 metres (1,970 ft) in diameter.[33] The circular town is presumably an indigenous Central Asian innovation, deriving from earlier prototypes such as Dashli 3 (illus. 17), and marks a major development in the history of town planning broadly. New Hellenistic settlements in Bactria, such as Emshi Tepe and Jiga Tepe, adopted the form, and recent surveys of the Balkh plain based upon satellite imagery by a team from the University of Chicago have picked up many more such circular settlement plans not previously recorded.[34] The circular form became a feature of later Iranian urban planning, such as for the Sasanian cities of Firuzabad and Darabgerd, and satellite imagery has revealed circular town plans underneath the later orthogonal plans of Sasanian Bishapur and Jundi Shapur as well.[35]

Related to the Central Asian tradition of circular city plans was the early development of massive defensive architecture. This may have been to defend against the hunter-gatherer tribes to the north, and the interaction between nomads and sedentary populations was a perennial theme in Central Asian culture. By the Iron Age in the first millennium we see some of the great cities of Afghanistan, such as Balkh and Kandahar, surrounded by substantial ramparts, often with great mud-built citadels (illus. 27, 30, 31). These fortifications are often characterized by casemate construction of linked rooms filled with packed earth, square towers at regular intervals and lines of arrow slits on several levels. This tradition of massive defensive works of architecture was to develop over time in Central Asia on an even vaster scale, more extensive than anywhere else in the world outside China, with entire regions being walled. Again, this probably developed from the desire to defend against nomads.

The two Achaemenid palaces at Altin 10 included features that were to have important later histories. One palace consisted of two porticoed courtyards with roofs supported by massive brick pillars, the other comprised a single courtyard dominated by a wide central entrance on one side (illus. 29). Both features subsequently evolved into two important architectural elements of the Middle East: the columned hall and the monumental portal or *iwan*. The *iwan* is a monumental entrance, usually in the form of a great arch or portico. From modest beginnings in Central Asia to the great central arches that dominate the courtyards of successive Parthian, Sasanian and Islamic monumental buildings and the simpler dwelling houses on the Iranian and Central Asian plateaus today, the *iwan* is one of the most persistent features of Central Asian and Persian architecture as a whole. The columned hall is seen in its full developed form at Persepolis.

The first millennium BC, therefore, was one in which the prototypes of certain basic architectural features were established: the circular form, monumental platforms, the columned hall and the monumental portal. That so many standard architectural elements of Afghanistan and neighbouring Iran were formulated in Afghanistan assumes significance in light of the Central Asian origins of the Iranians themselves: when they arrived on the Iranian plateau, they already had a developed and vigorous architectural tradition.

There is little to see of Achaemenid standing remains in Afghanistan today apart from the massive bulk of the citadel and fortifications of Kandahar (illus. 31). The legacy, however, was enormous. For the Achaemenid Empire was the world's first truly multinational empire. A massive new system of organization and administration was instigated: provincial government, roads, taxation, banking – all solid new institutions that survived the eclipse of this brilliant empire by many centuries. This internationalism unified the divergent worlds of India, Central Asia, the Middle East and the Mediterranean, a phenomenon expressed so vividly in the Persepolis reliefs (illus. 32), and this integration underpinned subsequent historical developments for a thousand years, long after the empire itself had collapsed. Without it there would have been no Alexander the Great, no Graeco-Bactrian kingdom and no Gandharan art, and even empires as contrasting in time and place as the Mauryan Empire in India, the Roman Empire in the Mediterranean and the Arab Caliphate in the Middle East would have been substantially different.

34 Alexander of Macedon at the Battle of Gaugamela, depicted on the 'Alexander Mosaic', *c.* late 2nd century BC, originally from the House of the Faun in Pompeii.

4

Hellenism Transformed: Macedonian Invasion to Greek Kingdoms

Many years ago over some evening drinks, the following question was posed to a gathered group, myself among those present: who is the most famous person in all history? Leaving aside religious leaders such as Jesus or Muhammad – who perhaps belong to a different category than sheer fame – whose name has been a household word in most countries of the world for centuries? A lively discussion ensued with various names mentioned, until the answer became obvious: Alexander the Great (illus. 34). Especially obvious given the circumstances where the question was posed: the group in question were members of an archaeological team excavating the site of Kandahar in Afghanistan. Not only was this one of the supposed 'Alexandrias' founded in the wake of the great man's conquests, but looking for traces of his legacy was one of the reasons for the dig.[1] And as if to emphasize the point, three members of the team were named after him: there was a Scot called Alastair, an Italian called Sandro and the Afghan government representative was called Sikandarpur, the eastern Persian variation of the name.

Indeed, many are named after this superhero: from the Alexanders, Sandys and Alastairs of Scotland; to the Alexeis, Sandörs and Sandros of Europe; to the Iskandars, Sikandars and Sikandarpurs of Asia; not to mention the female Alexandras, Alexandrinas and Sandras. And not only boys and girls, but kings, emperors, popes and sultans have been named after this single great conqueror. Cities too: up to 48 'Alexandrias' were supposedly founded at the time. Of course, modern history is littered with its Fort Williams, Washingtons, Leningrads, Leninabads and Leninakens, not to mention its Bolivias and Saudi Arabias – even America itself is named after a person. But Alexander is still talked about today when Amerigo Vespucci is all but forgotten. There are Alexandrias in Australia, Canada and the United States, thousands of years after the original city's founding, and the rash of Alexandrias in Australia and Canada, the United States and other parts of the New World demonstrates the continued popularity of the name when Leningrad and its namesakes have faded into history.

When one looks more closely, however, much is illusory. Of the 'Alexandrias' supposedly founded by the Macedonian ruler, most on examination turn out, at best, to have been named long after he died; at worst, their origins are entirely fictitious.[2] Furthermore, nearly all were not new foundations at all, but renamings of cities that had existed long before. Searches for the reality behind the great man himself prove even more ephemeral despite the vast outpouring of books written (and still being written) about Alexander, for contemporary sources are all but non-existent: a temple inscription from Anatolia, a scrap of parchment from Bactria, little else (illus. 36). The so-called 'sources' for Alexander were written long after the events they recount, in most cases centuries later. This makes any reconstruction of the events surrounding his conquests highly interpretive, and there are now increasing revisionist readings of Alexander that question much of his reputation: one recent book is even entitled *Alexander the Great Failure*,[3] and one of the world's most prominent authorities on ancient Greek art and archaeology now writes of Alexander 'the Great' in inverted commas.[4]

But how is this relevant to Afghanistan? Nowhere has Alexander's great adventure excited Western imagination more than where it relates to Afghanistan, from Kipling's tale of Alexander's long-lost city to myths of descendants of his army still living there to this day. 'Looking for Alexander' has been behind much of the archaeological research in Afghanistan. Alexander's campaign in Afghanistan and the establishment of Greek kingdoms there are undoubted facts, but the actual cause and effect are not so obvious. The emergence of the undoubtedly Greek-influenced art, discussed in Chapter Seven, is even more complex.

Invasion by Alexander III, King of Macedon

If one were to slightly rephrase the question that opened this chapter to 'who was the greatest Greek of all', most would agree that it was Alexander. They would be wrong. For Alexander was not Greek: he was Macedonian. This might seem like splitting hairs, and Greeks for thousands of years have made Alexander their own. But the difference was fundamental, for the Greeks themselves

> regarded Macedonians in general as semi-savages, uncouth of speech and dialect, retrograde in their political institutions, negligible as fighters, and habitual oath-breakers, who dressed in their bear-pelts and were much given to deep and swinish potations, tempered with regular bouts of assassination and incest ... a loud, clamorous male world of rough, professional soldiers, who rode or drank or fought or fornicated with the same rude energy and enthusiasm.[5]

These differences were especially relevant to the foundation of Greek Bactria, as we shall see.

The Persian Empire was destroyed in the late fourth century when a king from the little-known northwestern frontier of the empire invaded. To the civilized lands of the Persian Empire the invasion of Alexander of Macedon was a barbarian invasion on a par with those that later overthrew the Roman Empire, and in Persian tradition Alexander is known as 'the Demon King'. It certainly brought about a Dark Age in Iran itself but, like the Germanic invasions of Europe, the Macedonian invasion also reinvigorated much of the peoples with whom the conquerors came into contact, resulting in several shifts of focus and reaffirmations of international connections. This was certainly so in Afghanistan. In the wake of Alexander's conquests Greek

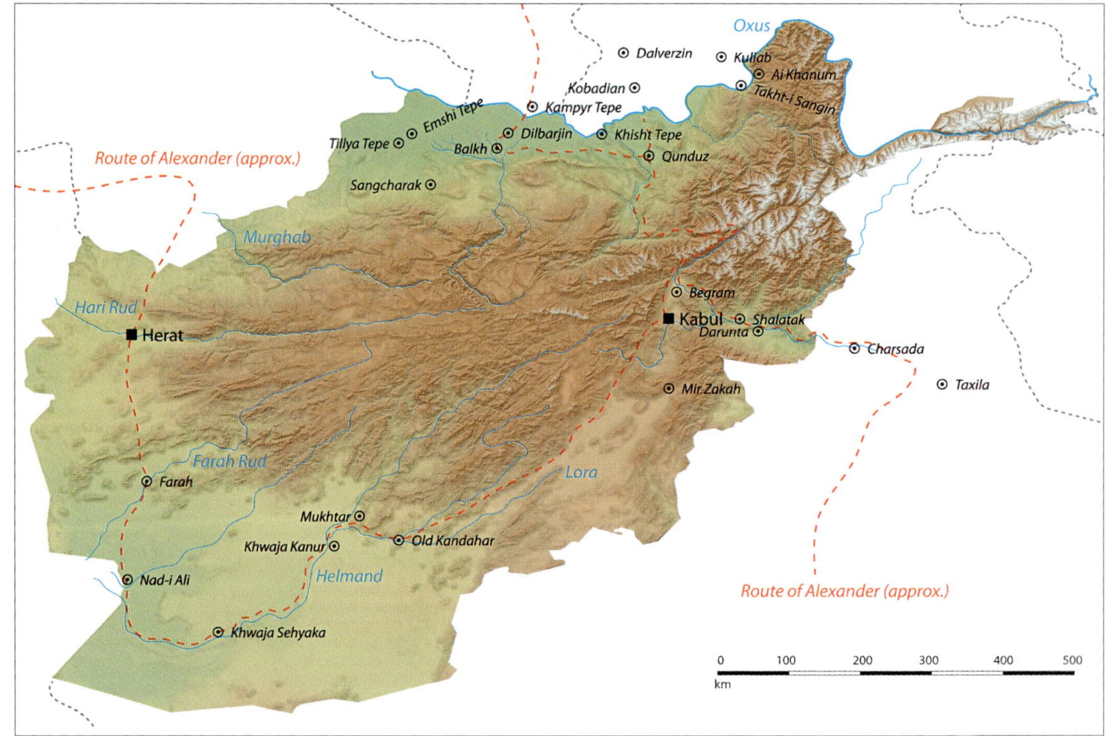

35 The route of Alexander through Afghanistan and the main sites mentioned in the text.

colonists established a new Hellenistic state in Bactria straddling the upper Oxus.

Alexander's conquest is deservedly one of the most famous military exploits in history. The bare outline can be summarized fairly quickly. Philip the Great, Alexander's father, had built up the Macedonian kingdom and its war machine. Following his death in 336 BC (in which Alexander was implicated), Alexander consolidated his hold on Macedon and Greece, wiping out one of Greek civilization's great centres, the city of Thebes, in the process. Then in 334 BC he crossed the Bosphorus into Asia to attack the Persian Empire. He first defeated the Persians at the Battle of Issus in Cilicia in 333 BC, then again more decisively at the Battle of Gaugamela in Mesopotamia two years later (illus. 34). In the lull between these two battles he marched down the Levantine coast in grand slaughter into Egypt, capturing the great Phoenician ports one by one. Tyre and Gaza were sacked, but Egypt fell without a blow. After Gaugamela, the rest of the Persian Empire lay open to him as he progressed through the royal capitals of Babylon, Susa, Persepolis (which he destroyed) and Hamadan, in pursuit of the Persian King of Kings Darius III, whom he finally caught up with on his death bed at Hecatompylos in northeastern Iran in 330 BC. However, the pursuit was not over with Darius' death: on the contrary, resistance began to harden. After a diversion into southern Afghanistan through Seistan and Kandahar, he turned north and crossed the Hindu Kush (illus. 35). Here, the rival pretenders to the Persian throne, at first Bessus and then Spitamenes, drew him deeper into Central Asia over the next two years. It was on this campaign that he married the legendary Roxana. Then, having completed his nuptials and mopping-up operations after Spitamenes' death, he returned across the Hindu Kush in 327 BC and entered the easternmost provinces of the Persian Empire in northwestern India (now Pakistan). The Indian campaign was a shambles. It involved a mutiny of his troops, the Macedonian army rampaging out of control and the near mortal wounding of Alexander himself. In the end it was his opponent, the Indian king Porus, who enlarged his kingdom, and Alexander was forced to make a disastrous retreat from India through the back door in 325 BC, returning to Persia across the deserts of Baluchistan, where his army, its leader and the legend almost perished.[6] Alexander then returned to the Persian royal capitals: Persepolis, Pasargadae, Susa (where he married the daughter of Darius III) and finally Babylon. Having not once stepped outside the borders of the Persian Empire – 'Not an inch of territory conquered by Alexander had not been held before him by the Achaemenians', as several authorities have emphasized[7] – it was here that he died on 10 June 323 BC, eleven years and two months after stepping foot on Asiatic soil for the first time. In the end it is perhaps Alexander's final words that ring truest, when he left his empire 'to the strongest' – ultimately, the words of a warlord, not of a wise ruler. His legacy was decades of more bloodshed as his successors fought over the spoils.

Alexander undoubtedly created a great empire but he destroyed an even greater one: Cyrus the Great's empire lasted nearly three hundred years, Alexander's a mere eleven (and that collapsed soon after he died). More important, Alexander's 'empire' was in any case a continuation of the Persian Empire under a new king: he merely conquered a functioning empire that Cyrus and his successors had created long before. The empire he inherited continued to be run on much the same lines: the old Persian system of provincial government – the satrapies – remained virtually unchanged; indeed, many of the governors themselves were simply reconfirmed in office (and in Anatolia several broke away and created 'neo-Persian' states). It was a similar situation with the road network, the administration and other institutions. After all, here was a great and ancient civilization, heir of the great Near Eastern empires that preceded it: the Babylonian, Assyrian and the Egyptian to the west, and the Iranian, Central Asian and Indian civilizations to the east. How could a backwater prince from Macedon – which even the Greeks regarded as barbaric – hope to match, let alone replace, all this?

There followed over twenty years of vicious civil warfare – twice as long as it took Alexander to conquer it all in the first place – while his generals fought each other for the spoils until the Battle of Ipsus in 301 BC. Out of it emerged four victors: Ptolemy, who took the jewel in the crown of Egypt; Seleucus, to whom fell the bulk of the empire in Asia stretching all the way to Bactria; Lysimachus, with Thrace and Asia Minor; and Cassander, with the original homeland in Macedon itself. In fact the Macedonian warlords and their successors continued at each others' throats until Rome arrived on the scene in the second and first centuries BC to knock heads together and eventually mop them up one by one. Alexander's son and wife were murdered and his empire – and what he had preserved of the Persian – was in tatters. But out of the tatters emerged new centres of Hellenism beyond Greece: Pergamon in Asia Minor, Alexandria in Egypt, Antioch in Syria – and Balkh in Afghanistan and ultimately even Taxila in Pakistan. It is the brilliant new civilization of the Graeco-Bactrian kingdom centred on

Balkh that mainly concerns us here. It combined elements of both Greek and Central Asian cultures which, with the addition of a further cultural strand from India, was to create the extraordinary eclectic civilization of Gandhara that would ultimately influence much of Asia for a thousand years and more after Alexander.

Resistance in Central Asia

At first sight, the conquests of Alexander and the emergence of Greek kingdoms in both Bactria and northwestern India with a rich Hellenistic culture seem to be a straightforward matter of cause and effect. But it was not so straightforward: as we have emphasized, Alexander was Macedonian, not Greek. The difference nowadays might appear both pedantic and irrelevant, so closely is Alexander identified with Greek civilization – indeed, he has become as great an icon for Greeks as Pericles or Homer are (witness the ongoing tug of war between Greece and Macedonia over his legacy). But at the time the difference was crucial, particularly when it came to the creation of Greek Bactria, as we shall see. For Alexander came as a destroyer of Greek culture, not its torch-bearer – indeed his tyranny and brutal autocracy that brooked no opposition were the very antithesis of the supposed ideals of Greek democracy and freedom. In Greece itself Alexander came as an outsider: the sheer savagery of his sack and destruction of Thebes, for example, shocked the Greeks. Not even the Persians had wreaked such devastation on Greek soil as Alexander did, and the Greeks both recognized and resented this. Alexander stood poised to wipe out Athens itself as well, and its citizens braced themselves for a holocaust. Alexander spared Athens, not through admiration of Greek culture, but simply because he was in a hurry to get on with his Asian campaign. The Athenians' horror at what had happened to Thebes convinced them in any case to surrender to Alexander (but not before the Athenian generals defected to the Persians).[8]

Indeed, it has become popular to present Alexander's campaign as a 'Greek crusade', but the figures for his army suggest the opposite.

Out of 43,000 infantry only 7,000 were Greek; out of 6,000 cavalry only 600 were Greek; of the 160 ships of his navy a mere 20 were supplied by Athens (which had over 300 at its disposal). The Persians had over six times more Greeks fighting on their side than Alexander did – and they remained loyal to Darius to the bitter end: 'the Greek exiles or their descendants, similar to the Greek mercenaries of Darius III, therefore stood firmly by the Great King's and his satraps' side'.[9] Even those few Greeks who did fight on Alexander's side were rarely used in battle, but were mainly for garrison and communication duty – and were released as soon as possible. Alexander had them chiefly as hostages rather than for real military value.

In other words, for much of Alexander's campaigns he was fighting Greeks as much as Persians: not only in Greece itself in his initial campaign, but sizeable Greek armies in the pay of the Persians, as well as experiencing frequent Greek revolts back home in his rear. Indeed, the death of Darius – Alexander's final victory over his Persian adversary – was marked not by rejoicing in Greece but by a major Greek uprising against Alexander led by Sparta. In the rash of new city foundations that sprang up all over the East in the wake of Alexander's conquest, it is notable that they are all either Macedonian dynastic names (Alexandria, Seleucia, Antioch, Ptolemais and so forth) or named after places in Macedon (Dium, Pella, Beroea), but there is not a single new city named after places in Greece. There would be new Pellas, but no new Athens, Thebes or Spartas.

This does not get us any closer to the explanation of how a Greek kingdom could emerge in Bactria – indeed, we seem to be further away from it than ever: if Alexander was so hostile to the Greeks, how could a Greek kingdom in Bactria be his legacy? And why Bactria? Why not Arachosia or Seistan or other parts of the Iranian world? To answer these questions, we must re-examine Alexander's campaigns in Bactria. Before his invasion of Bactria, Alexander's aims were limited to overthrowing Darius III, which he did in July 330 BC. With this, Alexander became ruler of the Persian Empire. But Darius, by the time Alexander caught up with him, was in the process of fleeing towards Bactria, the

36 Aramaic document from Balkh mentioning the provisioning of the resistance against Alexander's invasion.

original Iranian hinterland in Central Asia, where he could expect to find support. Alexander, therefore, could never be secure in his control of the empire while Bactria remained free. Indeed, it was in Central Asia that new commanders emerged to lead stiffened resistance against Alexander, at first under Bessus and then under Spitamenes, who were able to find firm support in the native Bactrians as well as in the remnants of the Persian army. Hence Alexander was drawn deeper into Central Asia between 330 and 327, despite his victory over Darius.[10]

A startling discovery has shed new light on Alexander's campaign in Bactria: a hoard of Achaemenid documents on leather and wooden strips, probably from Balkh, comprising some fifty texts, nearly all of them in official Achaemenid Aramaic, dated to between 353 and 324 BC. Five of them comprise official correspondence and administrative documents relating to Akhvamazda, the satrap of Bactria under Artaxerxes III (Darius III's successor), and Bagavant, the governor of Khulm (Tashkurghan) to the west of Balkh. These refer to the events surrounding Alexander's invasion of Bactria: one that mentions the regnal Year 1 of Bessus (under his regnal title of Artaxerxes) and another '15 Sivan of the Year 7' of Alexander, which equates to 8 June 324 BC (illus. 36). Most importantly, they relate to the provisioning of Bessus' army of resistance fighting Alexander's invasion, one of just a handful, if that, of contemporary documents for Alexander's reign.[11]

Alexander's first goal was the capital, ancient Bactris, modern Balkh, the key to control over Bactria. Before Alexander took it, however, an incident occurred that, while small enough in itself, sheds considerable light on the creation of Greek Bactria. On entering the great plains after crossing the Hindu Kush, Alexander's army encountered a town that was populated, to their astonishment, by Greek settlers: the 'Branchidae', Greeks from Asia Minor.[12] However, Alexander had the entire population slaughtered. There have been various later glosses put on this act, but in the present context it demonstrated two things. First, that Alexander was no torch-bearer for the Greeks. And second, that there were already Greek communities in Bactria *before* Alexander. Both of these facts we will have occasion to return to.

Bessus in the end was captured and executed, but with his death there emerged a new and formidable leader of the Central Asian resistance who was almost a match for Alexander. This was the brilliant guerrilla leader Spitamenes (who shared a family name with the prophet Zoroaster), whose tactics eventually forced Alexander to reappraise his entire Central Asian policy.[13] For the first time Alexander encountered serious resistance and even military defeat.[14] Alexander's advance to Maracanda (modern Samarkand) from Balkh provoked a general uprising of Bactria under Spitamenes. The ensuing fighting was a hard, vicious slog for the Macedonians: cities had to be systematically retaken one by one, and Alexander himself was wounded. Lightning guerrilla raids by Spitamenes had a devastating effect on the morale of the Macedonian soldiers, who could not hit back at forces which simply melted into the steppe. Denied military targets, the Macedonians carried out increasingly brutal reprisals against the rural inhabitants. In 329 BC an entire Macedonian division of Alexander's hitherto invincible army was annihilated in the Zarafshan Valley (near Samarkand) by Spitamenes. Alexander ordered a general massacre of the civilian population all along the Zarafshan Valley as a reprisal (120,000 slain, according to some sources),[15] but while his back was turned Spitamenes penetrated deep behind enemy lines and in a lightning raid scored a victory against the Macedonian garrison of Balkh itself, before retiring once more to the steppe. Members of Alexander's army were beginning to show their dissatisfaction: there were rumblings of mutiny; Alexander personally impaled Cleitus, one of his main lieutenants; and there is even a suggestion of an attempted suicide by Alexander himself. Clearly, the Central Asian campaign was not going well for Alexander, leaving him with little choice but to compromise.

Accordingly, he began to incorporate more Iranians and native Bactrians into his army, he increasingly adopted Persian ceremonies and customs in order to appear more acceptable to the Central Asians (to the horror of his Macedonian old guard), and he began to negotiate with local leaders rather than slaughter them. Even when the death of Spitamenes in 327 BC brought about an end to much of the resistance, Alexander realized that only through local support could he rule. In the end, Alexander cemented his new-found alliance with a dynastic marriage into a Bactrian aristocratic family, marrying the daughter of Oxyartes, one of his former opponents. Legend has embellished the Alexander–Roxana story into a romance, but there is little doubt that it was political expediency.

It was also in Bactria that, with the end of the resistance, the last remnants of the Persian grand army surrendered to Alexander. Here we have the seeds of Graeco-Bactria. Most of this army were, of course, Iranians, and many of these soldiers were incorporated into Alexander's own army. But included in the Persian army was a contingent of Greek 'mercenaries', which some estimates put as high as 23,000. While this figure might be an exaggeration, the number was nonetheless clearly large. The term 'mercenary' furthermore is technically incorrect, as the Persian Empire incorporated the Greek-speaking parts of Asia Minor, probably a greater population of Greeks than in Greece itself, so they would have formed as integral – and as loyal – a part of the Persian army as contingents from any other part of the empire would (hence the high number). Indeed, Greeks had a long tradition of fighting alongside Persians. A significant portion joined Xerxes in his invasion of Greece, for example, and the march of Xenophon's 10,000 Greek soldiers who fought on the side of Cyrus the Younger in a Persian civil war has become legendary. These 'Irano-Greek' soldiers presented Alexander with a quandary. He could hardly incorporate them into his own army: the long history of discord between Greek and Macedonian proved that he could not trust the former, not only for opposing him in Greece itself, but for raising the standard of revolt in his rear and fighting alongside the Persians in his front. He therefore settled them in the newly pacified territories in Bactria as garrisons, thus forming the kernel of what later became the Greek kingdom.

There is also the possibility that Bactria had absorbed some Greek cultural elements before Alexander. This controversial argument has been put forward by some as the only way to explain how thoroughly Greeks were able to put down roots in Bactria, and not in other parts of the Iranian east.[16] There are several ways in which this might have happened. One is the presence of Greek colonies settled there by the Persians – and the existence of major Greek populations within the Persian Empire (in western Anatolia) has already been noted. The massacre of a Greek community there by Alexander has also been emphasized, and the ancient sources refer to other communities throughout the Persian Empire, either political exiles or merely traders – and Greeks had long traditions as traders throughout the known world. Greek influence might also have arrived indirectly via the Scythians of Central Asia, who absorbed many cultural elements from the Greek colonies they came into contact with in the Black Sea region.[17] It is certainly notable that the main great Hellenistic centres that emerged after Alexander's conquests – Alexandria in Egypt, Antioch in Syria, Pergamon in Asia Minor – had had a Greek presence before: Naucratis on the Nile Delta, al-Beidha on the Syrian coast and the Ionian cities in Asia Minor. One might well expect some pre-existing presence in Bactria as well, which the Greeks in the Persian army would naturally be drawn to.

The Formation of a Greek Kingdom in Bactria

Alexander died in Babylon in 323 BC. News of his death was received with joy by the Greek garrisons in Bactria, sparking off a general revolt against the Macedonians (as, indeed, earlier rumours of his death while on campaign in India had). According to some sources all the rebels were butchered by the Macedonians, almost certainly an exaggeration, but it is nonetheless evidence of the deep mutual hatred between Macedonian and Greek. The region of Afghanistan then came under the new empire created by Seleucus, one of Alexander's generals. On the whole, Seleucus' rule was one of reconciliation and reassertion of stability. He reinstated Macedonian control over Bactria in 308 BC, enjoying good relations with the native Bactrians because of his marriage to Apama, the daughter of Spitamenes, the Bactrian leader who had so heroically resisted Alexander. This marriage was the only one to have survived the mass rape of captive Iranian women by Alexander's army in Susa, so was presumably a genuine match.[18] It is not difficult to detect Apama's hand behind Seleucus' relations with the Bactrians. Seleucus also had the wisdom to establish good relations with Chandragupta Maurya, the powerful new ruler of India who founded the Mauryan Empire. This relationship between Indian and Hellenic cultures was to have enormous repercussions for the subsequent development of art forms over much of Asia.

Accordingly, Bactria prospered. The initial core of Greek military colonizers was reinforced by new settlers arriving from the Hellenistic west, as well as by intermarriage with the local Bactrian population. Many of the new settlers – Greek, Macedonian, Iranian, Anatolian and Near Eastern – were doubtless refugees fleeing the interminable rounds of wars by the Macedonian successor states of the west, attracted to the stability of Bactria. Bactria in any case had a secure infrastructure ensuring its prosperity from long before: as we have observed, the region had major cities and sophisticated irrigation going back to the Bronze Age. The prosperity that attracted these new settlers, therefore, must be viewed in terms of both continuity from the Achaemenid period and good relations between incomers and the older Bactrian population. In the latter context it must be remembered that the Greeks (as opposed to the Macedonians) arrived not as conquerors and enemies, but as allies and friends of the Bactrians, so that the mutual dislike by conquered peoples for the Macedonians would have created a bond between Greek and Bactrian.

Relations between the Greek settlers of Bactria and their far-off Seleucid rulers in Antioch began to seriously deteriorate towards the middle of the third century BC during the rule of Antiochus III, who became involved in a series of increasingly costly wars with the rival Macedonian state of Ptolemaic Egypt. The distant but prosperous province of Bactria was an attractive source of revenue, and increased exactions were enforced to pay for Antiochus' wars. The consequent resentment by the Greeks once more erupted into open revolt against the Macedonians, but this time it was successful. The Greek governor of Bactria, Diodotus, declared his independence in about 256 BC and became king. Thus, out of the long record of discord, distrust and dislike of Alexander and his Macedonians by the Greeks, a new Greek kingdom in Bactria was born.[19]

Mauryan and Parthian Empires

The Greeks certainly added a new overlay to the existing cultures of Afghanistan. Yet another new cultural overlay was soon added from India. Not long after Alexander's conquest a new empire had emerged in India, founded in about 322 BC by Chandragupta Maurya. The capital was at Pataliputra (modern Patna) in northeastern India, and the empire soon extended northwestwards into eastern Afghanistan. Its greatest emperor, Ashoka, the grandson of Chandragupta, enthusiastically adopted Buddhism. This was the most important cultural element brought by the Mauryans to Afghanistan, through which Afghanistan was to have a dramatic effect on the world. The development of Buddhism in the Indian subcontinent after 500 BC, with its emphasis on proselytization and outwardness generally, will be examined in the next chapter.

For the moment, edicts proclaiming the Buddhist message were set up and missions were sent throughout the empire and well beyond to the countries of the Hellenistic West. Such diplomatic overtures to the Greeks in the West were reciprocated. Several missions by the Seleucid diplomat Megasthenes to the Mauryan court in Pataliputra, for example, are recorded. Speculation on Mauryan missionary activities in Greek-speaking communities received graphic confirmation in 1958 with the discovery of a bilingual Ashokan edict in Greek and Aramaic at Kandahar and another of the edicts, solely in Greek, in 1963. The Mauryan Empire declined soon after the death of Ashoka, but Buddhism had found fertile ground in the Hellenistic climate of the subsequent Graeco-Bactrian and Indo-Greek kingdoms, so that Ashoka's great reforms long outlasted him. Accordingly, Greek artistic forms soon fused with Indian philosophical ideas to produce one of Buddhism's major artistic expressions. Out of it, the art of Gandhara was born.

The next major power to emerge on the Afghan stage represented the last major movement of Iranian tribes from Central Asia: the Parthians. Like the Medes and Persians before them, the Parthians were initially little more than a tribal confederation in what is now Turkmenistan, until in about 238 BC they seized control of the trans-Caspian territories of the Seleucid Empire under the founder of their dynasty, Arsaces. Building up a power base in what is now Turkmenistan and ruling first from Nisa (near Ashkhabad), by the middle of the second century the Parthians had invaded Seleucid Iran. This culminated in Mithradates I becoming the ruler of a new Iranian empire in the old Persian capital, Babylon, in 141 BC. An Iranian renaissance was dawning. The Parthians soon re-established most of the old Persian Empire, restoring Iranian self-confidence after the humiliation it had received from the Macedonians, a revival that would later culminate in a Persian renaissance after the third century AD under the Sasanian dynasty. In the meantime, the Parthians expanded into western Afghanistan around Herat – the ancient satrapy of Aria – and into Seistan in the south and eastwards as far as Kandahar. Seistan became a major Parthian power base, where Parthian princes eventually outlasted the collapse of the main dynasty. Although the Parthians never expanded into Bactria, the effect upon the Greeks of Bactria was enormous: it cut them off from the Greeks of the west. Far from extinguishing Hellenism in Bactria it had the opposite effect: Bactria flowered into a new Hellenistic kingdom.

A Greek Kingdom in Bactria

The Graeco-Bactrian kingdom, together with its offshoot Greek kingdom in India, is one of the most extraordinary episodes in history. For it appears to have passed almost unnoticed by the Greeks further west. While we have copious written source material for the Seleucid and Ptolemaic kingdoms, no histories have survived of the Graeco-Bactrian and Indo-Greek kingdoms. The numismatist Frank L. Holt translates the entire Greek and Roman sources for the Bactrian kingdom in less than seven pages.[20] The few inscriptions that have been found – mostly at Ai Khanoum and Kandahar – do not add much more. Native texts in the Bactrian language are copious, but are mainly later, as are Chinese sources, which otherwise shed some light on the history of Afghanistan. Yet the effect of Greek Bactria was, if anything, greater than that of the Hellenistic kingdoms of the west, ultimately influencing subsequent cultural developments in South Asia and even China and the Far East. Furthermore, the difference between Greek Bactria and the other Hellenistic successor states of the west was that the core elements were *Greek* rather than Macedonian. This difference is often glossed over, but – particularly in Greek Bactria – it was important, indeed crucial. This distinction between 'Greek' and 'Macedonian' was actually spelt out by the first-century BC/AD geographer Strabo, on whom we rely for much of our history of the region. Strabo writes in the context of the Bactrian revolt against the Seleucids, 'the Greeks who caused Bactriana to revolt from the Syrian [that is, Macedonian] kings who succeeded Seleucus Nicator, say that when those [Greek] kings had grown in power they also attacked India . . . [and] those kings subdued more of India than the Macedonians [did].'[21] Strabo's perspective was an important one: he was a Greek native of Anatolia of part-Persian descent (his great-uncle, Moaphernes, was Persian) during the period of Roman rule.

To compensate for the lack of written sources, vast quantities of magnificent coins – the most splendid of the Hellenistic world – have survived, and so a significant proportion of the historical evidence for Graeco-Bactria and the ensuing period is numismatic.[22] Coins have provided satisfyingly detailed lists of kings with the over-strikes suggesting successions. However, the evidence only goes so far: the sheer quantities and glib nature of the coins have occasionally led to too much being pinned on them. Coins are by their very nature intrinsically valuable, so that their lifespan and circulation go far beyond the reigns and reach of the kings they depict. This limits the evidence of coin hoards in particular: nobody would take a Kushan coin hoard in Africa, to take an extreme example, as evidence of Kushan rule there,[23] but a similar coin hoard closer to home might not necessarily mean much more either. Movement of highly portable coins is not the same as movement of peoples or political power. Ancient coinage is further obfuscated by not being limited to single rulers or states: princes often issued their own coins concurrently with the king as well, creating uncertainty as to who ruled whom, where and when. Numismatics *are* an invaluable tool for the historian – and nowhere more so than Afghanistan – but their limitations must be recognized.

The history of Graeco-Bactria, such as it is, can therefore be told fairly quickly. It must be emphasized, however, that names, dates and successions are controversial and are constantly changing as new discoveries, new research and new arguments by numismatists emerge. Diodotus I founded the Greek kingdom of Bactria with its capital at Balkh. He was succeeded by his son, Diodotus II, but the kingdom was usurped by a Greek settler, Euthydemus, who instigated the rule of his own dynasty (and there might have been a king Antiochus between Diodotus I and Euthydemus). Euthydemus I (about 230–200 BC) consolidated and expanded the Graeco-Bactrian kingdom, extending as far as the Jaxartes (Syr Darya) River and perhaps beyond. He resisted the invasion of Antiochus III, who sought to reincorporate the breakaway province into the Seleucid Empire between 208 and 206 BC. When he died he left behind a kingdom that had been established on a secure footing: its independence had received recognition by the Seleucids, it had expanded and it prospered.

Euthydemus' son, Demetrius, crossed the Hindu Kush in the early second century BC and extended Graeco-Bactrian rule briefly into Arachosia, thus covering virtually all the area of eastern Afghanistan. He followed this up by invading northwestern India (although this might have been a second Demetrius – the numismatic evidence is unclear): an incipient Graeco-Bactrian empire seemed in the making. Several more kings of the Euthydemid dynasty ruled: there is numismatic evidence of a second Euthydemus, as well as kings named Agathacles, Pantaleon, Antimachus, Apollodotus and perhaps several more. The order is uncertain and the situation is confused by there being several kings of the same name as well as kings (issuing coins) ruling north and south of the Hindu Kush concurrently. Then, in one of the bouts of in-fighting that characterized the Graeco-Bactrian principalities, the Euthydemid dynasty was overthrown in about 170 by the greatest of the Graeco-Bactrian leaders, Eucratides, who established strong centralized rule on both sides of the Hindu Kush. The magnificent giant gold coin of Eucratides was the largest gold coin ever minted in the ancient world, weighing 169 grams (illus. 37).[24] Eucratides was killed at the height of his power in the mid-second century BC, after which the Bactrian kingdom began to split into separate parts, albeit still ruled by Greek princes. Their names are known from the coins, but their relationships – both dynastic and political – are uncertain, as there is practically no evidence outside numismatics. The date of Eucratides' death coincides approximately with the abandonment of Ai Khanoum (discussed below),

37 Giant gold coin of Eucratides, the Greek king of Bactria.

probably as a result of advancing nomads. The strongest power to emerge was a new, separate Greek kingdom in Pakistan and northwestern India, with its eventual capital at the ancient Persian and subsequent Mauryan provincial capital at Taxila in Gandhara (illus. 42). The last Greek king known to have ruled in the Kabul region was Hermaeus, who ruled between about 90 and 70 BC.

The subsequent Indo-Greek kingdom lasted longer. Its greatest king was Menander (*c.* 150–135 BC), who ruled a large kingdom covering much of Afghanistan south of the Hindu Kush and most of the area of modern Pakistan, and his campaigns penetrated deep into India. Menander was, furthermore, known to be favourably disposed towards Buddhism, and the *Milindapanha*, or 'Questions of Menander', a dialogue between King Menander and a Buddhist monk, survives as one of the most ancient sacred texts of Buddhism. Of all the Hellenistic successor states that sprang up after Alexander, it was the least known that survived the longest: the last Greek king in India, Strato II, still ruled from his capital at Sagala (modern Sialkot) in Panjab until about AD 10. It thus survived its parent kingdom of Graeco-Bactria by some eighty years and thus survived the best-known and longest-lasting Hellenistic kingdom in the west, Ptolemaic Egypt (which was absorbed into the Roman Empire following the death of Cleopatra in 30 BC), by some forty years.

The Buildings of Hellenistic Afghanistan

The inadequacy of historical sources, both native (Bactrian) and secondary (Classical and Chinese), and the problems of the numismatic sources leave us with only one other source: archaeology. The capital of the Graeco-Bactrian kingdom was the ancient Persian satrapal seat for Bactria, Balkh, which was also Alexander's military headquarters during his Central Asian campaign. Just how 'Greek' Balkh became remains uncertain, as a high water table has always prevented excavation down to lower layers. Balkh was in any case presumably a large and well-established city long before the arrival of the Greeks (indeed, the 'mother of all cities', according to later Islamic tradition), so 'Greek Balkh' would have been little more than a mere taking over of the upper echelons of administration and defence, rather than the founding and laying out of a whole new Greek city. Indeed, ever since disappointing initial soundings in the 1920s, the Hellenistic presence at the presumed capital of the Graeco-Bactrian kingdom has proved frustratingly elusive – appropriately dubbed a 'Bactrian mirage' by the first French archaeologists. However, its elusiveness was dramatically overturned by excavations in the early 2000s within the walls of Balkh, where fluted columns and Corinthian and Ionic capitals confirmed the existence of a temple whose Hellenistic credentials could not be in doubt. Reused masonry remains, similar to those at Ai Khanoum, suggests further Hellenistic-style monumental buildings awaiting discovery. The irrigation system in the Balkh oasis also reached its greatest extent in this period, with channels traced far into what is now desert to the north.[25]

Perhaps because Balkh was the satrapal capital of the former Achaemenids with a strong Bactrian character, an entirely new Greek city was founded fairly early in the Seleucid period to accommodate the new settlers. This was at the site of Ai Khanoum on the upper Oxus on a bluff overlooking its junctions with the Kokcha River (illus. 38, 39), a short distance downstream from a circular city of the Achaemenid period (illus. 33). It was laid out on a colossal scale surrounded by ramparts, with the main north–south thoroughfare 1.5 kilometres long (just under a mile) and settlement eventually spreading well beyond the ramparts. The layout conformed to standard Hellenistic town-planning principles with its grid system of streets and includes familiar Hellenistic monumental buildings: a palace, temples, a gymnasium, a theatre, an agora, a propylaeum, colonnades and other imports from the Hellenic world. Some fifty inscriptions in Greek were excavated, including one of a famous Delphic maxim copied from Delphi itself and brought to Ai Khanoum by Kineas – presumably a colonist – and set up in the sanctuary that he dedicated. However, the city also included important local elements, the beginnings of a syncretic style.

38 The site of Ai Khanoum from the citadel.

The gridded planned layout, for example, might just as easily be local – we have already observed how planned urban layouts began in the Iron Age – or imported from India, where the gridded plan developed in the Harappan Civilization a millennium earlier. The division into citadel and lower town might also be seen as a local influence, the classic Central Asian *ark* (citadel) and *shahristan* (lower town). While structural elements at Ai Khanoum were of stone – colonnades, door jambs, thresholds, lintels – the overall building material was in the local mud-brick. The main temple, the 'Temple of Indented Niches', resembled Iranian prototypes and not the pedimented and colonnaded temples of Greece, although the foot of a giant statue, possibly of Zeus, found inside was characteristically Greek. The palace at Ai Khanoum, while embellished with Corinthian colonnades (in fact among the earliest Corinthian capitals recorded in the Hellenistic world), in overall plan was closer to Achaemenid prototypes, with monumental portals opening into columned halls. With its predominant mud-brick construction and flat roofs the view from the acropolis would have resembled a Central Asian city, still familiar today, rather than an ancient Greek one.[26]

39 Statuette from the 'Temple of Indented Niches' at Ai Khanoum.

Ai Khanoum remains somewhat of an enigma. As an essentially 'Greek' city, despite local elements, it is unique in Afghanistan and is likely to remain so, despite initial hopes for Kandahar (discussed below) or other unexcavated urban sites. Indeed, there is nothing quite like it in the Hellenistic world. That it represents a city of Greek colonists is without doubt, but why lay it out on such a grandiose scale even before the independent kingdom of Graeco-Bactria was founded? The palatial complex was huge, probably larger than any other palace in the Hellenistic world (with the exception of Alexandria in Egypt), presumably a royal seat – although the capital was in Balkh. This was no mere settlement of army veterans; it was something special, attracting pilgrims all the way from Delphi, Greece's most sacred centre. Even its name remains unknown: Alexandria Oxiana or Eucratidea have been suggested, but without conclusive evidence (the modern name Ai Khanoum is the local Turkish name meaning 'Lady Moon'). Who filled the 6,000 seats in the theatre, and what did they watch? Who manned the vast extent of the city walls?[27] The sheer scale suggests the founding of a new capital in a foreign country by a colonial power: indeed, it bears some comparison to the British foundation of the new Imperial Delhi designed by Edwin Lutyens with Herbert Baker in the twentieth century. Like Ai Khanoum, the architecture of New Delhi is essentially that of the imperial power (British Neoclassical) but incorporating local elements; both Ai Khanoum and New Delhi were founded next to older cities: the Achaemenid circular city of Kuhna Qal'a nearby in the case of Ai Khanoum, Shahjahanabad and earlier cities in the case of New Delhi. The vast palace, built after the city's foundation, presumably by a local ruler (possibly Eucratides) to display both his ego and Hellenistic credentials, seems far beyond the needs of what is, after all, a provincial city, not a capital. This is reminiscent of the Roman emperor Septimius Severus' massive monumentalization of his home town of Leptis Magna in Libya, or the massive new temple in Jerusalem built by Herod to display the Judaic credentials that his family lacked. We will never know: Ai Khanoum has been almost completely destroyed by looters, another of the cultural casualties of, on the one hand, the total breakdown of law and order in Afghanistan and, on the other hand, the insatiable worldwide demand for collectable antiquities.

Evidence of major conflagrations at Ai Khanoum in about 130 BC and again in 90 BC points to the final destruction of the city by invaders, possibly the Scythians. But the unique blend of Western and Eastern elements found at the site continued to influence the subsequent cultures of Afghanistan for almost a millennium – and the illiterate newcomers adopted the Greek alphabet for the Bactrian language. Many elements of Greek architecture remained particularly tenacious: pilasters, column bases, the Corinthian order, entablatures, decorative elements, and others. Equally tenacious – if not more so – was the persistence of Greek sculptural and artistic forms. This is examined separately in Chapter Six. Until the discovery and excavation of Ai Khanoum in the 1960s and '70s, knowledge of this important formative period when the two cultures first became fused had been almost non-existent. It has to be said, however, that the Greek presence in Afghanistan remains intangible, despite Ai Khanoum, and no other Greek city has yet been found in Afghanistan despite historical references to other 'Alexandrias'. Most important, while the idea has long been dismissed that it was Alexander and his successors who brought the blessings of urbanism to Afghanistan, giving rise to Bactria's reputation as a 'land of a thousand cities', archaeology has conclusively demonstrated that the Hellenistic period was very much a part of a settlement continuum.

The evidence for Greek settlement elsewhere in Afghanistan, albeit elusive, is unsurprisingly mainly in Bactria. The best documented is the hinterland of Ai Khanoum itself, which has been intensively surveyed, where a dense pattern of settlements was recorded and the irrigations system, first built in the Bronze Age, was extended. These, however, almost certainly represent the work of pre-existing local populations rather than Greek settlement, although a large fort, Kafir Qal'a, seems to have been built in the Hellenistic period and so might represent Greek settlers.[28]

In the Balkh plain several important sites dating from the Hellenistic period have been excavated. The extensive urban site of Dilbarjin dates mainly later from the Kushan period, but earlier remains included a fragmentary painting of the Dioscuri, suggesting the existence of a Hellenistic temple dedicated to that cult. At Emshi Tepe a completely circular town founded in the Hellenistic period that continued until the fourth or fifth century AD was excavated, continuing a town-planning principle from the Achaemenid period that was to have a long duration in the Iranian world (illus. 40). A circular plan also characterized what appears to be a massive temple at Jiga Tepe nearby. Both Emshi Tepe and Jiga Tepe also produced Greek ostraca. Other sites are promising but have not been thoroughly investigated, such as the extensive urban site of Nimlik west of Balkh, where a sherd with a Greek inscription was found. Whether these sites can be evidence of actual Greek settlement is uncertain, but the evidence of the coins suggests the existence of semi-independent Greek princes as well as the kings ruling from Balkh, so such sites might represent their estates.[29]

Greek Bactria, of course, straddled the present border of Afghanistan with Uzbekistan and Tajikistan, where Hellenistic remains have also been found. Although it is not possible to summarize them here, mention must be made of Takht-i Sangin in Tajikistan, a major Hellenistic site near the Oxus. This is the site of the second-century BC Temple of the Oxus, built of mud-brick but with Ionic columns, altar and other elements in stone, a style similar to that of Ai Khanoum. It was dedicated to the Oxus river god, although the layout resembles later Zoroastrian fire temples. Pits associated with the temple contained over 5,000 dedicatory objects, many of them precious. This has led many to believe that Takht-i Sangin might be the find-spot of the Oxus Treasure (discussed in the previous chapter), although Takht-i Kuwad further south on an ancient crossing point of the Oxus is more favoured. A fortified Hellenistic settlement has also been excavated at Sakhsanokhur on the Afghan border, also in Tajikistan, which included stone architectural elements that may have been reused from Ai Khanoum 36 kilometres (22 mi.) to the southwest.[30]

Elsewhere in Afghanistan evidence of a Hellenistic presence – mainly coins and pottery – have been found at many sites, such as at the later Kushan capital, Begram (which might have been another 'Alexandria'), and the later still Turk dynastic centre, Bamiyan.[31] These do not necessarily add up to Greek principalities or even settlements, but more likely Greek influence on local populations in the Hellenistic period. Otherwise, the main candidate outside Ai Khanoum for a substantial Greek presence has been Kandahar, almost certainly identified with Alexandria Arachosia, even though it was only under Greek rule

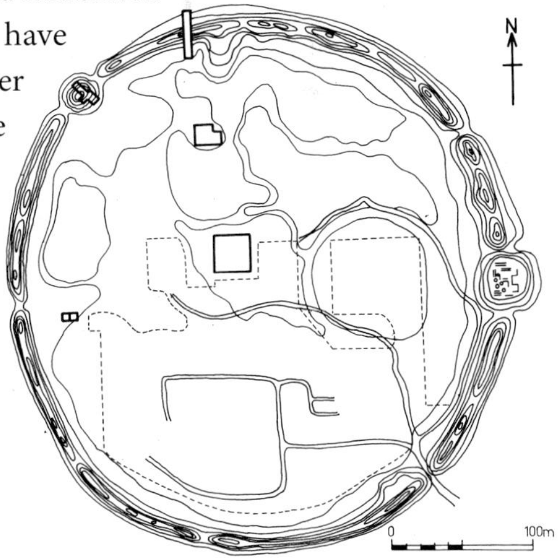

40 Plan of the circular Hellenistic city of Emshi Tepe on the Balkh plain.

very briefly before being ceded to the Mauryans. This was the first site in Afghanistan to produce important inscriptions in Greek. The first to be discovered, in 1958, was the bilingual Greek and Aramaic inscription of the third century BC giving the text of one of Emperor Ashoka's pious proclamations. The second was an inscription in Greek discovered in 1963, again proclaiming edicts of Ashoka, and another Ashokan edict inscription, this time only in Aramaic, was purchased in the Kandahar bazaar in the same year. In 1978 another Greek inscription excavated by British archaeologists referred to a certain 'son of Aristonax'. Another inscription appeared on the international antiquities market in the early 2000s that originally came from Kandahar commemorating in perfect literary Greek one Sophytos son of Naratos.[32]

Despite the promise held by the Greek inscriptions, the excavations at Kandahar proved elusive for the Hellenistic period. The Greek inscriptions have led to some overblown speculations of Greek communities and the Greek nature of Kandahar, with even agoras, gymnasia, theatres and other trappings of a Greek *polis* conjured up out of thin air. This should not blind one to the other elements revealed by the inscriptions, two of which were also in Aramaic, the administrative language of the former Persian Empire: the inscriptions equally therefore address surviving Iranian communities in Kandahar. Most of all, it must be remembered that three of the five inscriptions are edicts of the Indian emperor who ruled Kandahar at the time of the inscriptions – and even Sophytos and Naratos turn out, on analysis, to be not Greek names but Indian, the 'perfect' literary Greek of the inscription notwithstanding.[33] Aristonax at least is a Greek name, which *may* indicate the existence of a Greek-speaking trading minority. But despite important results of the excavations, Kandahar is no 'southern Ai Khanoum' (and the Aristonax inscription was from a redeposited context, not from any supposed Greek monument). Greek inscriptions admit no more than the existence of Greek as a lingua franca, in much the same way as bilingual signs in Persian and English in Afghanistan do today – and the evidence of the inscriptions in any case suggests a mainly Indian rather than Greek element.

Intriguing Hellenistic material has been found elsewhere in southern Afghanistan. At Mukhtar, northeast of Bust, a large Hellenistic temple on a high, stepped, artificial platform has been recorded (illus. 41). At Khwaja Kanur, a short distance from Mukhtar, is a site covered in fluted columns and balustrade fragments, together with fragments of a large terracotta frieze of Hellenized busts and acanthus leaves. No architectural remains were detected, however, despite it being surveyed three times, and it was suggested that the objects were redeposited from Mukhtar. Further down the Helmand at Khwaja Ali Sehyaka the remains of a Hellenistic temple with a colonnaded portico *in antis* and an inner sanctuary together with associated structures have been excavated. Objects recovered included Greek and Aramaic inscriptions and Classical architectural fragments such as column bases and acanthus leaves (implying Corinthian capitals). The Greek inscription includes the name 'Frahat', presumably a reference to Phraates, one of several Parthian kings of that name, and the fragmentary Aramaic texts include references to Zoroastrian Ahura Mazda and a temple. Dated to the period of Parthian rule in southern Afghanistan, this important sanctuary and its inscriptions still remains to be fully assessed.[34] It is significant that both Mukhtar and Sehyaka are isolated and not associated with urban remains, implying that they had important religious associations in their own right. Sehyaka in particular might have been a place of pilgrimage.

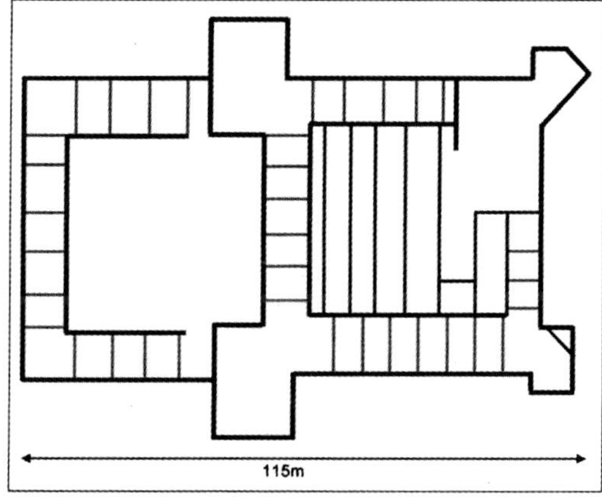

41 Sketch plan of the Hellenistic temple at Mukhtar.

Hellenistic remains in western Afghanistan remain extremely elusive, despite the long assumed identification of Herat with Alexandria Areia. Excavations in the early 2000s at Herat revealed evidence for Achaemenid settlement at Herat, but with nothing after the fifth century BC until the Sasanian period: of the Hellenistic city of Alexandria

Areia there is not a trace. This absence appears astonishing in view of the prominence attributed to Greek Areia in the literature.[35]

Although well outside the present borders of Afghanistan, the site of Taxila in Pakistan not far from Rawalpindi is also important for the Hellenistic period. Its origins lie in the legends of the epics *Ramayana* and *Mahabharata*, and the oldest part of this vast site (known as Hathial) dates from the Harappan period. That part of the site known as Bhir Mound was successively an Achaemenid and then a Mauryan provincial capital. In the late second century BC Taxila became capital of the Indo-Greek kingdom that expanded throughout Pakistan and northwestern India. A new city was founded at Taxila, known today as Sirkap, alongside Bhir Mound, consisting of a grid network of streets punctuated by a main central north–south thoroughfare, an acropolis in the southwestern corner, and the whole surrounded by walls

42 Ionic temple of Jandial at Taxila in Pakistan.

punctuated by four gates at the cardinal points. Just outside Sirkap is the temple at Jandial, whose architecture belongs to Greek prototypes, consisting of an outer peristyle surrounding a central *naos*, with two Ionic columns *in antis* (illus. 42). The temple is not, however, to any Greek deity, nor even to Buddha, but appears to be a fire temple, showing Zoroastrian influence. It has been fully excavated, as have large portions of the city of Sirkap. Most of the excavated structures, however, date from the Indo-Parthians and Kushans after the first century AD, although Taxila and other centres still retained many Hellenistic cultural elements.[36]

A Question of Identity

The frequently cited rumours of descendants of Alexander still living in remote areas of the Hindu Kush were examined in Chapter One and dismissed as, at best, wishful thinking, at worst entirely fictional. Fictional descendants aside, just how 'Greek' was Afghanistan in the Hellenistic period? Even in Bactria it would be a mistake to overstate the Hellenic character of the Graeco-Bactrian kingdom – indeed, its Hellenism never matched the other Hellenistic centres such as Pergamon or Ptolemaic Alexandria, both of which became centres of Greek learning that outstripped Athens, Bactria's Greek (as opposed to Macedonian) credentials notwithstanding. It was always a mixed population with a mixed culture, gradually becoming more localized as time wore on and isolation from the main centres of Hellenism in the west became more pronounced. Many citizens, it is true, made a point of clinging to their Hellenism: Delphic maxims were imported all the way from Greece and lovingly set up in their public places, Greek was the language of inscriptions, buildings were embellished in the Corinthian and Ionic orders, people went to Greek theatres to listen to Greek drama (doubtless in an accent that would have made an Athenian cringe). But behind their Hellenism one senses a desperation, almost pathetically so, born of an anxiety to not be confused with 'those barbarians'. One is reminded of the words of the modern Alexandrian

Greek poet C. P. Cavafy, of a man who 'assumed a Greek name, dressed like the Greeks,/ learned to behave more or less like a Greek;/ and all the time he was terrified he'd spoil/ his reasonably good image/ by coming out with barbaric howlers in Greek'.[37]

For the citizens, isolated thousands of miles from the Greek homelands, Hellenism was a way of underlining their difference from their local neighbours. Even though the population would have become ethnically mixed through intermarriage, Hellenism, however thinly it hung, was a statement: we are still 'us', not 'them'. (One is reminded of the Anglo-Indian community under the British Raj.) But by being so underlined, it took root and lasted a thousand years after the collapse of this extraordinary kingdom. While the facts of its history remain obscure, the evidence of its legacy holds its own.

The Western fixation with Alexander and perceived 'Greekness' concerned investigators almost obsessively, to such an extent that Greek presences were conjured up on little evidence (non-existent 'agoras' at Kandahar, for example) and much of the archaeological work in Afghanistan was dominated by 'looking for Alexander' – or at least for Greeks. It is true that with the discovery of Greek inscriptions at Kandahar and Ai Khanoum Greeks were at last 'found'. But there is a tendency to load far too much on inscriptions away from their original linguistic homeland. The classicist Rachel Mairs writes, 'When is a Corinthian column in the Hellenistic Far East a sign of Greek identity, and when is it simply something that supports a roof?'[38] No one knows. The majority of the population would have remained indigenous throughout. The Romans left their linguistic trace in a vast swathe right across Europe, from the Danube to the Atlantic; the Greeks in the Hellenistic Far East left hardly a word in later languages of the region.[39] The question of identity in Hellenistic Afghanistan therefore is easily answered: all evidence suggests that it was overwhelmingly local, whatever that might have been in ethnic or linguistic terms. Like the use of English throughout the world today, the use of a particular foreign language carries a certain cachet, a language of fashion, of internationalism. Perhaps the greatest legacy of Alexander's momentous passage through Afghanistan in the fourth century BC was not so much the Hellenization of Central Asia, but the huge stimulus it has given to archaeological research there in the twentieth and twenty-first centuries AD.

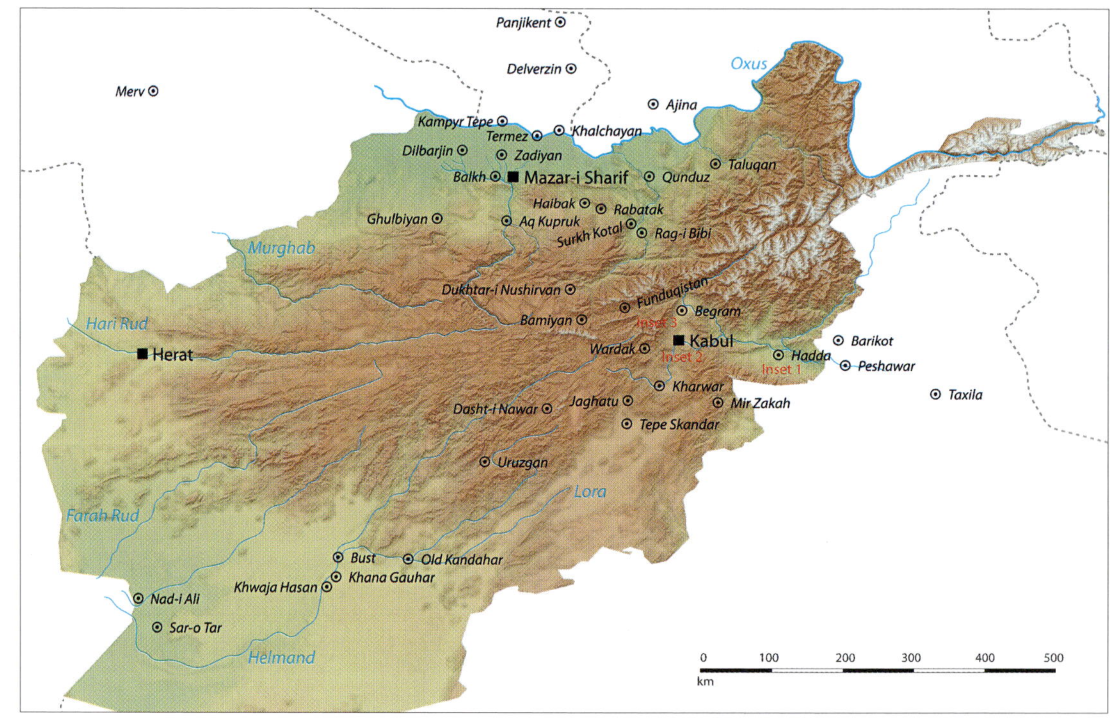

43 The main Parthian and Kushan sites.

5

A Forgotten Empire: From Hunted Nomad Chiefs to Kushan Emperors

In the first few centuries AD, almost all the Eurasian continent was dominated by just four great powers: the Roman Empire; the Parthian Empire; the Han Empire of China; and the Kushan Empire in Afghanistan, Central Asia and India. Much has been written about the first three empires: histories of the Roman Empire alone would fill a library (think of Edward Gibbon). But of histories of the Kushan Empire, there is practically nothing – indeed, few have even heard of it.[1] There is, of course, a vast corpus of specialist studies scattered across academic journals and libraries, but nothing really accessible for the non-specialist. The reasons for this lack are complex. In discussing the problems of writing Kushan history, the historian John M. Rosenfield wrote,

> Writing Kuṣāṇa [Kushan] history is like reconstructing a giant mosaic. Scholars have pieced together parts of the outer frame and a few internal configurations, but whole areas are still empty, and many fragments are abraded and ambiguous in meaning. Much progress has been made, but the inherent difficulties in the field are truly daunting. Evidence from one discipline often seems to contradict or conflict with that from another, and . . . lively debates abound . . . The occasional discovery of new evidence sometimes speeds up the process of reconstruction, but substantial gains in Kuṣāṇa studies have often been the result of small, incremental steps.[2]

The archaeologist Henri-Paul Francfort notes further that

> the Kushan empire is divided between indologists, iranologists, hellenists, sinologists, even turcologists, etc., in short, divided by the academic disciplines as they exist since the 18th century, dominated by linguistics, philology and history. Moreover, the lack of sources (few texts and not much of epigraphy) make things difficult for numismatists and archaeologists.[3]

Of course, the Kushans are included in many books covering broader subjects such as numismatics and the arts, and in more general discussions (such as this one), as well as in specialist excavation reports of particular archaeological sites (notably Surkh Kotal, discussed below). But the legacy of the Kushan Empire in terms of subsequent cultural events was as great as that of the other empires – and its story even more extraordinary, from a group of tribal refugees hounded out of China to eventually founding a great empire. This was when the territory of Afghanistan first truly became the centre of events that affected much of Asia. While the Roman, Persian and Chinese empires are common knowledge, few other than specialists have even heard of the Kushan Empire: truly the 'forgotten empire'.[4]

The end of the Graeco-Bactrian kingdom was brought about by a series of 'invasions' by nomad groups from the steppe. But, like the 'barbarian invasions' that were to bring about the end of the Roman Empire in the West, the Graeco-Bactrian kingdom might already have been in a state of terminal decline and infighting. The nomads simply added nails to the coffin, with the 'invasions' described more accurately as movements that were not always necessarily aggressive. Be that as it may, during the last few centuries BC a series of disruptions on the Eurasian steppe resulted in large-scale displacement and mass movement of different peoples – the classic 'knock-on' effect of the Eurasian steppe where one group would displace another – culminating in what one scholar described as 'an avalanche in Transoxiana [Bactria]'.[5] These events, pieced together from often contradictory sources, are very confusing. The names of the different peoples involved are even more so, exacerbated by many of the same peoples being known under different names in different sources. It involves apparently unrelated and often conflicting events as far off as China in one direction and Ukraine in the other. But the reader is asked to bear with us: these shadowy events lie behind a series of movements that brought about an end of the Greek kingdoms in Afghanistan to fundamentally change it once more, culminating in perhaps the greatest civilization that took place on Afghan soil – and a great empire was the result.

But first a note of caution. One must guard against the terms 'hordes', 'invasions', 'waves' – and certainly 'avalanches' – often used to describe such steppe movements.[6] Such terms give a false impression of violent and sudden movements that were as often as not gradual, usually taking place over several generations, with assimilation and accommodation on the way, even though the end result might be long-term change. It is rare that a single definable culture or people emerges on the steppe, despite the tribal and national names that litter the pages of history; such names were usually just that of a prominent group that incorporated many other groups.

The Steppe Background

From the end of the second century BC right through the first millennium AD, Afghanistan was frequently affected and disrupted by movements of nomadic groups from the steppe, most of them familiar from Western sources: Scythians, Huns and Turks. There was also a little-known group known in Chinese sources as far back as the seventh century BC as the *Da Yuezhi*, a group of horse-riding nomads on the northwestern borderlands of China in Gansu.[7] It is this latter, less familiar, group that concerns us here. In order to understand how and why these came about it is worth summarizing the steppe background.

The steppe is a belt of temperate-climate grasslands between 400 and 700 kilometres (250 and 435 mi.) wide that stretches from Hungary to eastern Siberia. The environment has severe limitations for both stockbreeding and pastoralism. However, occasional fertile years can result in a sudden increase in animals which, by the following years when conditions revert to normal, can with equal suddenness simply not be supported by the steppe. There is consequent overpopulation and hence urgent need for more pasture – and hence outward movement, often with cataclysmic results. Whenever this cycle was upset the balance between different nomad groups would be disrupted. One group would be forced beyond its traditional pasture lands into conflict with the next. This in turn would disrupt the next group, occasionally resulting in the weaker group being absorbed and large-scale steppe confederations coming into being. Either way it would set in motion a chain reaction throughout the steppe. Such a 'billiard ball' or 'domino' effect is often dismissed by historians and anthropologists, but the pattern did occur. The original cause would usually be unknown, but the effects would be felt right across the Eurasian land mass, sometimes generations after the event that prompted it. The spark that initially ignites a movement might be a drying-up of pastures, a change in climate, overpopulation, a war by a neighbouring tribe or a political event far removed from the event that sets it in motion; the causes are many, there can even be none, and they are usually unknown. Nomadic ('barbaric' in the sources) invasions of Europe, Russia, Iran, India and China at different times have often been the result of this pattern.

Throughout history, nomad societies have paradoxically often been militarily superior to the more sophisticated – and supposedly more powerful – sedentary nations, even great empires with their massive standing armies. Russia, China, Persia, parts of India, Rome, all at different times have been overthrown – or at least threatened – by ostensibly less developed nomadic groups. This apparent paradox is perfectly plausible. In steppe society, 'military'-style training is a part of the everyday lifestyle from birth. Children – girls as well as boys – learn to ride as soon as they walk, simply because it is essential to their lifestyle. The extremely harsh life of the steppe into which the nomad is born automatically makes them resilient. It is a life both in a camp and of forced marches, often through adverse conditions and extremes of weather. Resilience is inherent to the nomadic lifestyle.

This kept the nomads' moveable effects to a minimum, so they could travel light and rapidly: the extraordinary mobility of nomad armies was as natural for them as their way of life. This was reinforced by the animal that underpinned the steppe economy: the tough steppe pony, capable of travelling greater distances than other breeds of horse and of enduring greater extremes. Indeed, animals were a major factor in the military success of the steppe nomad, both directly as a means of transport and indirectly as source of food. The predominantly meat diet of the steppe nomad did give them one great advantage over their sedentary opponents: they carried all their food with them. It was on the hoof, either the horses they rode or the flocks and herds they drove. Less carnivorous armies were more dependent upon cereals for their diet; hence vast cumbersome logistics were required simply to supply the quantities of grain to feed an army on the march, not to mention the need to demobilize and return from campaign to gather in the harvest.

Animals played another major factor in steppe prowess, for the natural activity of the steppe nomad was hunting. Hunting is the nearest activity to warfare. It involves the use of the bow and accurate shooting, often at full gallop, and a hunt would involve all members of a tribe, including women. All nomads, in other words, were 'soldiers' and precision organization and manoeuvring were everyday matters. Furthermore, the very lifestyle of the nomad was dependent upon strong charismatic leaders – 'captains' – in whom the members of the tribe could trust implicitly. This was simply the only way that the tribe could operate and survive. Without boundaries and fixed establishments, such as those that a sedentary state would have, nomadic societies had to place far more emphasis on social structure, cohesion and strictly enforced chains of command, hence their generally greater military prowess. It was a ready-made army of which most commanders of more conventional forces could only dream. Furthermore, since women had to lead exactly the same lifestyle, sharing with the men the skills necessary for survival, the women could be soldiers too. Sexual inequality and seclusion of women would not only have been unthinkable on the steppe; they would have been impossible for practical purposes.

The Scythians

In the early first millennium BC the Eurasian steppe is broadly designated 'Scythian', characterized by similar styles of arms, horse harnesses and the 'animal style' of art that was common to steppe culture from Hungary through to Siberia and the northern zone of China. It would be a mistake, however, to consider these peoples and their culture 'Scythian' in too great an ethnic sense – and most certainly not an 'empire' or indeed any single unit, as some recently have characterized them.[8] To some extent, the name 'Scythian' was a general blanket term used by the sources to refer to all of the nomadic groups on the Eurasian steppes; it may have included Sarmatians, Huns and other similar nomadic groups, and ultimately would end up almost as ethnically meaningless an appellation as 'Hun', 'Frank', 'African' or 'Indian'. As well as in the Classical sources, the Scythians appear in Assyrian and biblical sources as the *Ashkenaz*, in Iranian and Indian sources as the *Saka*, in Arabic as the *Saqlab* and in Chinese as the *Sai*. The Scythian language was Iranian-related. The last few centuries BC witnessed several main movements of Scythian groups into Afghanistan.

Various Scythian groups were well known to the Achaemenids (as the Saka) in the sixth and fifth centuries, when they are depicted on the Persepolis reliefs (illus. 44). Their first movement into Afghanistan has been linked to the end of the Graeco-Bactrian kingdom in the second century BC. However, the Saka had been present in the Bactrian population as far back as the Achaemenids and presumably continued to form a significant but integral part of the Graeco-Bactrian state. The overthrow of the Graeco-Bactrian kingdom therefore was not as simple as was previously believed. It has even been suggested that the fall of the Graeco-Bactrian kingdom was caused by rival Graeco-Bactrian

44 Scythians depicted on the Persepolis reliefs.

elements in alliance with the Saka,[9] with the Saka invasions a result of the decline rather than its cause, a final death blow to a kingdom already in decay. Saka weapons in any case were included in the Ai Khanoum arsenal, and a Greek document refers to the payment of a hundred silver drachms to hire forty Scythian mercenaries during the reign of Antimachus.[10] Such details suggest that the Scythians had long lived alongside the Greeks in Bactria. Whether or not invasion was involved, the site of Ai Khanoum was probably abandoned some time in the latter half of the second century BC.[11] It is not known what became of these Saka: they may have been absorbed into the local population, or they might have joined further Saka migrations southwards (reviewed below). But it created a vacuum in Bactria, soon to be filled by other tribes from the steppe.

Another Scythian group settled in the southern oasis towns of Xinjiang in the second century BC, identified with the Sai of Chinese sources and the Saka of Persian sources. These Sai/Saka founded an important group of city states south of the Taklamakan Desert over the following five centuries or so, at times semi-independent and at other times coming under the sway of neighbouring kingdoms. Groups of Saka from Xinjiang migrated through the Karakoram mountain passes of northern Pakistan into the northwestern Indian subcontinent, probably in the late second century BC. By the first century BC they had founded another kingdom based at Taxila, not far from Rawalpindi, that covered much of eastern Afghanistan and northern Pakistan. Much of the evidence is numismatic, particularly from the vast hoards of coins discovered at Mir Zakah in eastern Afghanistan, as well as the occasional mention in Indian sources. Its first king, from about 75 BC, known from his coinage as Maues, was ruling when there were still Greek princes present (albeit in pockets). As mentioned earlier, the last Indo-Greek 'king', Strato II, died in about AD 10 at Sagala, by which time a new Scythian dynasty had been founded by Azes. The line of Azes and other kings of the same or similar name (such as Azilises) in the dynasty ruled much of northern Pakistan and eastern Afghanistan. This branch of the Scythians was probably descended from those who entered via the Karakoram passes.

This Scythian kingdom probably only lasted until about AD 30 with the death of the last king, Azes II, although there are many imitations of the coins of Azes II until the end of the century. But they left their mark in place names in the region, such as Sajawand or Sakawand in eastern Afghanistan near Gardez. Significantly, this is near Mir Zakah, the site of the greatest coin hoard ever found anywhere in the world, first of some 11,000 coins in 1947 and then an astonishing further two tons of coins in the 1990s. A significant portion of these are Saka.[12] They have also left a linguistic mark on the Wakhi language, the language spoken today by a small minority found mainly in the Wakhan corridor high up in the Pamir mountains of northeastern Afghanistan, as well as in neighbouring districts in Tajikistan, China and Pakistan. Since these were the passes through which the Saka presumably entered northwestern India, the Wakhis are probably a remnant Scythian group and their communities the only places now in the world where this once widely spoken language has survived.[13]

The northern Scythian kingdom is distinct from the Scythians of southern Afghanistan and the lower Indus, and the two are often confused. The southern kingdom was probably the end result of yet another Scythian group moving out of Central Asia who may have been more nomadic, so less likely to issue coinage. This group moved into southwestern Afghanistan sometime in the second century BC, probably taking advantage of a weakening of Parthian rule in the area. They settled in the Iran–Afghan borderlands known as Seistan, deriving from *Sakastan*, 'Land of the Saka' in Persian. From Seistan the Saka conquered much of southern Afghanistan. The fortress city of Kandahar, one of the few places where a Saka presence has been identified archaeologically, might have formed a base for further Saka incursions into South Asia in the first century BC. There they formed a kingdom in the region of Sind in the southern Indus, known in Hellenistic sources as 'Indo-Scythia' and in Indian sources as *Saka-dvipa*, 'Land of the Scythians' in Sanskrit. Indo-Scythia lasted into the first century AD, although the chronology is very imprecise. They became patrons of Buddhism, leaving their mark on a number of Buddhist monastery complexes in the region. They may also have left their mark in the characteristic Saka Central Asian style of dress, consisting of baggy trousers and long shirt, still worn in Afghanistan and Pakistan today (illus. 13, 14). Both northern and southern Saka kingdoms were probably absorbed by a subsequent state that ruled in northwestern India that scholars have labelled the Indo-Parthian kingdom (of which more below).[14]

From China to Bactria

The next movement of nomads into Afghanistan was a result of events far off in China. In the last few centuries BC the Han Chinese empire had expanded towards Central Asia. This was to evict a particularly warlike nomadic nation known as the *Xiongnu* (*Hsiung-nu*), usually identified with the Huns, from the northern borders of China (explored in the next chapter). Chinese efforts to evict the Xiongnu also resulted in the long-term displacement of many other tribal groups and was to have a knock-on effect all over the Eurasian continent. The Xiongnu founded a huge nomadic empire in northern Central Asia under the formidable warrior king Maodun after about 200 BC, expanding westwards into Gansu, where they came into conflict with a group of tribes known in the Chinese sources as the *Da Yuezhi*. The Yuezhi probably spoke an Indo-European language and have been identified by most authorities with the Tocharoi or Tocharians of Classical Greek sources. There were further conflicts between the Yuezhi and the Xiongnu when the Yuezhi king himself was killed (Maodun made his skull into a cup), forcing the Yuezhi to flee Gansu in the second century BC to the area around the Ili River (in present-day eastern Kazakhstan). It was here that they collided with the Scythians. Their arrival dislodged the latter, deflecting them southwest towards Bactria and thus bringing about the end of the Graeco-Bactrian kingdom, as we have seen. That kingdom's collapse created a power vacuum in Bactria, drawing in Yuezhi tribes in the wake of the Scythians.[15]

At this point the Classical sources take up the story, giving confused accounts of different tribes coming into Bactria in the late second and early first centuries BC: *Tocharoi*, *Asii*, *Sacaraucae*, *Iaitoi* and others, who were fleeing the Xiongnu/Huns. The situation was similar to the different tribes – Alans, Goths, Vandals and others – who poured into the Roman Empire in late antiquity with, again, the Huns in pursuit. Equating these tribes with names in the Chinese sources on the one hand and Greek and Indian on the other has been notoriously difficult, and there is still no consensus on the details of these population movements.

With the departure of the Scythians to southwestern Afghanistan, the way was open for the Yuezhi to enter Bactria. Whether these Yuezhi invaders were the same people as those who spoke the ancient Indo-European language in Xinjiang that has been labelled 'Tocharian' by philologists remains confusing: the language has been recorded in the northwestern oases of Xinjiang, but the Yuezhi were from further east in Gansu.[16] The Tocharian name survives in the name of the region of Tukharistan – the name for eastern Bactria in the medieval Muslim sources – which became the modern province of Takhar in northeastern Afghanistan. The Yuezhi were a confederation of five tribes, the most powerful of whom were known in the Chinese sources as the *Guishuang*, better known from Indian sources as the Kushans.

The second and first centuries BC therefore saw a number of nomadic groups enter Afghanistan from several directions: Scythians in Bactria, another Scythian group in Seistan and southern Afghanistan, yet another Scythian group in eastern Afghanistan, and finally the Yuezhi/Kushans in Bactria. It is a confusing period of different peoples at different times in different parts of Afghanistan, with overlaps of both times and places. Often described as 'invasions', they might well have been more gradual migrations, as they did not extinguish Hellenistic culture in Afghanistan – far from it. For by this time the culture of the Greek colonists had taken root, fusing with the native Bactrian and Indian cultures to form a stronger, eclectic new culture. The nomad incursions reinvigorated the sedentary peoples they encountered. Having little sedentary cultural traditions of their own, they adopted and encouraged the Graeco-Bactrian and Indo-Greek culture of the lands they entered.

The Kushan Empire

At first, the Kushan presence would have been little more than groups of Yuezhi and other nomads or semi-nomads, ruled by their respective chiefs, both society and lifestyle differing little from the years of wandering ever since they were first evicted from Gansu. Their movements into northern Bactria and subsequently across the Oxus into Afghanistan might not even have been grand invasions, but largely peaceful nomadic migrations into the political vacuum created by earlier tribal movements and the collapse of the central rule of the Graeco-Bactrian state. Indeed, the collapse might even have invited invasion, rather than been caused by it.

But it was in Afghanistan that the wanderings of the Yuezhi people finally came to an end. Here, from the mid-first century AD, the Kushans formed a great empire.[17] The leader of the Kushan tribe who united the four other Yuezhi tribes and first entered Bactria in the latter half of the first century AD was Kujula Kadphises, generally regarded as the first of the Kushan kings. Under him and his son,

45 The greatest extent of the Kushan Empire by the mid-2nd century AD.

Wema (or Vima) Takto, the Kushans conquered eastern Afghanistan and extended the empire into Pakistan and northwestern India. They adopted the local Bactrian language and adapted the Greek alphabet to write it, which then became the language of the empire. The Bactrian language was also written in Kharoshthi, an Indian script based on Sanskrit ultimately derived from the Aramaic script, but these were mainly in Buddhist religious contexts. The language of the Kushan rulers themselves, however, was not used on coins or official inscriptions. They adopted the local Bactrian language (which belongs to an eastern Iranian group) but their own language might have been an obscure related branch, known only from a few inscriptions, that has just recently been identified.[18]

Vima Takto was succeeded by Vima Kadphises, but the greatest Kushan emperor was Kanishka (illus. 46), the son of Vima Kadphises.

Under Kanishka the Kushan Empire became a great power covering northwestern India, Pakistan, most of Afghanistan and much of Central Asia (illus. 45). It was ruled initially from Balkh and subsequently from Peshawar (ancient Purushapura), but Begram in Afghanistan was expanded and rapidly became a major centre.[19] After centuries of being harried through Asia by enemies, the wanderings of the Yuezhi refugees from Gansu seems finally, at this point, to have come to an end and reached spectacular fruition.[20]

Unlike other empires of antiquity – notably Rome and China – the Kushans left very little history of themselves behind. The little we have is derived from coins, reliquary texts and monumental inscriptions at the dynastic centres of Surkh Kotal and Rabatak in Afghanistan, as well as several more in Tajikistan, Uzbekistan, Pakistan and India (a Bactrian inscription has even been found as far away as the island of Socotra off the coast of Yemen).[21] Despite this, there has been confusion over the relationships and sequence of the Kushan emperors, and even more over their dates. In particular, the date for the accession of Kanishka was for many years one of the most disputed chronological minefields of Afghan studies, with dates as divergent as AD 78 and 278 being proposed, along with several in between – this would be akin to not knowing the date of Augustus' accession within a two-hundred-year range. However, the consensus now favours a date of AD 127/8. Following the discovery of the Rabatak inscription in the 1990s, which identified the 'Nameless King' – for years a red herring – with Wema Takto, it is now known that the first four emperors until Kanishka were a clear father-to-son succession line. After Kanishka, however, the picture is less certain, and has been based on the different interpretations of coins and inscriptions.

46 Statue of Kanishka from Surkh Kotal, today in the National Museum of Afghanistan.

However, following extensive (mainly numismatic) studies, our understanding is now improved and can be summed up in the table opposite (illus. 47), although disagreements among specialists still occur.[22]

From the outset, Kushan civilization was eclectic, combining many different cultures, as befitted their years of wandering. Their imperial titles, for example, combined the Chinese 'Son of Heaven', the Iranian 'King of Kings' and even the Roman 'Caesar'. Although it marks a new era in Afghanistan, there was considerable continuity from the previous period. The Greek script was used for the native Bactrian language, which suggests that Greek settlers still remained in the region – indeed, one of the monumental inscriptions at Kanishka's dynastic sanctuary at Surkh Kotal was signed by a Greek, Palamedes. This suggests that the Kushan 'invasion' was probably more a peaceful takeover and merger with the existing population rather than a violent displacement. Its eclecticism is reflected even more in Kushan religion. At the time of their invasion the main religion in Central Asia was probably Zoroastrianism (or at least a form of it), but this was by no means the only one. During the Graeco-Bactrian kingdom the Greek pantheon was worshipped, and under the Kushans many of the Greek gods were transformed by being assimilated to local deities. Heracles, for example, was particularly popular through assimilation with Verethragna, an Iranian deity, as well as a Bactrian deity, Oesho (illus. 48, top). Zeus became identified with Ahura Mazda (illus. 48, bottom), Apollo with Iranian Mazda or Indian Surya, and Artemis with Nana or Anahita, an Iranian water goddess. A popular cult in Bactria was that of the river god Vakhshu (from which the name Oxus derives, as well as some of its tributaries, such as the Vaksh, the Varakhsha and possibly the Kokcha, as well as the region of Wakhan).

The Kushans also adopted Indian religions. The cult of Shiva seems to have been established even before the Kushans extended their rule into India. The Indian goddess Hairiti also became widespread. Such Indian cults are hardly surprising: Indian influence in Afghanistan is known from as early as the second millennium BC (the Harappan colony of Shortughai, for example) and was reinforced by the Mauryan

BC/AD	Bactria	Begram/ Kabul	Gandhara	Taxila
AD 10	Da Yuezhi	Indo-Scythians	Indo-Scythian	Indo-Scythians
20			Indo-Parthian	
30			Gondophares	Satraps
40	Kushans	Kushans		
50	Kujula Kadphises			
60			Abdagases	Kushans
70				
80			Sasan	
90	Wima Takto			Indo-Parthians
100			Kushans	Kushans
110	Wima Kadphises			
120	Kanishka I			
130				
140				
150	Huvishka			
160				
170				
180				
190	Vasudeva I			
200				
210				
220				
230	Kushanshahs	Kanishka II		
240	?Ardashir	Vasishka		
250	Peroz I			
260		Kushanshahs	disputed by Kushans and Kushanshahs	Kanishka III/VD II
270	Hormizd I			Vasudeva II
280				
290				
300	Hormizd II			Mahi
310	Peroz II			Shaka
320	Varahran			
330	Kidarite Huns			Kipunadha
340	Kirada/ Peroz/ Kidara	Sasanian	Kidarite Huns	Kidarite Huns
350		Shapur II		
360				
370				
380		Ardashir II/ Shapur III		

47 The approximate framework for rulers of Gandhara and adjacent regions.

conquest in the third century BC; there is still a Hindu minority in Afghanistan today. But by far the biggest import from India was Buddhism, which, from its transformation in Afghanistan, became not only a major religion of a major empire, but eventually a world religion that remains prevalent and popular today. This is discussed more below.

In depicting so many deities on their coinage, the Kushan emperors displayed religious tolerance – or at least disinterest – but also attempted to forge a syncretic official pantheon. This official syncretism was given concrete monumental form in a series of dynastic cult centres at Khalchayan in Uzbekistan, Mathura in India and – most spectacularly – Surkh Kotal in Afghanistan (discussed below). The official religious syncretism that these coins and cult centres expressed is perhaps the greatest single achievement of Kushan civilization.

48 Paintings of the Kushan deities Oesho (*top*) and Ahura Mazda (*bottom*) on terracotta votive panels, *c*. 3rd century AD.

The period also saw an upsurge in prosperity, international connections and stability generally. Under the resulting 'Pax Kushanica' the eclectic Hellenistic civilization of Central Asia was given powerful political expression. Chinese painting fused with Hellenistic and Iranian styles to form the characteristic Central Asian painting, which eventually resurfaced, after the fragmentation of the Mongols, in Persian painting. There was an expansion of existing cities and the creation of new ones. There was a great increase in irrigation – a tradition going back to the Bronze Age in Afghanistan, as we have seen – which created agricultural wealth. The Kushan economy was one of only three gold-based currencies in the world at the time (the others being the Roman and the Ethiopian). Such stability and wealth encouraged trade on an international scale. Works of art from all over the known world – the Mediterranean, India and China – flowed into the Kushan Empire and such works have been discovered at Begram (discussed below). Kushan gold flowed out to pay for such luxuries: Kushan gold coin hoards have been found as far away as Ethiopia.[23]

The end of the Kushan Empire was brought about by a resurgent Persia under its vigorous new dynasty of Sasanian kings in the third century. In a series of campaigns by its founder emperor, Ardashir, and his great conqueror son, Shapur, the Sasanians extended their rule deep into Afghanistan, Central Asia and the borderlands of India. Shapur's spectacular conquests were celebrated in the victory relief of Rag-i Bibi that was symbolically carved into the rock near the Kushans' own dynastic centre, Surkh Kotal (illus. 49). However, the Sasanian conquest changed very little: it was neither the disruptive conquest of steppe conquerors such as the Mongols, nor the reinvigorating conquest of peoples such as the Kushans or Arabs. The Sasanian conquest was more one of continuity.[24] The Kushan dynasty survived, albeit as vassals of the Sasanians until about AD 350 (and Kushan princes continued to reign independently in India beyond Sasanian rule). Thereafter the region was governed on Sasanian behalf by rulers known as the *Kushanshahs* or Kushano-Sasanians. Otherwise, there appears to be no break in the archaeological record in Afghanistan, so the Sasanian conquest should be viewed as a continuation of Kushan civilization, albeit less international in scale. Buddhist monastery complexes continued to be built and embellished with the same Gandharan sculptural styles that characterized the Kushan period. Indeed, there even seems to be an increase in building activity and artistic productivity in some Buddhist centres, such as Hadda in eastern Afghanistan.

49 Sasanian relief at Rag-i Bibi.

Before we examine such building activity and artistic productivity, it is necessary to look at another power that ruled much of southern Afghanistan and for a time overlapped with the rule of the Kushans: the Indo-Parthians. For this we must retrace our steps a little to the vacuum left behind by the Scythian tribes in Seistan.

The Indo-Parthians

The Indo-Parthians, who displaced the Scythians, are similarly elusive, even though they ruled over a wide area of the Indo-Iranian borderlands in the first two centuries AD. The Indo-Parthians were originally a branch of Parthians who had settled in Seistan. In the wake of the Scythian migrations eastwards to India in the later first century BC, these Seistani Parthian families, probably under the leadership of an aristocratic Parthian family known in Iranian tradition as the Surens, seized power and extended their rule over most of southern Afghanistan. The legendary Iranian hero Rustam may have been a member of this family. Seistan was the homeland of Rustam, one of the great heroes of the epic *Shahnameh* or *Book of Kings* compiled by Firdausi in the eleventh century. The 'Rustam cycle' in the *Shahnameh* (part of which was popularized in English by Matthew Arnold's epic poem *Sohrab and Rustum*) is generally recognized to be Seistani in origin (although whether it is Parthian or Scythian is disputed). The Suren family survived the overthrow of the main Parthian dynasty of Iran by the Sasanian dynasty in the third century as autonomous princes in Seistan.[25]

One Indo-Parthian prince, Gondophares – his connection to the Surens, if any, is not known – followed the Scythian invasion route into India in the first century AD and established himself on the upper Indus, displacing the Scythian Azes dynasty ruling at Taxila. Gondophares' dynasty became known in Indian sources as the Pallavas. Gondophares is known in biblical tradition as the object of St Thomas' apocryphal journey to India. Other Indo-Parthian kings are known mainly from their coins. The line of Indo-Parthian kings in Taxila came to an end with the conquest by the Kushans in the mid-first century AD, although Indo-Parthians continued to rule over southern Afghanistan for the first two centuries AD.

While we know little of their political history, the Indo-Parthian period was an expansive one. Large numbers of settlements have been recorded in southern Afghanistan extending from Seistan in the southwest and along the Helmand River to Kandahar (which remained a key site for this period). This suggests a dense population – probably denser than today, at least in Seistan – and a high level of prosperity. Many were substantial fortifications, mainly along the Helmand (although exact dating remains uncertain).[26] Substantial cities are also recorded at Kandahar and at Nad-i Ali and (probably) Shahr-i Ghulghula in Seistan (which later became the capital of the Saffarid dynasty in the Islamic period).[27]

The period also sees diverse religious monuments in southern Afghanistan, indicating a mixed population. The Hellenistic-style

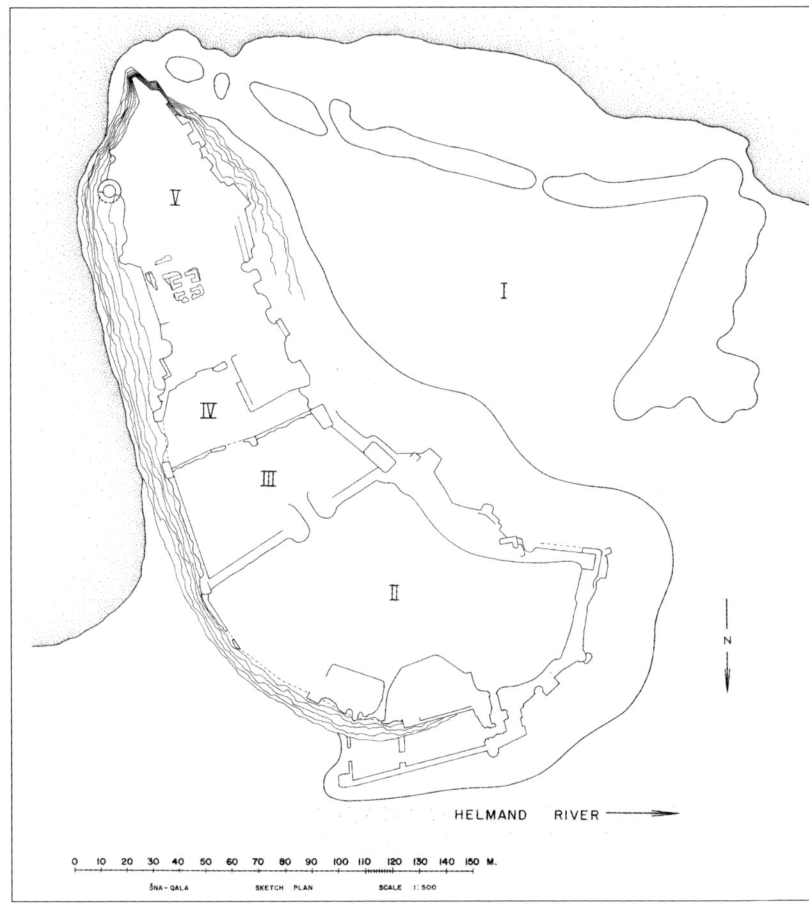

50 Plan of the Parthian fire temple complex at Sna Qal'a.

temples of Khwaja Kanur and Khwaja Ali Sehyaka (discussed in the last chapter) date from this period, the latter with possible Zoroastrian associations. Added to this are a number of fire temples (presumed to be Zoroastrian) in Seistan that have only recently been published. At Sna Qal'a on the right bank of the lower Helmand is a large and substantial fire temple complex of the Parthian and Sasanian periods on top of a hill approached by a series of terraced and walled platforms cut out of the hill (illus. 50).[28] This recalls the near contemporary Kushan dynastic centre of Surkh Kotal, discussed below, in the Hindu Kush to the north as well as the huge Parthian fire temple complex of

Kuh-i Khwaja just across the border in Iranian Seistan to the east, so would appear to be a major Zoroastrian centre, presumably a pilgrimage destination. Some scholars locate Zoroaster's homeland in Seistan (although this is not now widely accepted).[29] Several more fire temples in the Sar-o Tar area of Seistan were also founded in the Parthian period.[30] These have obvious implications for the history of Zoroastrianism, and add substantially to the increasing number of such temples now recorded in the eastern Iranian–Afghan–Central Asian borderlands (formerly found mainly in western Iran). More intriguingly, two Buddhist monuments have been recorded on the Helmand (although dates are uncertain): an excavated Buddhist stupa and associated artificial caves at Khana Gauhar near Lashkargah and another stupa further down the Helmand at Khwaja Hasan.[31]

The Expansion of Buddhism

We think of Buddhism today primarily as a religion of the Far East. Originating in the northeast of India on the borders of Nepal in the sixth or fifth century BC, it is found today mainly in China, Japan and Southeast Asia – ostensibly a straightforward spread from its origins in northeastern India to where it is currently practised. But it is important to emphasize that Buddhism's first outward drive was towards the *west*, not the east, where it only arrived by spreading westwards first. In the development and dissemination of Buddhism in antiquity to become the major religion that it is today, the position of Afghanistan was crucial – indeed, it is probably true to say that Buddhism would not have become what it is now if it had not flourished in Afghanistan first.

Buddhism remained little more than a local cult until it received its first major stimulus in the third century BC when it was adopted by the Mauryan Emperor Ashoka. The empire had been established by Ashoka's grandfather, Chandragupta Maurya, but under Ashoka virtually all of the Indian subcontinent was brought under his control. Ashoka was an enthusiastic supporter of Buddhism and summoned a general Buddhist Council at Pataliputra (modern Patna), usually regarded as the Third Buddhist Council, where it was decided that missionaries should be sent out to all the known world. Accordingly, edicts proclaiming the Buddhist message were set up (three of which were at Kandahar), and missionaries went forth throughout the empire and beyond. The former Achaemenid satrapal capital in the northwest, Taxila, where Ashoka had been posted as his father's representative, became a major Buddhist centre and Buddhism was presumably established in Afghanistan at this time (although the first Buddhist monuments are dated to the first century AD).

It next received a major political stimulus under the Kushans. Kanishka (or it may have been Kanishka II, who was a supporter of Buddhism) emulated Emperor Ashoka several centuries previously and convened the Fourth Buddhist Council in Kashmir. From this, Buddhism diverged into two main schools of thought, Mahayana and Hinayana, the 'Greater and the Lesser Vehicles'. Although not a 'state religion' in the modern sense, Buddhism thus became a major religion of a major empire and there was consequently an explosion of Buddhist building throughout the Kushan Empire, extending into Central Asia. With the persistence of Greek styles of sculpture and the arrival of new Roman forms borrowed from the Mediterranean, this transformed style of Indian Buddhist art spread eastwards through Kushan trade routes in its new Kushano-Hellenistic guise, ultimately to influence China, Japan and Southeast Asia.

Although there were earlier Buddhist centres in India, it was in Afghanistan during the first millennium AD therefore that Buddhist civilization reached its peak. It was here in Afghanistan that the great Chinese pilgrim Xuanzang came in the seventh century in search of spiritual truth (recounted in his *Journey to the West*) and major chapters in the development of Buddhism were played out. This was during the last – and probably the greatest – upsurge in Buddhism in Afghanistan under the Western Turk Empire, which lasted well into the Islamic period, as late as the ninth or even the eleventh century by some reckoning (see Chapter Seven). The fact that Buddhism is today viewed largely an 'Eastern' religion, therefore, is due more to historical circumstances than to its initial place of origin.

In emphasizing that the initial outward expansion of Buddhism was towards the west, not the east, we might ask if it ever spread further westwards from Afghanistan? One of Ashoka's edicts even claims specific Hellenistic kingdoms in the eastern Mediterranean that were converted to Buddhism: Seleucid Syria, Ptolemaic Egypt, Macedon, Cyrene in North Africa and Epirus on the Adriatic. Of course, we know from Western sources that these well-documented Hellenistic kingdoms did not become Buddhist. But speculation on Mauryan missionary activities in Greek-speaking communities received graphic confirmation in 1958 with the discovery of the Ashokan Buddhist edict proclaiming the Buddhist message in the Greek language at Kandahar in Afghanistan. Buddhism then continued at Kandahar into Islamic times. The third-century AD inscription of the Zoroastrian high priest of the Sasanian Empire, Kartir, carved in stone near Persepolis, actually refers to Buddhists in the empire at the time, while the great eleventh-century Central Asian polymath al-Biruni wrote, 'In former times, Khurasan [northeastern Iran and Central Asia], Persia, Iraq, Mosul, and the country up to the frontier of Syria, was Buddhist.'[32] A series of artificial cave complexes along the Persian Gulf of Iran, together with some historical evidence, has led to speculation that these might have been Buddhist.[33] The two Buddhist monuments on the Helmand discussed above are the westernmost Buddhist monuments so far discovered in Afghanistan. Their occurrence on one of the main ancient communication routes into Iran adds considerably to the question of whether Buddhism spread further west in antiquity. Although fairly modest Buddhist remains compared to the spectacular monuments of Hadda or Bamiyan, these Helmand stupas add an important chapter to the major position played by Afghanistan in the development of one of the world's great religions.

Treasures and Monuments of the Kushan Empire

The Kushan period saw what was probably the greatest building upsurge in Afghanistan's history, leaving behind a bewildering number of monuments, cities, dynastic enclaves and even entire sacred landscapes. But before describing this it is necessary to discuss what was probably the most spectacular discovery of gold artefacts in the world of the latter half of the twentieth century, which, it has been suggested, was associated with the arrival of the Yuezhi in Afghanistan. This was the discoveries at Tillya (or strictly speaking Tilla) Tepe near Balkh in 1978 of six undisturbed burials of five females and one male adorned with some 20,000 gold objects: bracelets, bowls, clasps, buttons, weapons, statuary jewellery and other objects.[34] The richness and nature of the burials suggest a king or chief and his consorts (illus. 51). After 2004 the Tillya Tepe treasure formed the main focus of a worldwide touring exhibition.[35] The objects represent a mixture of Indian, Central Asian, Iranian and Hellenistic styles, as well as local Bactrian, dated to the later first century AD. Some of the gold objects at least were of local manufacture; some appeared Greek, and may even have been imports from the Mediterranean; others were of Chinese manufacture, such as mirrors – indeed, the placing of mirrors over the chests of three of the female burials follows Chinese practice in keeping with the origin of the Yuezhi in Gansu. Of particular interest were many that reflect the 'Scythian' art of the steppes, the so-called 'animal style'. The eclectic nature, together with similarities to some of the art of the steppes, led the excavators to associate the burials with an elite group of the Yuezhi tribes (perhaps even the Guishuang tribe, who eventually became the Kushan rulers). However, the Scythian 'animal style' of art did not continue in Afghanistan, where older artistic imports from India and the Mediterranean resurfaced.

The first Kushan administrative centres were Balkh and then Begram, north of Kabul. Subsequently the capital was moved to Peshawar (ancient Purushapura) and Taxila in Pakistan and eventually to Mathura in India – a reflection, perhaps, of the original nomadic

51 Gold pendant of the so-called 'dragon king' from Tillya Tepe.

52 Tepe Rustam at Balkh, site of the stupa of Nau Bahar.

nature of the Kushans (illus. 45)? Limited excavations at Balkh show virtually continuous occupation from the Iron Age, but the huge overburden of later material (combined with a high water table) has made it difficult for archaeologists to recover earlier remains, or to ascertain how much of it was Kushan.

To the south of the city walls are two large mounds, Tepe Rustam and Takht-i Rustam, representing the remains of the major Buddhist stupa and its associated monastery of Nau Bahar (illus. 52). Nau Bahar, derived from the Sanskrit *nawa vihara* meaning 'new [Buddhist] monastery', was the most famous Buddhist institution of Central Asia, and its origins probably lie in the Kushan period (although this has not been tested by excavation). The monastery was administered by a caste of hereditary Buddhist high priests whose family, the Barmakids, after conversion to Islam, later became important viziers and governors for the Abbasid Caliphate in Baghdad in the eighth and ninth centuries.[36] According to a recent study this Buddhist monastery complex with its hereditary high priests formed the core of a 'sacred landscape' combining Buddhist, biblical and Iranian mythical traditions that continued well into the Islamic period.[37] This is an astonishing survival of Afghanistan's Buddhist past, but is not the only instance of the continuity of sacred landscapes in Afghanistan, as we will see. In a history so often characterized by violent disruptions, that of Balkh speaks powerfully that it can equally be characterized by continuity and memories of its past.

Investigations by French archaeologists in the 2000s, as well as older surveys by Soviet archaeologists in the 1970s, have documented Kushan fortifications in the Balkh oasis on a truly gigantic scale, indeed among the most extensive in the ancient world. These investigations, enhanced by satellite imagery, have revealed a vast early Kushan military camp near Zadiyan, northeast of Balkh. It measures over 16 square kilometres (6 sq. mi.) surrounded by ramparts preserved up to 7 metres (23 ft) high in places (illus. 54). In the exact centre of the enclosure is the large square citadel mound measuring approximately 200 square metres (2,150 sq. ft) with walls standing up to 12 metres (39 ft) high surrounded by a ditch.[38]

53 Outer wall of the Kushan military camp at Zadiyan.

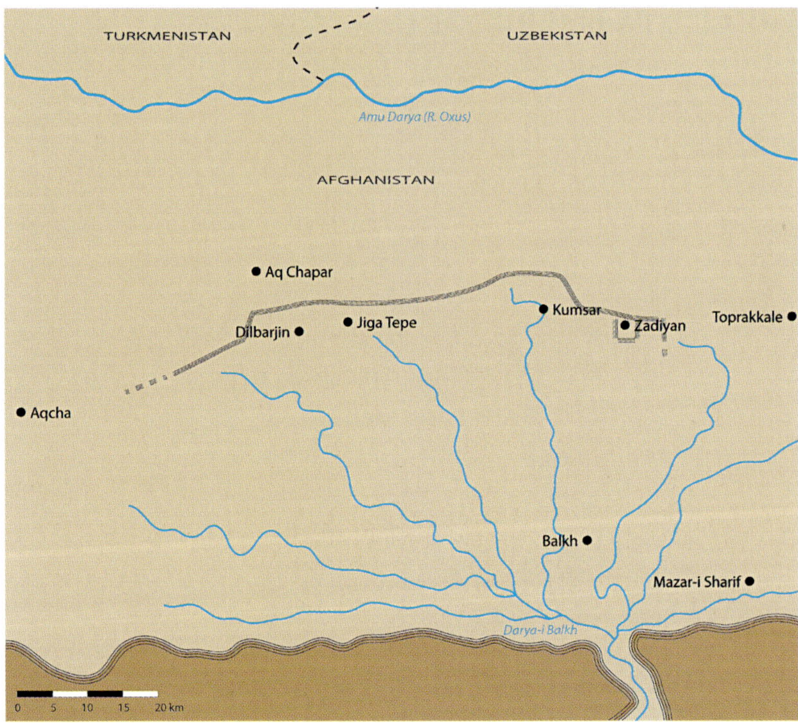

54 The Balkh oasis wall.

A structure linked to the Zadiyan enclosure and recorded by archaeologists was a long fortification wall up to 3 metres (10 ft) high stretching for more than 60 kilometres (37 mi.) from a few kilometres to the east of Zadiyan right across the northern edge of the Balkh oasis to just short of Aqcha (illus. 54, 55). The eastern and western limits of the wall have not been determined, so the total length would have been longer. Radiocarbon tests showed a date between AD 134 and 334.[39] Although much work still remains to be done on this very intriguing complex of 'great wall' and military camp, it is one of the most important – and certainly the largest – work of Kushan architecture. Following the absorption of Bactria into the Sasanian Empire in the fourth century, the Zadiyan complex might well have been the inspiration for a similarly massive military complex in Iran: the Gorgan Wall, a 200-kilometre (124 mi.) wall, along which was lined and associated forts and military camps, stretching across northeastern Iran east of the Caspian Sea and constructed to defend against the Huns.[40]

The eastern Bactria survey of the 1970s has further recorded large numbers of settlements, many substantial, often fortified and often in continuous occupation from older periods. Notable is another vast fortified enclosure at Qal'a-i Zal further east measuring 1,800 by 900 metres (5,905 by 2,950 ft), a scale comparable to that of Zadiyan.[41] This and many of the other fortifications recorded in Bactria seem to belong to a broader and older tradition of massive fortifications recorded elsewhere in Central Asia where entire oases would be walled. The extensive irrigation system from earlier periods was also maintained.

Balkh's Graeco-Bactrian and Kushan past still remains elusive, but far more has been discovered at the site of the other Kushan capital, Begram, just south of the Hindu Kush on the plain north of Kabul. It has been identified with the site of Alexandria ad Caucasum of the Classical sources, becoming the city known as Kapisa in the Kushan period. It is a large urban site consisting of a fortified area made up of

55 Distant view of the Balkh oasis wall.

56, 57 Indian ivories from Begram.

two walled enclosures: the Burj-i Abdullah to the north and the 'new royal city' to the south, where most of the excavations have taken place. There is, in addition, a third, purely urban, area to the south of that. In the nineteenth century, Begram was a favourite collecting ground for many travellers, with bronzes, seals, sculptures and other works of art, in addition to vast numbers of coins, being found.[42]

Between 1937 and 1942 French archaeologists uncovered parts of the bazaar, the fortifications, the entrance and the palace. It is most famous for just two rooms in the palace which contained an astonishing treasure that comprised an eclectic collection of works of art from all over Asia. It included stuccoes and bronzes, as well as ivories from India (illus. 56, 57), lacquers from China and among the most impressive collections of Roman glassware that have ever been discovered (illus. 58, 59). The treasure has been interpreted variously, mainly as either a private royal collection by the Kushan kings for aesthetic purposes – an ancient 'museum' – or as tax in kind of the luxury goods that were traded through Begram, with the rooms in which they were found some sort of bonded warehouse. As the equally spectacular Tillya Tepe treasures demonstrated, the Kushan princes certainly had a taste for art treasures (if indeed the Tillya Tepe treasures were early Kushan). The objects range over a long period, making any date for their deposition difficult. Most opinion favours deposition in the mid-third century AD.

58 Roman glass from Begram.

Four kilometres (2½ mi.) north of Begram is the small Kushan Buddhist monastery complex of Shotorak, which consisted of some seven or eight stupas.[43] The main stupa was surrounded by a cloistered courtyard and decorated in schist sculptures and reliefs, many of them major works of Gandharan art (illus. 60), and large numbers of clay stupa models. It has been suggested that Shotorak may have been the site of a Chinese community. In addition, many more stupa-monastery complexes were built in the Kuh-i Daman plain surrounding Begram, usually in the foothills, evidence of flourishing Buddhist communities during the first few centuries AD.

59 Roman glass from Begram.

There can be no doubts about the sacred nature of the landscape surrounding Jalalabad on the main road eastwards out of Afghanistan towards the Khyber Pass (illus. 61). This comprises an extensive area of stupas, monasteries and artificial cave complexes stretching over an area of nearly 20 kilometres (12 mi.) that reached its height under the Kushans (although many were founded in the Scythian period immediately prior). The main site of Hadda is one of the more significant Buddhist sites – and sources of Buddhist art – in the Gandhara region and is probably the site of ancient Nagarahara, one of the most important Buddhist religious and pilgrimage centres in Asia (the name survives as the modern province of Ningahar).[44] In the centre of the Jalalabad plain at Dasht-i Bagram is an extensive area of low mounds that may be the ancient city of Nagarahara, though it remains unexcavated. Adjacent is the very large stupa of Nagara Ghundi some 30 metres (98 ft) in diameter that

60 Schist relief from Shotorak.

might be identified with the Nagarahara stupa described by Xuanzang in the seventh century. Nearly all of the sites are stupa-monastery complexes, usually located in the foothills to the west and south of Jalalabad. A surprising number of the dedicatees on the reliquary inscriptions had Hindu names rather than Buddhist. Hadda itself produced an immense artistic wealth of clay and stucco sculpture (illus. 85, 86); many gold, silver and steatite reliquaries; large numbers of coins; several Kharoshthi inscriptions; and many other articles of gold, silver and precious stone.[45] The Hadda area actually comprised some ten main stupa-monasteries, often with more than one main stupa and always with many votive stupas. At Prates, for example, some 2 kilometres (just over a mile) to the southeast of the main Hadda complex, is a group of some sixty stupas covering an area of 19 by 40 metres (62 by 131 ft) dominated by four large stupas. The most spectacular finds came from Tepe Kalan (illus. 62), which produced a gold reliquary studded with emeralds and sapphires, and from Tepe Shutur, where reliefs included a very Classical-style statue of Heracles (illus. 83).

There is a particularly large number of stupas bordering the plain to the west of Hadda. Most were investigated in the nineteenth century,

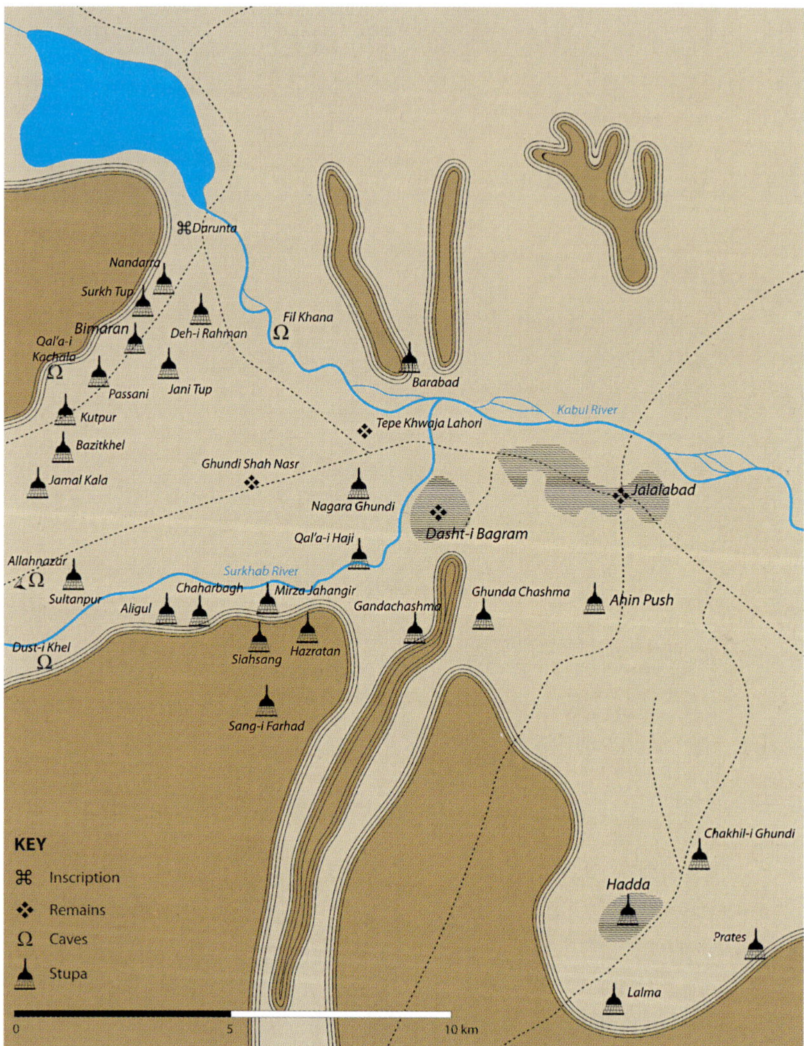

61 Buddhist sites in the Hadda-Jalalabad area.

with many more that were scientifically studied in the twentieth century by French and Japanese missions. Many contained gold coins and reliquaries, usually of steatite, but the most important was the stupa of Bimaran, which contained a gold reliquary studded with rubies, with what might be the earliest known depiction of the Buddha (illus. 77).[46] The date remains controversial, but the consensus is for the late first century AD. There are also many artificial cave complexes, usually associated with the stupa-monasteries (which is perhaps why so many are located in the foothills at the edge of the plain). Many of the caves are decorated, and some have stucco decoration, paintings and sculptural fragments.

Although not as extensive as the Jalalabad remains, the large number of remains in and around Kabul attests to its importance as a major urban site since the Kushan period or earlier. Much of the evidence has been due to accidental discoveries, exacerbated by modern building in the old city, which obscures the nature of earlier remains. This has meant that each discovery has usually been discussed in isolation. However, when all are put together, in particular in the light of recent excavations on the hills overlooking the city, Kabul emerges as a pre-Islamic religious and urban centre second to none in Afghanistan. Much of this was in the final upsurge in Buddhism during the early years of Islam, so will be discussed more in the next chapter. However, skirting the plain to the southeast of Kabul in the foothills are a string of important stupas at Yakhdarra, Shiwaki, Kamari and Seh Tupan, with the major well-preserved stupa-monastery complex of Guldarra dominating a side valley (illus. 63, 70).[47] These monuments might be considered a part of greater ancient Kabul.

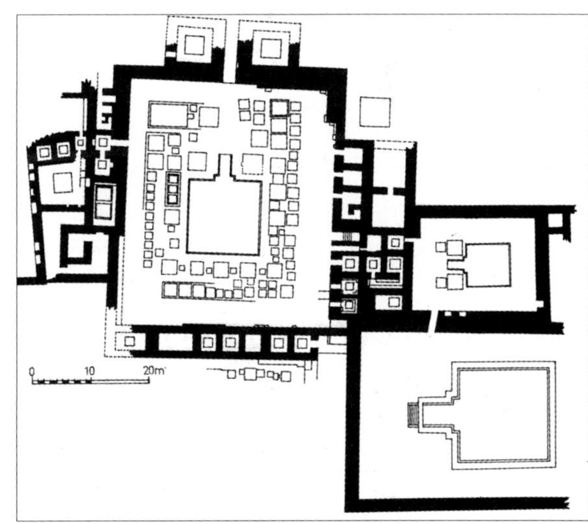

62 Plan of the Buddhist monastery complex of Tepe Kalan at Hadda.

Another site in the Kabul region that has revealed considerable new information on the Kushan period has been the subject of rescue excavations in advance of large-scale copper mining. This is Mes Aynak, to the south of Kabul, where occupation has been traced back to the Bronze Age. Scattered over

63 The Buddhist stupa at Guldarra.

the hills are masonry terrace walls, and mud-brick structures mark the remains of a substantial monastic settlement and associated town covering some 40 hectares (100 ac). Some four hundred Buddha statues have been recovered, and excavations have revealed several Buddhist monasteries, substantial Buddhist sculptures and paintings, and gold and semi-precious objects.[48]

Kushan Dynasticism

In addition to their administrative capitals, the Kushans instituted a series of dynastic centres, which have been identified at Khalchayan in Tajikistan, Mathura in India and Surkh Kotal and Rabatak north of the Hindu Kush near Baghlan in Afghanistan. Surkh Kotal is approached by a monumental brick and masonry staircase, flanked by four massive terraces, cut out of the hillside.[49] The main temple, in the centre of a paved courtyard, has a cella facing east, enclosed by a corridor on the three other sides. In the centre is a square masonry altar with the remains of four Hellenistic column bases at each corner. The sanctuary is surrounded by massive mud walls decorated with Hellenistic pilasters in stone and stucco. Abutting the south side of the temple is a later complex of two small fire temples linked by a courtyard. These each have a square central sanctuary enclosed by corridors (illus. 64, 65).

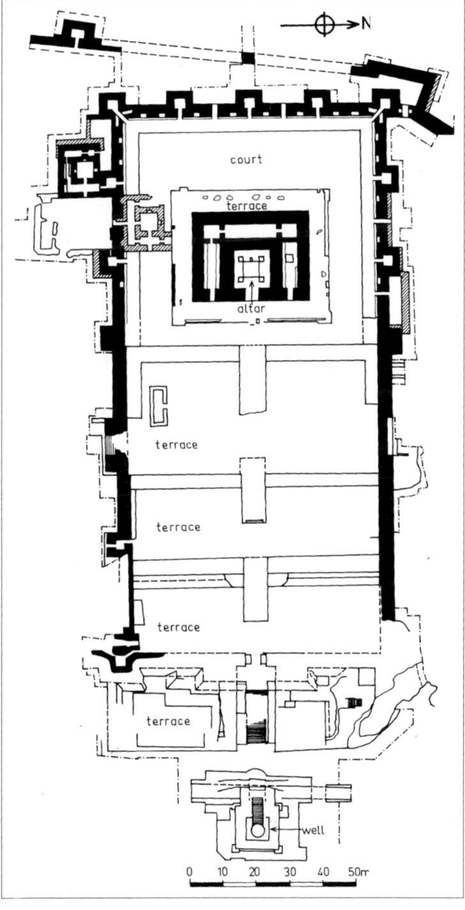

64 Plan of the Kushan dynastic complex of Surkh Kotal.

The most important finds have been epigraphic. The most notable one is the monumental foundation inscription in the Greek script but in the Bactrian language, made up of a series of stone blocks that originally lined the front of the third terrace. Another, also in the Bactrian language, is an elaborate inscription in three versions, which describes the construction and restoration of the complex by an official called Nokonzok in the year 31 of the Kanishka era (probably about AD 158). A life-size (but headless) statue of Kanishka I confirms Surkh Kotal's foundation by him (illus. 46). Other finds include several more inscriptions, including one written by a resident Greek named Palamedes (albeit in the Bactrian language), as well as many coins and various sculptural fragments in stone and stucco.

The Bactrian word for the Surkh Kotal sanctuary was *bagolaggo*, and survives in the region as the modern town of Baghlan nearby.[50] In 1993 a new Bactrian inscription of the early Kushan period was recovered from Rabatak about 15 kilometres (9 mi.) northwest of Surkh Kotal, dedicated by Kanishka I to his ancestors.[51] The site itself was another dynastic sanctuary, probably similar to Surkh Kotal in that it consisted of a series of terraces. The two were possibly a part of a single overall dynastic scheme. Not far off the main north–south road between Kabul and northern Afghanistan and 5 kilometres (3 mi.) south of Surkh Kotal is the Sasanian rock relief of Rag-i Bibi depicting a Sasanian emperor, suggested to be Shapur I, dated to the middle decades of the third century. Shapur is depicted hunting rhinoceros, hence commemorating the Sasanian advance to the Indus.[52] It also depicts a captive, possibly a Kushan king, and so marks the Sasanian conquest of the Kushan Empire (illus. 49). This was both a pointed symbol of the victory of the new dynasty and a reassertion of the importance of the older dynastic centre. This suggests continuity of Kushan traditions in the region; the carving of the Sasanian rock relief of Rag-i Bibi not far from Surkh Kotal might be seen to confirm such continuity. The surrounding region of Surkh Kotal and Rabatak has been identified with a region mentioned in fourth- to late eighth-century Bactrian documents as *Kadagstan*, which means 'land of the [royal] family' governed by a *kadag-bed*, meaning *kagan* or khan.[53] It has been suggested that this meant that it was a special enclave for the Kushan kings, a status that the construction of the Rag-i Bibi relief implicitly

65 The Kushan dynastic site of Surkh Kotal.

continued under the Sasanian kings, thus marking dynastic continuity: a dynastic landscape.

The associations with fire worship at Surkh Kotal have obvious Zoroastrian affinities, the ambulatory in the form of corridors around the sanctuary is a feature of Buddhist architecture, and the pilasters adorning the court and the column bases supporting the canopy over the altar are Hellenistic. The syncretic fusion of different religious ideas and architectural elements into a cult focused on the person of the emperor was intended to symbolize the unity of different cultures of the empire. The Kushan emphasis on dynasticism expressed in monumental architecture presumably derives from the Persian tradition, expressed so powerfully at Persepolis as well as elsewhere in the Iranian world. But a cult of tribal leadership was a characteristic of the inner Asian nomads, from whom the Kushans themselves derived, so it might equally be a part of their own nomadic past.[54] Although such nomads had no architecture, the cult of leadership was expressed in the massive and elaborate 'royal' burials, the *kurgans*, that characterize the Eurasian nomads, and such burials – often numbers of burials spread over particular localities – have been suggested to have assumed the status of sacred and/or dynastic enclaves.[55]

It is perhaps appropriate to end our survey of the Kushans by returning to the steppe traditions of the Inner Asian nomads, whence they came. Originally refugees from the borders of China fleeing the Huns, then homeless nomads of the Inner Asian steppe and eventually masters of a great empire, theirs is one of the more remarkable stories in history. We return to the steppe in Chapter Seven, where we explore what became of their pursuers: the Huns. But first in the next chapter we explore the extraordinarily eclectic art that was formed in the Kushan Empire.

66, 67 A relief in the Lahore Museum from a Buddhist monastery (*top*) compared with a Roman sarcophagus in the Antalya Museum (*bottom*).

6

Buddhist Art: Greek, Roman and Indian Styles Merge in Afghanistan

Sometimes the similarity in stance and gesture between the classical and Gandharan figures is almost uncanny.

PETER STEWART[1]

If one were to draw a north–south line through the exact middle of a map of Eurasia, the region of Gandhara, comprising eastern Afghanistan and northern Pakistan, is seen to be precisely in the centre (illus. 68). Of course, such a device is entirely artificial and completely meaningless: in antiquity such a concept of 'Eurasia' (let alone its boundaries) would have been unknown. But it does at least illustrate how – and perhaps explain why – Gandhara received, transmitted and spread influences over much of that area.

Gandhara was originally the name of the ancient Persian satrapy in northern Pakistan extending into eastern Afghanistan, with its capital at Taxila. The region was the heart of the ancient Greek kingdom of India founded by the Greeks of Bactria in the middle of the third century BC. Other centres were the Swat Valley to the north and Hadda, near Jalalabad in Afghanistan, to the west. Gandhara gave its name to the rich Buddhist art of the first few centuries AD that was discovered in the region in the nineteenth century and, with the discoveries of the same styles of art soon after in eastern Afghanistan, the term 'Gandharan art' was expanded to include this broader region, at times broadening to include discoveries in southern Central Asia as well. Gandharan art was hybrid, a mix mainly of

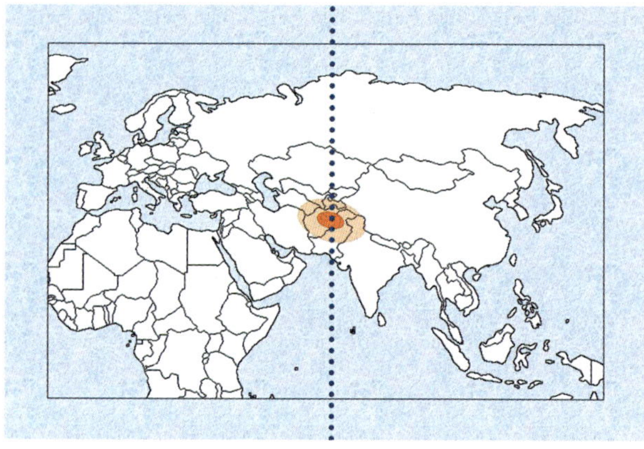

68 Eurasia, with Gandhara in the centre.

Classical and Indian styles, as well as Central Asian, Iranian and local influences. Its predominant elements were the Buddhist religion and Classical art. The fusion of these two completely foreign elements produced the Gandharan art style. Here we discuss mainly discoveries in eastern Afghanistan, but it must be emphasized that the styles and objects apply equally to northern Pakistan. We also include the late resurgence of 'Gandharan' art of the first few centuries of Islam in Afghanistan.

A less artificial and more meaningful *what-if* than a line through Eurasia is that if one were to place a second-century AD sculpture from a Buddhist monument in Gandhara alongside a Roman sculpture from the Mediterranean of the same period, the differences would be indistinguishable to anybody but the specialist (illus. 66; see also illus. 78, 88), 'an artistic relationship that should not exist', in the words of one expert.[2] The undoubted 'Roman' appearance of much of the Buddhist art in the first few centuries AD has exerted a fascination that is very different from other art categories: ancient Near Eastern art, for example, or modern art, or even (dare one say) mainstream Classical art. For the interest in Gandharan art is that it comprised Classical and Classical-derived art found thousands of miles away from where it should be in the Mediterranean. Classical art in the Mediterranean requires no explanation; Classical art in the Hindu Kush defies explanation. No other art form in the ancient world has travelled so far and exerted so wide an influence. It was eventually reflected in art as far away as the Far East and Indonesia (illus. 97). It is this more than anything else that has prompted misinterpretations, abuses, misappropriations – and explains its allure.

An obvious explanation that might occur is, of course, Alexander the Great, bringing the light of Greek culture to darkest Asia. Alexander is a part of the story, but only indirectly and no more than, say, Emperor Wudi of China in the second to first century BC: both launched chains of events that culminated in Gandharan art hundreds of years later, one by invading Bactria, the other by evicting the Huns from the borders of China that brought the Kushans into Afghanistan under whom Gandharan art flourished.

Gandharan art is almost exclusively an architectural art adorning religious buildings. So before examining the art itself, it is important to examine the types of building that it adorned.

The Buddhist Stupa-Monastery Complex

The arrival of the Yuezhi from Central Asia added a new element to the already eclectic nature of the architecture of Afghanistan. The establishment of the Kushan Empire invigorated existing traditions and reasserted international connections, particularly between the Indian subcontinent and Central Asia, and the widely divergent traditions of architecture in Afghanistan became a cultural and political whole under a powerful empire. Buddhism became the dominant religion in Afghanistan (at least in the east and the north), and the main architectural manifestation of Buddhism, the stupa, is one of the most distinctive monuments of eastern Afghanistan. In the long, complex evolution of the stupa form, Afghanistan played a key role, not least because contact with Hellenism gave rise to the distinctive art and architectural style of Gandhara. New forms of Buddhist architecture evolved, the Buddha image was given artistic and architectural expression, and numerous monastic complexes were built in the regions roughly east of a line between Kandahar and Balkh. Most importantly, it was during this formative period that Buddhism and its associated architecture spread from Afghanistan northwards into Central Asia and ultimately eastwards to China and Japan, rather than directly from its northeastern Indian origin.

Originally, stupas were built to hold a relic of the Buddha himself – a monumental reliquary. Relics were rarely meant to be taken out for ritual, as in Christian practice, but would usually be permanently sealed in a chamber in the core of the stupa. The first stupas were built in northeastern India to house relics associated with the Buddha soon after his death. These were no more than earth mounds or tumuli, which gave the stupa its characteristic dome-like form. But they probably did not become objects of veneration or achieve any architectural distinction until after the Third Buddhist Council in the third century BC, when the Maurya emperor Ashoka had these original stupas opened and the relics subdivided to be given to missionaries in order to spread the faith further afield. Thus was disseminated not only the religion, but the peculiar building type associated with the worship of its relics. Eventually stupas came to house the relics of any Buddhist ascetic and not necessarily of Buddha himself, becoming centres of veneration in their own right and increasingly of monastic communities.

69 Votive stupas from Tepe Kalan, Hadda.

Often, the original central stupa of a monastic complex would be relatively small, but subsequently enlarged by being encased a second or even a third time. The stupa would be the physical centre of a Buddhist community, but eventually came to be surrounded by smaller 'model' or votive stupas donated by worshippers as acts of veneration (illus. 62, 69). Hence the stupa came to have a more spiritual meaning as well. Building or endowing a stupa would in itself be an act of religious merit, so that a monastic community might end up with thousands of them: in courtyards, in side niches, in assembly halls and chapels, even painted onto wall surfaces or onto the surfaces of the large stupas themselves. Ultimately, the stupa came to symbolize Buddhism itself, becoming its main architectural expression, eventually evolving into the pagodas of China and Japan (illus. 94).

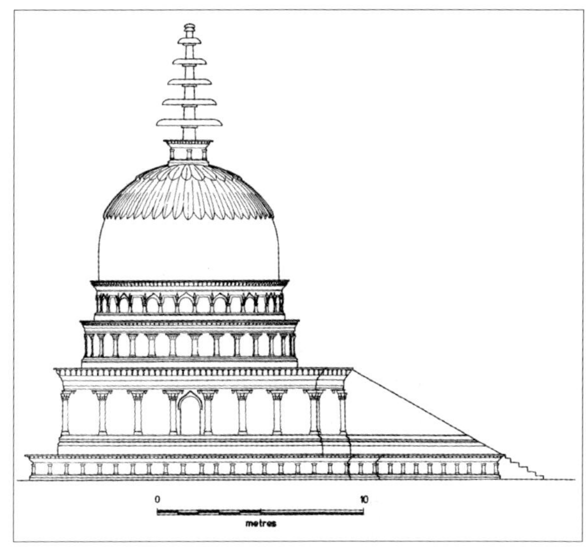

70 Reconstructed elevation of the stupa at Guldarra.

It became the custom to deposit the 'seven jewels' of Buddhism in the stupas as well as the relic itself: gold, silver, pearl, crystal, lapis, diamond and coral. In practice this was not always possible, especially in Gandhara, where such commodities were not always available, but some form of jewellery at least usually formed stupa deposits, as well as precious metals. The precious metals (usually gold and/or silver) furthermore had to be wrought rather than in their raw form (illus. 77). In practice this generally meant coins, which had the great benefit for archaeologists of providing dates (although a coin could be hundreds of years old at the time of deposition, especially if it was precious).

In keeping with the tumulus origin of the first stupas, the early ones were simply large domed masonry structures, usually sitting on a circular plinth such as the famous third-century BC stupa at Sanchi in India. The dome would be surmounted by a square balcony known as a *harmika* and then a mast of seven 'umbrella-shaped' superimposed discs known as a *chakra* (illus. 70). Eventually, the mast would dwarf the stupa itself. In the Gandharan region the stupa form was transformed by Hellenistic styles. Typically, the dome was elevated on one or two drums, the whole further elevated on a high, square platform and socle, which it is suggested are a borrowing from Roman architecture (illus. 63, 70), with a stairway either at the front or on all four sides. The internal radiating construction of many of the domes, it is also suggested, may have been Roman-influenced.[3] As the stupa form moved north and eastwards, the square podium became more and more elevated, eventually evolving into the square 'pagodas' of the Far East (illus. 94). The characteristic construction is the distinctive 'diaper masonry' that is the hallmark of architecture of the Gandharan period throughout the region: large stones, dressed on one side, with small flat stones filling the interstices. This, however, would not originally have been visible, as stupas were usually covered in plaster. The platform and drums are decorated with rows of ogival or polygonal blind arcades – a style that originated in India – that would frame seated Buddha images, but the niches would be divided by 'Indo-Corinthian' pilasters, a local variation of the Greek prototype (illus. 75, 78). The various horizontal elements – socle, platform, drums and dome – would be further divided by Classical-style entablatures.

Stupas, then, became both the centre for great monastic communities and the symbol of religious and philosophical ideas. In eastern Afghanistan stupas number in hundreds, if not thousands. The stupa was never isolated but invariably the focal point of large monastic complexes. They would be surrounded by a circumambulatory, an essential feature of Buddhist ritual (with the stupa kept to the right), and usually enclosed within a courtyard. The courtyard would, over a period of time, acquire miniature votive stupas eventually numbering dozens or even hundreds, giving older stupa complexes a somewhat cluttered appearance (illus. 62). A monastery would be an integral part of the stupa, usually comprising a courtyard surrounded by an ambulatory and cells for monks. The courtyard may contain a secondary stupa in the centre as well as smaller votive stupas. Facing both monastery courtyard and stupa courtyard would often be subsidiary chapels containing Buddha images, smaller stupas and reliefs. The entire complex – stupa, monastery walls, chapels – would usually be liberally covered in painted and sculptured decoration, either in stone or in stucco (depending upon the local availability of materials) depicting scenes of Buddhist iconography as well as statues of the Buddha and bodhisattvas (usually 'one who is on the path to Buddhahood'). This *horror vacui*, an almost profligate encrustation of entire monuments with sculptures and reliefs – even on minor surfaces such as stair risers – is one of the main characteristics of Buddhist architecture and virtually the sole source of Gandharan art. Major monastic complexes, such as Hadda near Jalalabad, expanded to comprise dozens of major stupas, monasteries and artificial cave complexes extending for considerable distances, eventually expanding to comprise an entire 'sacred area' of approximately 39 square kilometres (15 sq. mi.), for example, in the case of the Hadda–Jalalabad region.

Cave Complexes

The other main characteristic of Buddhist architecture is artificial caves. There are no particular religious reasons for this, although the Buddhist emphasis on places of retreat, contemplation and seclusion for its monks might naturally lead to the use of isolated caves. The tradition followed Buddhism from India, where cave temples had an older history – at Ajanta in western India, for example. In Afghanistan they soon became one of the main – almost essential – features of Buddhist monastic communities, continuing to follow Buddhism eastwards into China: the (successively later) caves at Kizil, Dunhuang, Maijishan and Yungang, for example. The greatest cave complex in Afghanistan, of course, is Bamiyan (discussed in the next chapter), but there are numerous other cave complexes elsewhere, although nowhere as extensive, as decorated or as elaborate as at Bamiyan. There are many around Jalalabad, probably because of the existence of the major Buddhist centre at Hadda. A particularly elaborate complex at Takht-i Rustam in the north includes a large stupa cut entirely out of the rock (illus. 71). Caves usually consist of just monks' cells, but at Bamiyan at least there are also assembly halls (*chaitya* halls), chapels and, of course, the famous Buddha statues (illus. 99, 100). Buddha statues can be standing or seated, and include space around them for ritual circumambulation. Many are elaborately decorated, with either sculptures from the bedrock, applied stucco, paintings (illus. 106) or combinations of all three. In some cases the applied stucco would be made to resemble wooden structures (illus. 73). Painted decoration in particular came to be a hallmark of Buddhist

71 The entirely rock-cut stupa at Takht-i Rustam.

72 Painting from Bamiyan.

cave architecture. In addition to Bamiyan it occurs at Kakrak, Fuladi and Dukhtar-i Nushirvan in Afghanistan as well as at the Hadda monasteries (illus. 72, 74), becoming the most famous feature of Buddhist architecture in Xinjiang.

Although Afghanistan was incorporated into the Sasanian Empire in the third century AD, under the Kushano-Sasanian rulers local cultural forms continued uninterrupted, albeit displaying increasing Sasanian artistic influence. The Hephthalite Huns (discussed in the next chapter) are often associated with great destruction, but in Afghanistan the Buddhist civilization not only continued but flourished following their invasion. Indeed, it is often difficult to distinguish

73 Stucco decoration in one of the Bamiyan caves made to imitate wooden construction.

any differences in the material culture of the Kushan, Sasanian and Hephthalite periods.

Greek, Roman, Indian: The Art of Gandhara

Gandharan art evolved out of the confused period between the first century BC and the first century AD. Politically, the old Graeco-Bactrian and Indo-Greek kingdoms had collapsed in the face of successive Scythian, Parthian and Kushan incomers from the north. Both Scythians and Kushans adopted the Hellenistic art and the Buddhist religion of the lands they conquered, providing Gandharan art with political expression. Gandharan art – usually sculpture – is almost entirely Buddhist in subject-matter but displays undeniably Classical styles. The term 'Romano-Buddhist' was first coined in 1876 to describe this synthesis (although the term is now less used, being too culturally loaded). The characteristic style consists of relief panels adorning virtually every wall surface of stupas, as well as associated chapels and monasteries. These wall surfaces are often divided horizontally by Classical entablatures, with relief panels separated by pilasters, usually in the Corinthian order (see illus. 75, 78, 93). These pilasters are evolved orders, either Corinthian or 'Persepolitan' from Iran. Both the entablatures and the Corinthian capitals are often heavily debased and in themselves may not reflect direct Roman influence.[4]

More 'Roman' in style is the sculpture itself. Its characteristic technique of depicting a story in relief as a series of episodic panels is suggested to have derived from Roman models (for example, the Column of Trajan), rather than Indian, where continuous narrative was the norm. On the other hand, episodic panels occur on the relief sculptures of Persepolis: either, both or neither might have been the origin of the style. A more important iconographical element purported to be from the West is the Buddha image itself. Before about AD 100 (the date is subject to dispute), the Buddha was depicted in Indian art in the abstract, for example as a footprint. The first Buddha images appeared after this date, one of the first being the seated Buddha depicted on the first-century AD gold reliquary from Bimaran in Afghanistan (illus. 77), regarded to be modelled ultimately upon Classical prototypes (although Indian prototypes have also been discussed). The current consensus for the date of this important work

74 Painting from Bagh Gai, Hadda.

75 Schist 'Indo-Corinthian' pilaster from the Gandhara region.

of art is from the second half of the first century to the first half of the second century AD for the deposition of the casket, based on a combination of stylistic analysis and the dates of the coins buried with it, although a precise date still remains controversial.[5] A gold coin from Tillya Tepe is another possible early or earlier depiction of Buddha,

76 Seated Buddha from Tepe Kalan, Hadda.

also in a Classical style.[6] The seated Buddha has since become the most familiar image of Buddhist iconography (illus. 76, 101).

Almost as familiar is the standing Buddha, often with his right hand raised in the *abhayamudra* or 'gesture of fearlessness' stance, believed to have been modelled after the stance in statues of the Roman emperors as *pontifex maximus*: iconographically, the authority of the founder (illus. 80). In this way the Buddha in Buddhist art is linked to the Roman cult of the emperor. This is a predominant theme in Buddhist art, also found on the reverse of many of Kanishka's coins.[7] The strongest links are not so much the iconographic concepts but the actual appearance of the sculpture itself. The resemblance is astonishing, and many of the reliefs might almost be from the pages of a book on Roman art (illus. 66, 67 and 78). The sarcophagus art of the Roman world probably provides the closest similarities to Gandharan art, with many motifs 'clearly lifted from the iconographic repertoire of Roman sarcophagi' (illus. 67).[8] Other recurring motifs include beings from Greek mythology, such as ichthyocentaurs, tritons, gryphons; Atlas figures, often depicted supporting Classical entablatures (illus. 79); cupids; garlanding and other details of Classical ornament, such as tendrils, bead and reels, egg and darts, and palmettes; and the almost universal use of the Corinthian order. Many Indian deities are depicted in well-known Classical guise: Vajrapani, for example, is depicted as Heracles (illus. 83) and Hairiti as Tyche, and Dionysiac imagery constantly recurs. There is even an extraordinary relief today in the British Museum depicting Cassandra

77 Gold reliquary from Bimaran, inset with garnets, *c.* 1st century AD.

78 Reliefs from a Buddhist stupa in Gandhara.

79 Painted Atlas figures from Tepe Kafiriha, Hadda.

above: 80, 81, 82 Standing Buddha statues from Bamiyan and Gandhara compared to a statue of Augustus (not to scale).
below: 83, 84 Relief of Hercules from Tepe Shotor, Hadda, compared to the Farnese Hercules (*right*) in the National Museum in Naples.

and the Trojan Horse that could only have been inspired by Virgil rather than Homer.[9] Such works bear almost no relation to contemporary or earlier Indian sculpture, and almost as little to the Hellenized art of Palmyra or Parthia.[10]

Perhaps the most striking are the large numbers of portrait busts in Gandharan sculpture, particularly the stucco sculpture from Hadda in Afghanistan (illus. 86). Some, such as the Heracles relief from Tepe Shotor (illus. 83), appear almost identical to Roman art in Asia Minor or Syria of the first to second centuries AD (or indeed of the famous Farnese Heracles in the National Museum in Naples). Most of the Hadda stuccoes are generally thought to be later, occurring after the third century, although there are problems with dating. One authority sees these stuccoes as 'essentially Greek figures, executed by artists fully conversant with far more than the externals of the classical style'.[11] They are usually heads of Buddhas or bodhisattvas which form part of a relief narrative, but now occur mainly in isolation in museum collections. Such busts closely resemble Roman portrait sculpture – the resemblance of one bodhisattva to the 'Antinous' sculptures of the Hadrianic period is a particularly famous example (dubbed the 'Gandharan Antinous': illus. 85). These stucco busts are thought to be the result of mass production, the stucco medium lending itself more easily than stone to imitative workshops. The dominance of Alexandrian stucco workshops is emphasized in this context. Much of the 'Roman' style of Hadda appears to anticipate European Romanesque and Gothic art a thousand

85 The so-called 'Gandharan Antinous' from Tepe Kalan, Hadda.

86 Stucco portrait busts from Bagha Gai, Hadda.

years later: just as late Roman art in the West evolved into Gothic, late Romano-Buddhist art in the East evolved into the 'so-called Gothic art of Hadda.'[12]

From West to East

There are three channels from which this 'Roman' art might be derived: first, as a natural evolution of the Hellenistic art of the same area (Bactrian Greek), a parallel evolution to the development of Roman art itself in the West; second, as direct influence by itinerant groups of artists from the Roman Empire; and third, as indirect influence stemming from Romanizing elements in Iranian art.[13]

Its evolution from Greek art of the same region – the Hellenistic successor states of Bactria and India – at first appears the most plausible. After all, the Hellenism was undoubtedly there, and the Roman appearance of the later art seems as logical an evolution as Roman art in the West, which evolved similarly from Hellenistic art. It has certainly won eminent supporters, including the scholar who, perhaps more than most, rediscovered Gandharan art, Alfred Foucher.[14] The main objection, however, is that the Greek kingdoms disappeared long before the appearance of the first syncretic Gandharan art style, with the Hellenism of Bactria virtually disappearing; there seems no smooth, artistic transition such as occurred between Hellenistic and Roman art in the West. Consequently, there are too many missing links to enable a convincing evolution to be documented, and only the arrival of entirely new contacts with the West can explain the style. There is almost no Buddhist art, for example, at Taxila before about AD 50. Arguments, therefore, have revolved around efforts to date many of the pieces with demonstrable Western influence as early as possible.

After the initial discovery of Gandharan art, these arguments gradually gave way to those who favoured a more direct Roman origin for the style. But the evolutionary argument still has much to recommend it. To begin with, the post-Hellenistic invasions – Scythian, Parthian, Kushan – that brought the Hellenistic kingdoms to an end were neither a 'dark age' nor a material break: the Greek script remained in use; there were still Greeks living under the new rulers (such as Palamedes, who signed one of the Surkh Kotal inscriptions); and the Corinthian order continued to be used, again such as at Surkh Kotal.

The archaeological record indicates far stronger continuity in the region than was previously believed, with the invaders promoting and continuing Hellenism rather than extinguishing it. The absence of artistic links, therefore, does not mean that such links never existed. They may yet be found – indeed, our knowledge of the archaeology of Afghanistan is still notoriously inadequate. The discovery and excavation of the Greek city of Ai Khanoum has demonstrated beyond doubt that Greek art did take root in the region, fusing with local elements. Finally, relatively recent studies have focused on a hitherto neglected aspect of Gandharan art. These are the so-called palettes or 'toilet trays', dated between the late second century BC and the first century AD, belonging to a Hellenistic tradition that originated in Anatolia or Alexandria (illus. 87). The art of these stone palettes has contributed much towards filling gaps in the evolution of Gandharan art (although this has since been questioned).[15]

87 The so-called 'toilet trays' or palettes from Begram, *c.* late 2nd century BC–1st century AD.

Most discussion, however, has centred on the second hypothesis, that the art must have been a product of journeymen craftsmen from the Roman world – and the schools which they founded – working in northwestern India after the first century AD.[16] Only such direct influence can explain the close similarities. Studies of the sculptures have shown that the artisans were 'very conversant not only with the classical repertoire but also with western carving modes', prompting speculation that they must have been trained in the West or were even craftsmen imported from the West.[17] Hence anonymous Roman sculptors have been postulated arriving in Afghanistan, either forming entourages in official diplomatic delegations or travelling independently. While no such delegations are known, the reverse is attested, such as the 'embassy' to Emperor Antoninus mentioned by Aurelius Victor. This is interpreted as coming from one of the Kushan emperors, either Kanishka or Vasishka. It is suggested that such a delegation might have returned from Rome with sculptors for the specific intention of lending an appropriately 'imperial tone' to Kushan sculpture, our worthy Kushan rustics having doubtless been bowled over by the glories they saw in Rome itself. A sculptor in the wake of such a delegation might have trained an assistant who was responsible for the undoubted Roman influence in many of the Gandharan friezes.[18] Support for such hypothetical Roman sculptors roaming the East is seen in the Yavana (the Indian word for 'Greek' derived from 'Ionian', presumed Roman in this case) artisans mentioned in southern Indian literature at the time, or the apocryphal story of the journey of St Thomas – a carpenter – to Taxila in the first century AD. The collection of such a travelling artist's stock of finished and unfinished Graeco-Persian gems was found at Taxila.[19] The spectacular discovery of the hoard of Roman glass at Begram in Afghanistan certainly demonstrated links with the art of the Roman world (illus. 58, 59). While these were merely trade items, and not Roman works of art produced locally, Begram and the other trade links may provide a background for the possibilities of artists arriving in the wake of the objects. There is a huge amount of evidence for Roman trade with India, but this is almost entirely with the *southern* tip of India, from where the distance to Gandhara is almost the same as from the eastern Mediterranean. Roman influence on the art of southern India is in any case virtually negligible.

A re-examination of the Roman glassware and other Roman-related objects at Begram dated them to the first and early second centuries AD rather than the mid-third century as was originally thought. A date of the late first or early second century was then also preferred for the ivories.[20] Thus the Roman objects at Begram now provide us with the required Roman 'missing link' before the formative period of Gandharan art. Indeed, the Roman-inspired plaster palettes from Begram might well have formed a part of samplers of a Western craftsman at the Kushan court (illus. 87). Against this, it must be borne in mind that such efforts to re-date the Begram treasure have focused almost exclusively on the date of the objects themselves rather the date of their deposition; a more recent study now dates this to the mid-third century AD.[21]

Other speculation has emphasized the importance of Hellenistic elements in Iranian and Near Eastern art of the same period. The sculpture at Palmyra in Syria and Hatra in Iraq, as well as the paintings at Dura Europos in Syria, belong to this 'Irano-Hellenistic' style. Here, the frontality of the art, as well as the dress, the ornament and the framing of the reliefs, are seen to be essentially Iranian variations on an underlying Hellenistic theme. These variations are also found in Gandharan art and are, therefore, seen to be a development. In this context the precarious nature of Greek art in Bactria has been emphasized as well as, perhaps, its shallowness, in contrast to the remarkably more durable arts of Iran.[22] The stucco medium of, for example, the Hadda busts, which are generally late, is also thought to be inspired by Iranian art, which favoured the stucco medium, particularly after the Sasanian occupation of Gandhara in 241.[23] But while such connections undoubtedly exist, the Roman element in Gandharan art is far more pronounced than the Parthian – or even Palmyrene – calling for more complex explanations which suggest more direct links.

The real problem lies in the state of Gandharan art itself. The story of its rediscovery since the nineteenth century is a sad tale of despoliation of sites, looting and accidental discoveries. By far the majority of objects in museum collections are divorced from their contexts, with few from controlled excavations. It is a problem that continues today more than ever before: the destruction and looting of the National Museum in Kabul and the ongoing illicit excavations in Afghanistan are merely the latest episodes in a long and sorry story. Consequently, it is impossible to date much of the sculpture closer than the first to sixth centuries AD, and chronology is the biggest problem that continues to plague the study of Gandharan art – estimated dates for some sculptures can vary by as much as four centuries.[24] Most is divorced both from its sculptural and archaeological contexts, as well as from the broader social and historical contexts that might provide us with the information to fill the many gaps in its evolution. Even when recovered from scientifically conducted archaeological excavations, sculptures might often be much older than the contexts where they were found: reused, in other words, as sacred relics. Gandharan art and the academic questions which surround it, perhaps more than most other art styles, are a victim of their own intrinsic collectability and value.

Much discussion has concerned the conceptual origins of the Buddha image. In particular, it has been argued that this was inspired by the Roman cult of the emperor, as we have noted, central to the Buddhist iconographical cult of the authority of Buddha (illus. 80–82). The origins of such a cult, however, whether of the Roman emperor or of the Buddha authority, lie not in Roman art but in Persian. The cult of the Great King is one of the predominant themes of Achaemenid art, emphasized at Persepolis and continuing as a major Iranian artistic theme in the rock reliefs of the Sasanian emperors. It has also been argued that the development of the Buddha image occurred entirely within the religious development of Buddhism in India, and not as a response to any Western ruler concepts.[25] The episodic style of Gandharan reliefs, believed to derive from Roman art, also occurs earlier in the Persepolis reliefs.

In postulating how Roman artisans might have arrived in Afghanistan and India, speculation has centred around the various delegations to Rome from 'Bactria' and elsewhere in the East that the historical sources mention, such as those which came to Augustus.[26] It is suggested that such delegations might have brought back groups of artists with them. But the central point of these delegations is that, if anything, they are evidence of a movement from *east to west*, not the reverse: we have virtually no evidence that such delegations were reciprocated by Rome; our only evidence is for Indians or Bactrians coming to Rome. Other speculations on the artistic links have looked to the Roman trade with southern India, mentioned above, for an explanation. Ancient southern Indian sources certainly mention Yavana artisans working in southern India. But even if the Yavanas were Romans (and it is unlikely the term was so precise, as we have noted), no 'Romano-Indian' art has been found in the south, where all the archaeological evidence, such as it is, suggests that it should be. It is all in the northwest, which had few links with the south – and even fewer links, apart from artistic, with the Roman world. Indian literature furthermore makes no mention of Yavanas – craftsmen or otherwise – in the north at this time.

The similarities between Roman and Gandharan sculpture are self-evident – and overwhelmingly persuasive enough to be convincing of artistic links. But the 'missing links' that have been put forward – a hoard of Roman glass here, an unexplained series of stuccoes there, the occasional intaglio elsewhere – are not enough. What is lacking is sculptures themselves to provide missing links, as it is in sculptural art that the similarities exist, not glassware or other objects. What is more lacking, however, is any convincing historical framework that would have allowed such links to form. Central to the argument is the existence of 'journeymen craftsmen' from the Roman world. The idea that a hypothetical sculptor in an entirely hypothetical entourage of an equally hypothetical Roman delegation to the Kushan court might have trained local craftsmen in Roman sculpture to influence a subcontinent is so ridiculously tenuous as to appear unworthy of serious consideration. The picture of itinerant groups of Roman sculptors – swags of samplers, patterns and tools over their backs, wandering around from court to court in parts of remotest Asia that few of even the best-educated

Romans had ever heard of, teaching the natives how to sculpt in languages mutually incomprehensible, heads brimful of abstruse iconographical concepts – somehow lacks conviction. Even more lacking is any cast-iron archaeological or social context in which the hypothesis might be placed.

Most of all, it must be pointed out that the controversies over Graeco-Bactrian versus direct Roman versus Irano-Hellenistic origins for Gandharan art are not in conflict: *all* hypotheses must be substantially correct. None of the hypotheses can by themselves account for the unquestionably Western character of the style. But the combination of *all* forces and influences is the only possible explanation for perhaps the most extraordinary syncretism in art history. To argue for one hypothesis over the others is to miss the point.[27]

88, 89, 90, 91
Gandharan Corinthian capitals. Top to bottom: Hadda (Musée Guimet), Hadda (Musée Guimet), Takht-i Bahi (Lahore Museum), Airtam (Hermitage). Not to scale.

From East Back to West?

The spread of art is always a two-way flow, and Gandharan art transmitted as well as received. The transmission is usually viewed as towards the east: to India and to Inner Asia, China and Japan. But did it go west as well? One variant of the Corinthian capital that is thought to have been a uniquely Gandharan development from the first century onwards is of a figure – in a Gandharan context the Buddha figure – framed by the acanthus leaves of the capital (illus. 88–91), perhaps inspired by the legend of Gautama seated under the bodhi tree.[28] This treatment is little known in the Classical art of the West, so that when it appears in late Classical and early Gothic art of Italy and France, where it becomes a regular motif, it might be evidence of an East–West flow. Although plausible, it is difficult to substantiate. Such developments can in any case evolve quite independently.

Another example comes from the architecture of the eastern provinces of the Roman Empire. In a seminal study, Margaret Lyttelton discussed an essentially Eastern variant of Roman architecture dubbed 'Roman Baroque'.[29] Using the parallel of the conventional definition of Baroque, as applied to the architecture of seventeenth- and eighteenth-century Europe, the 'Baroque' style was applied to the more flamboyant forms of Graeco-Roman architecture, particularly in the areas of decoration, in contrast with the more strict, 'Classic' forms. While Roman Baroque occurred throughout the empire it was more a feature of the eastern provinces, particularly Syria, than of the western. Nearly all of the examples were drawn from here in Lyttelton's study.

Features of this style are the highly elaborate, flowing and curved facades, often conveying a sense of movement. Entablatures are alternatively recessed and breaking forward, as are the pediments. Decoration is liberal to the point of profligacy – indeed, such facades can appear almost organic. This is almost literally true for the most famous Baroque facades, those at Petra, which are cut from the living bedrock. Niches and miniature pediments are used as additional embellishments, usually having no function other than decorative. Often, such niches are framed by pilasters and a pediment, a decorative feature known as the 'Syrian niche', one of the most distinctive Syrian features of Roman Baroque architecture (illus. 92). This is a niche set into a wall – often to house a statue – framed by a pair of engaged colonnettes supporting a miniature pediment and often repeated in continuous rows over entire facades. They were used to great – and elaborate – effect to adorn facades, most notably in the temenos walls of Baalbek and Palmyra.

Gandharan architecture, although not included in Lyttelton's study, is almost textbook 'Classical Baroque' in these terms. The tradition of framed niches first occurs in the Buddhist architecture of Mauryan India, where they are used – like the Syrian niches – simply as a repeated, recurring decorative motif to adorn wall surfaces. They occur, for

92 Rows of the so-called 'Syrian niche' decorating the courtyard of the temple of Baalbek.

93 Votive stupas at Taxila.

94 The 7th-century Big Goose Pagoda in Xian, displaying distant descendants of Hellenistic pilasters and entablatures.

example, on the second- to first-century BC facades at Bharhut, Sanchi and Bhaja, becoming characteristic of the cave architecture of Karli and Ajanta between the first and fifth centuries.[30] The importance of the framed niche in Gandharan art is iconographical, deriving from the reverence for the Buddha image. This is one of the commonest features of Buddhist art, where the Buddha image typically occurs within a frame. The earliest occurrence is on the possibly early first-century AD gold Bimaran reliquary discussed earlier (illus. 77). Thereafter, it becomes characteristic in Gandharan art, where Buddhist narrative reliefs or rows of seated Buddhas in niches are divided by Corinthian columns (illus. 93). Such resemblance might well be illusory, but John Boardman has emphasized the underlying unity of the Achaemenid Empire over this entire region, a unity that long outlasted its collapse, and that the 'remarkably durable arts of Persia' not only survived but underpinned the formation and movement of other forms.[31] The importance of the Achaemenid Empire from the sixth to the fourth century BC for internationalism and the transmission of artistic ideas cannot be emphasized too strongly. Against this background, the western spread of Gandharan art to influence elements of Roman art is just as plausible as the eastern spread of Roman art to influence Gandhara – and in turn for the distant descendants of Gandhara to reappear in the later architecture of China (illus. 94). If nothing else, it demonstrates just how central the Afghan melting pot was to the arts of Eurasia.

7

The Great Buddhas of Bamiyan and Beyond: Huns, Turks and Hindus

It is difficult to think of Afghanistan or Buddhism without Bamiyan.

ALKA PATEL[1]

In the West today, Turks are almost solely associated with Turkey, rarely with Afghanistan. But Afghanistan's most famous monument is certainly associated with the Turks. This, of course, is Bamiyan, the main subject of this chapter, famous even before the great Buddhas were notoriously and publicly blown up in 2001. It might seem surprising to ask of Bamiyan – one of the best-known monuments of antiquity – what is it and why is it there? And more than anything else, why was Bamiyan so special? To answer this, like so much of Afghanistan's history, one must go back once more to the Inner Asian steppe.

The Steppe Background Again

From a little before the middle of the first millennium AD, groups of people speaking entirely unrelated languages started coming to the fore in Central Asia, where they still remain. These were people speaking various Uralic and Altaic languages, the main one being Turkish. Ultimately this would result in an almost complete linguistic displacement of the indigenous Indo-Iranian speakers in Central Asia apart from the Tajiks. The first of these non-Indo-European speakers to appear were the Huns. Although there is practically no evidence for the Hun language, it is assumed that they spoke an Altaic-related language.

The Huns were probably the same as the Xiongnu of the Chinese sources, and their eruption into Central Asia and eventually Europe a long-term consequence of the Chinese expansion into Inner Asia. The identification of the Xiongnu with the people known variously as Huns, Chionites and Hephthalites is subject to dispute. They are also identified with the *Hayatila*, *Hyaona* and *Hyon* of the Iranian sources and with the *Hunas* of Indian sources (the general term 'Hunnic' is used here to lump them all together), the cause of as much disruption in both Europe and India as they were in China.[2] The Xiongnu are first recorded in the Chinese sources as a 'barbarian' group in the late third

95 The Bamiyan Valley with the 53-metre (174 ft) Buddha on the left and the 38-metre (125 ft) Buddha on the right.

century BC, roughly in the area of Mongolia. In the second century BC the Xiongnu united the steppe tribes to form a huge nomadic empire under the formidable warrior king Maodun, who defeated the Yuezhi of Gansu (their descendants eventually founded the Kushan Empire, as we saw in Chapter Five). The Xiongnu 'empire' reached its height under Huhanye in the mid-first century BC. The term 'empire' here is probably a misnomer compared to the more organized and centrally ruled Chinese empire – or indeed the other great sedentary empires of antiquity, such as the Persian or Roman.[3] Chinese imperial policy in the final few centuries BC – it amounted to an obsession – was aimed at evicting the Xiongnu from their borders by diplomatic and military means; the construction of the Great Wall was the most visible manifestation of this policy. Eventually, the Xiongnu were driven away from China and onto the immense Eurasian steppe belt. This resulted in the long-term displacement of other tribal groups. It was to have immense ramifications all over Eurasia.

After the death of Huhanye the empire split into warring factions, out of which a chief known in Chinese sources as Zhizhi emerged as the ruler of the Northern Xiongnu. His 'empire', centred very roughly on modern Kazakhstan, seems to have been in a state of perpetual warfare with rival Xiongnu groups as well as with the Chinese. The Chinese eventually defeated the Northern Xiongnu in 35 BC when Zhizhi was killed, after which they became less of a problem for the Chinese. They presumably remained in the area as groups of nomadic tribes, however, as it was from this area that the Huns, the putative descendants of the Xiongnu, invaded both Europe, Iran and Afghanistan after the fourth century AD.

Whether or not the Xiongnu and the Huns are the same is unimportant. What is important is that the Chinese defeat of the Xiongnu resulted in a huge, long-term displacement of steppe nomads, a chain reaction that would have a knock-on effect right across Eurasia, 'the tide of emigration which impetuously rolled from the confines of China to those of Germany', in the words of Gibbon.[4] The early Turks were another group caught up in these events.

The Huns in Afghanistan and India

In the latter part of the fourth century a succession of Hunnic tribes appeared in Bactria and established control over the Hindu Kush mountains at Sasanian expense.[5] Formerly, these tribes were all referred to under the general term 'Hephthalites', but numismatic and historical studies refer to several distinct Hun groups: Chionites, Kidarites, Alkhans, Nezaks and the Hephthalites proper, sometimes termed 'Iranian Huns'. 'Chionites' might not refer to a separate group, but was a term in Greek sources referring to the Huns generally. Much of the chronology and relationships between the various groups is controversial, and there is also confusion between some of the groups.[6]

According to Greek sources it was the Chionites (from the Greek *Khion*, or 'Hun') who first invaded Bactria in about AD 350, displacing Sasanian rule there, but the name does not appear in the numismatic record. The Greek sources therefore are probably referring to the Kidarites, who were the first of the Hun groups to issue coins in Bactria from their capital at Balkh soon after the mid-fourth century (although dates are disputed). The group – presumed a Hun tribe – was named after their king, called Kidara, although he and his successors continued to use the title 'Kushan-shah', which has led to some confusion. They ruled north and south of the Hindu Kush from about the mid-fourth century to the mid-fifth. At about the same time as the Roman Empire was battling against Attila the Hun in Europe, Sasanian Iran was paying tribute to the Kidarites, and a Kidarite king styling himself 'King Uglarg the Kushan-shah' was ruling a kingdom that stretched from Samarkand to Gandhara.

From about AD 390 onwards another group of Huns known as the Alkhon or Alkhan began issuing coins south of the Hindu Kush in the Kabul area. Probably at first subordinate to the Kidarites, the Alkhans replaced them after the mid-fifth century and extended their conquests into northern India. A separate group of Huns with distinct coinage, the Nezak Shahs, emerged south of the Hindu Kush from about 560 until becoming absorbed by a Turk kingdom there in about 748. The last Hun group to emerge north of the Hindu Kush by about 484 were the Hephthalites (although they could have been part of the Alkhon), who established an 'empire' across Central Asia, absorbing the remnant Kidarite kingdom in Bactria.

Of the various Hun groups, the Hephthalites have left the most information in the sources. Their wars of the first half of the fifth century with the Sasanians were the greatest the Sasanians ever fought, greater than Sasanian wars with the Romans. They came near to bringing the Sasanian Empire to its knees: indeed, the Sasanians were tributary to the Hephthalites for a while. In 459 Emperor Peroz overthrew his brother Hormizd III with the aid of the Hephthalites, but later perished in a war against them in 484. Such was the threat that they posed to Sasanian Iran that a wall was built across northeastern Iran, the so-called 'Gorgan Wall', stretching from the Caspian Sea across the steppe for at least 195 kilometres (121 mi.), ending in the Kopet Dagh mountains forming the present border of Iran with Turkmenistan. The wall, including its associated roads, canals, fortresses and massive garrison encampments, was one of the largest and most elaborate defensive systems ever built in the ancient world.[7] Afghan Seistan also appears to have been heavily fortified during the Sasanian period. Although not matching the great linear barrier of the Gorgan Wall, chains of intervisible fortifications were erected during the Sasanian period (the so-called *qalas*), ranging from large numbers of relatively small towers 20 metres (66 ft) or so square to more substantial forts up to 100 metres square (1,075 sq. ft), typically with projecting circular towers on each corner and square or circular towers in the intermediate walls of the larger forts.[8]

In Afghanistan the Hephthalites absorbed the Alkhan Huns and established a major empire which extended from Central Asia to the Indus Valley. Known as the 'Huna' in Indian sources, they were at first resisted by the powerful Gupta emperor of India, Skandagupta, in 458. But after the death of Skandagupta his empire collapsed, partly as a result of Hun pressure. By the early sixth century, the Huns under Toramana had established their own rule over much of northern and western India and Afghanistan. This was consolidated by Toramana's son and successor Mihirakula, who has the reputation in Indian historical tradition of unmitigated cruelty – an eastern Attila. Hephthalite rule, however, did not last for long. King Yasovarman of Malwa led a confederacy to defeat the Huns in 528, forcing them to withdraw to Kashmir. In the mid-sixth century, the Oxus empire of the Huns was overthrown by the Turks allied to the Sasanians.

The Hun/Hephthalite invasion of Afghanistan, Pakistan and northwestern India has been described in Indian and Chinese sources as wreaking utter devastation, with cities and monasteries laid waste, many of them never to recover. This is regarded as the beginning of Buddhist decline in the region, and the Chinese pilgrim Xuanzang, who travelled through there in the mid-seventh century, writes of once flourishing Buddhist centres reduced as a result of Hun destruction. The archaeological record in Afghanistan at least does not entirely support this picture, with monasteries such as Tepe Maranjan near Kabul or Funduqistan in the Ghorband Valley not only flourishing during this period but producing some of the most delightful and vigorous new sculptural styles of Gandharan art (illus. 96, 97).[9] Some, at least, of the Hephthalite chiefs seem to have settled in the region and ruled wisely, becoming patrons of the local religion. After the collapse of the main Hephthalite kingdom, remnant Hephthalite petty states survived for a while longer in some places. It has been suggested that the warlike Rajput clans of later medieval western India are descended from these Huns. Tenth-century and later sources record

96 Sculpture from Funduqistan.

97 Sculpture from Funduqistan.

descendants of the Hephthalites known as the Khalaj, speaking a language that was distinct from either Turkish or Persian. The Khalaj were still recorded as a distinct tribe in the fourteenth century, although by that time their language had changed to Turkish. By the sixteenth century the name had become Khalji or Ghalji. They are still known today in the same region of eastern Afghanistan as the Ghilzai, according to some studies, although by now speaking only Pashtu, in common with the surrounding Pashtun tribes.[10]

Enter the Turks

In the sixth century, Sasanian rule was re-established in Afghanistan. This was largely due to a weakening of Hephthalite rule caused by the arrival of a new nomadic people whom Central Asia and history as a whole were to hear more and more about. These were the Turks.

To see how this new people arrived on the scene to eventually displace – at least linguistically – most of Central Asia (and ultimately Anatolia) we must return to Inner Asia once again. The collapse of the Xiongnu at the end of the first century AD resulted in various tribal movements, out of which the Turks were to emerge as a major force. Originally subject to the Xiongnu, we first encounter the Turks forming a state in China. Although this might appear irrelevant to later Turk movements into Afghanistan (and eventually beyond), the actions of a particular Turk tribe in China was to have huge ramifications in Afghanistan.[11]

An eastern Turk tribe, the Tuoba, had founded the Northern Wei dynasty of China, centred on Datong, in the late fourth century. The Northern Wei were enthusiastic supporters of Buddhism, being the first to elevate Buddhism to an official state level since the Kushans or even since Ashoka Maurya (the Kushans, although supporting Buddhism, probably did not make it a state religion). In particular, the Tuoba kings embraced the peculiarly Mahayana element in Buddhism, where the secular ruler is invested with the authority of the Buddha. This element took spectacular form in the Buddhist caves constructed throughout the fifth century by the Northern Wei dynasty at Yungang outside their capital at Pincheng (modern Datong), as well as at the Longmen caves near their later capital, Loyang, where each Tuoba king erected a giant statue of Buddha representing the Buddhist authority invested in himself: each giant Buddha statue, in effect, represented both Buddha and emperor. This was the first time that giganticism – colossal Buddha statues – had been introduced into Buddhist art, and was to have enormous consequences for both Buddhist and subsequent Turkish history (illus. 98).[12]

98 The giant Buddha statues at Yungang.

Meanwhile a new steppe confederation was emerging in the mid-fifth century of Turk-speaking tribes, described in Chinese accounts as a group in the Altai mountains. By 552 these Turk tribes were united by Bumin, who assumed the title of *kagan*. The Turks quickly filled the vacuum in the steppes, emerging as the First Turk Empire (or Kaganate) covering a vast area stretching from the borders of Manchuria to Bactria. The Turks had arrived on the threshold of world history.[13]

Bumin was the only kagan to rule over a united empire, for on his death he was succeeded by his two sons, Muhan (553–72), who ruled the eastern half of the empire, and Ishtemi (553–*c.* 575), who ruled the western half. Ishtemi, the kagan of the Western Turks, was one of the rulers who overthrew the Hephthalites of Central Asia, in alliance with the Sasanians of Iran. By about 555 his empire probably extended as far as the Aral Sea and possibly even as far as the River Don. Ishtemi was succeeded as emperor of the Western Turks by his son Tardu, who ruled until 603.

Meanwhile the kagan of the Eastern Turks, Muhan's successor Taspar (572–81), was converted to Buddhism by a Chinese monk. Buddhism then spread among the Turks in both eastern and western branches. On the whole, however, both kaganates were marked by religious tolerance, and Zoroastrianism, Christianity and Manichaeism also flourished under the Turk rulers, as well as the indigenous heaven worship of the steppe. However, there was increasing conflict between the western and eastern arms of the Turk Empire in the early seventh century, and the eastern branch collapsed with the death of its kagan Illig (619–30). The Western Turk Empire absorbed much of the Central Asian territories at Eastern expense.

The Western Turk Empire was expanding rapidly, particularly after the defeat of the Hephthalites. Despite a victory that was carried out in alliance with Sasanian Persia, by 616/17 a Turk army penetrated deep into Iran as far as Rayy, just south of Tehran. In 619 the most powerful of the Western Turk kagans succeeded to the throne, Tong Yabgu Kagan. Under Tong Yabgu the empire reached its greatest extent, incorporating Xinjiang, Ferghana in Central Asia, Bactria and parts of Afghanistan and northern Pakistan, with Tong Yabgu's armies advancing as far as the Indus in 625. But Tong Yabgu was killed in 630, after which the empire slowly disintegrated, and the last kagan of the Western Turks was killed in battle against the Chinese in 659.

With the collapse of both branches of the First Turk Kaganate there followed a period of fragmentation. The Turk tribes were reunited by Elterish Kutlugh (r. 682–92), who established the Second Turk Kaganate. Elterish was succeeded by his brother, Kapgan Kagan (r. 692–716), who consolidated the Second Kaganate and entered into a rapprochement with China. His rule is regarded as the height of the Second Turk Empire. Two more brothers succeeded Kapgan: Költegin and Bilgä Kagan (r. 716–34), who ruled together. Under them the Second Kaganate reached its greatest extent, but it collapsed quickly on the death of

Bilgä, with the last kagan killed in 745. The Second Turk Empire had lasted barely sixty years.

The period of the collapse corresponds to the expansion of the first Muslim Arab Empire into Central Asia, and this doubtless was a contributory cause. But it would be a mistake to overemphasize this. Nomadic empires were seldom more than loose tribal confederations on a large scale, which by their nature are subject to fragmentation: there was rarely the highly centralized rule that characterizes the great sedentary empires of antiquity. Hence it is likely that the Turk Empire would have collapsed even without the Muslim expansion.

At first sight the Turk Empire – in its various manifestations, First (*c.* 552–659) and Second (*c.* 682–*c.* 745), East and West – might appear yet another ephemeral steppe 'empire', leaving little in the way of material remains. This is not to say that it was merely a barbaric horde. More important, many of the Turk princes were cultured patrons of the arts and many subject peoples, such as the Sogdians in Central Asia, flourished under the Turk rulers. The Sogdians – an indigenous Central Asian people speaking an Iranian-related language, ancestors of the Tajiks – dominated much of the trade and commerce of the Turk Empire, their influence extending deep into China and west as far as the Black Sea.

But it was further south in Afghanistan that the Turk Empire had the greatest effect. Attention has been drawn to the fact that the first three centuries of Islam saw a sudden and massive increase in Buddhist art and architecture in eastern Afghanistan and that the Buddhist centres of Bamiyan, Kabul and Ghazni were part of a complex Buddhist communications network between the seventh and tenth centuries. This is attributed to the power of the Turk Kaganate.[14] For it was under the Kagan Tong Yabgu, who was known to be favourably inclined towards Buddhism, that the vigorous Buddhist art of Afghanistan and Central Asia underwent a revival. Many of the isolated mountain valleys of the Hindu Kush, as well as the plains surrounding them, came to be ruled by petty Turk princes. These princes not only absorbed the cultures they encountered but patronized them on a grand scale, and there was a consequent explosion of Buddhist art in the Hindu Kush area, a renaissance of the great days of Gandharan art. This has been confirmed by excavations of extensive Buddhist religious complexes in Kabul, which remained active probably as one of the main centres of Buddhism in Afghanistan at least until the ninth century. The most famous Buddhist monuments in Afghanistan, however, are the colossal Buddhas of Bamiyan and their associated cave and monastery complexes (illus. 95, 99–104), dating from the period of the first Turk Empire.

Bamiyan and the Last Flowering of Gandharan Civilization

The setting of the great Buddhas of Bamiyan is probably the most magnificent in Afghanistan – indeed, one of the most magnificent of any monument in Asia (illus. 95). It is in the heart of the Hindu Kush range in a valley just off one of the main routes connecting northern Afghanistan with Kabul, in ancient times one of the main routes between Central Asia and India. The main part of Bamiyan consists of an extensive area of remains along the foot of the cliffs bordering the north side of the valley.[15] For a length of about 1,800 metres (5,905 ft) the cliff face is honeycombed with some 750 artificial caves, all forming a part of an extensive Buddhist monastic centre, extending into the side valley of Fuladi where there were many more caves.[16] Some are very large and elaborately decorated in sculptures and paintings (illus. 103), and plaster applied to the bedrock to represent architectural details often in imitation of wooden prototypes (illus. 73). There were two giant standing statues of Buddha, one 53 metres (174 ft) and the other 38 metres (124½ ft) high, with a third seated Buddha between the two, carved out of niches in the cliff face in deep relief (illus. 99–101). Details of the robes were applied in stucco over a framework of ropes (representing the folds) attached to the bedrock with wooden pegs (illus. 100). In the niches surrounding the two standing Buddhas were the remains of paintings. At the foot of the cliffs many mounds cover structural remains, including a large stupa to the east of the 38-metre

99 The 53-metre (174 ft) Buddha at Bamiyan. Note the bench at its foot for scale.
100 The 38-metre (125 ft) Buddha at Bamiyan.

Buddha and a series of fortifications. Contrary to popular belief, the faces of the two giant Buddhas were not cut off by iconoclastic Muslims, but probably formed a part of the original structure, with the upper faces made of gilded wood and/or plaster.

In the architecture and art generally of Bamiyan there exists a surprising paradox. For Bamiyan was only a minor principality in the Western Turk federation, the capital of which was at Qunduz in north-eastern Afghanistan, where no monuments on such a scale have been discovered. The answer lies in the sheer scale, not only of the two gigantic Buddhas but of the entire built landscape surrounding them, besides which even the Buddhas look small. The two colossal figures form just a part of a much larger whole: three seated Buddha statues, a 19-metre (62 ft) sleeping Buddha uncovered in the early 2000s, the much larger and as yet unlocated sleeping Buddha recorded by Xuanzang, the hundreds of cave monasteries carved in the cliff face and the many built monasteries and stupas in the valley floor. There is also the urban mound of Shahr-i Ghulghula in the centre of the valley and what appears to be a tumulus cemetery nearby.[17] In the lateral valleys of Fuladi and Kakrak are many more cave monasteries, the latter with its 6-metre (19½ ft) standing Buddha (illus. 102).[18] Frequently discussed with Bamiyan is the Buddhist cave complex of Dukhtar-i Nushirwan with its important paintings in a pass approaching Bamiyan from the north.[19] Further afield are the Buddhist stupa-monastery complexes of Killigan and Tang-i Safidak in the approach from the west[20] – the

101 A seated Buddha at Bamiyan.
102 The standing Buddha at Kakrak in Bamiyan.

latter with a thirteen-line Bactrian inscription – and the monastery of Funduqistan in the Ghurband Valley approaching from the east, where numerous sculptures were recovered (illus. 96, 97).[21] In addition, numerous artificial cave complexes have been recorded, mainly leading out of Bamiyan to the north; some at least contained carved decoration consistent with the decorated Buddhist caves of Bamiyan. Bamiyan therefore is a part of a larger Buddhist sacred landscape, rivalling similar sacred landscapes such as Hadda in eastern Afghanistan or Swat in Pakistan.[22]

There is one other architectural feature that sets Bamiyan apart and does not often appear in discussions of its art: it is one of the most – if not *the* most – heavily fortified regions in Central and Western Asia: giganticism of another form (illus. 104). Surrounding the central valley overlooked by the Buddha statues are fortifications ranging from lines of single towers and fortlets to massive castles guarding the eastern, western and northern approaches into and out of the Bamiyan Valley.[23] The larger fortifications, such as Shahr-i Zuhak (illus. 105) and Sarkhushak guarding the eastern approaches,[24] or Shahr-i Barbar and Chehel Burj (illus. 106) guarding the western approaches,[25] are immense, and the fortress of Tala on the northern route is described as 'palatial'.[26] Dates are unfortunately imprecise, with most dated broadly 'seventh to thirteenth century' on stylistic and occasionally ceramic grounds, and so continued into the Islamic period when Bamiyan was a principality subject to the main Ghurid state to the west (discussed in the next chapter). Many others are merely recorded by aerial and satellite imagery or recorded by passing travellers. These have been put together in the *Archaeological Gazetteer of Afghanistan* so for the first time it is possible to grasp a picture of Bamiyan in its fullest context. In other words, it is both a fortified and a sacred landscape – but on a simply vast, almost unprecedented scale.[27]

Radiocarbon dates are AD 544 to 595 for the 38-metre Buddha and AD 591 to 644 for the 53-metre Buddha, with some of the paintings in the Buddha niches dated to the end of the ninth century and construction elsewhere in the valley (such as the 6-metre Kakrak Buddha)

103 Buddha niches and decoration in Cave II at Bamiyan.

continuing into the tenth century.[28] The main period of construction, therefore, was at the height of the empire of the Western Turks. A seminal study of Bamiyan recognized the Western Turks behind the colossal Buddhas and the Western Turk background is now widely accepted. It was further suggested that Bamiyan might have been a dynastic centre for the Western Turks.[29] With the combination of sacred landscape plus fortified landscape reviewed above, the suggestion seems entirely convincing.

But why locate a dynastic centre at Bamiyan? Bamiyan emerged as a Buddhist religious centre after the first century AD, but there were other Buddhist centres equally or more eligible, such as Hadda. So why not these other centres? In Chapter Five we emphasized the Kushan tradition of dynastic centres not far from Bamiyan as well as the continuity of Kushan traditions in the region to late antiquity. This is how Surkh Kotal, similarly not a capital, functioned for the Kushan kings several centuries previously, with a similarly iconic standing statue (albeit not on Bamiyan's colossal scale), so perhaps was a continuation of such a tradition of dynastic centres.

Might the Central Asian tradition of dynasticism generally and the Kushan tradition more specifically also stem ultimately from a nomad tradition? The nomadic element among the Kushans was also emphasized, being descended from the Yuezhi tribes who migrated over several centuries from Gansu in China. The Turks too originated from mainly nomadic Central Asian traditions. The cult of the nomad chief was a major element among nomadic societies. This took visible architectural form in the elaborate nomad burials, the *kurgans*, which could reach elaborate and gigantic size from the Altai of southern Siberia through to the southern Ukrainian steppe.[30]

Another reason why Bamiyan was selected over other Buddhist centres is that it possessed one feature that Hadda, Ghazni and other centres lacked: quite simply, those magnificent cliffs, large enough to accommodate a royal ego. In this respect the concept behind the colossal Buddhas at Bamiyan resembles that of the earlier Northern Wei colossal Buddhas at Yungang in China (illus. 98).[31] The decision

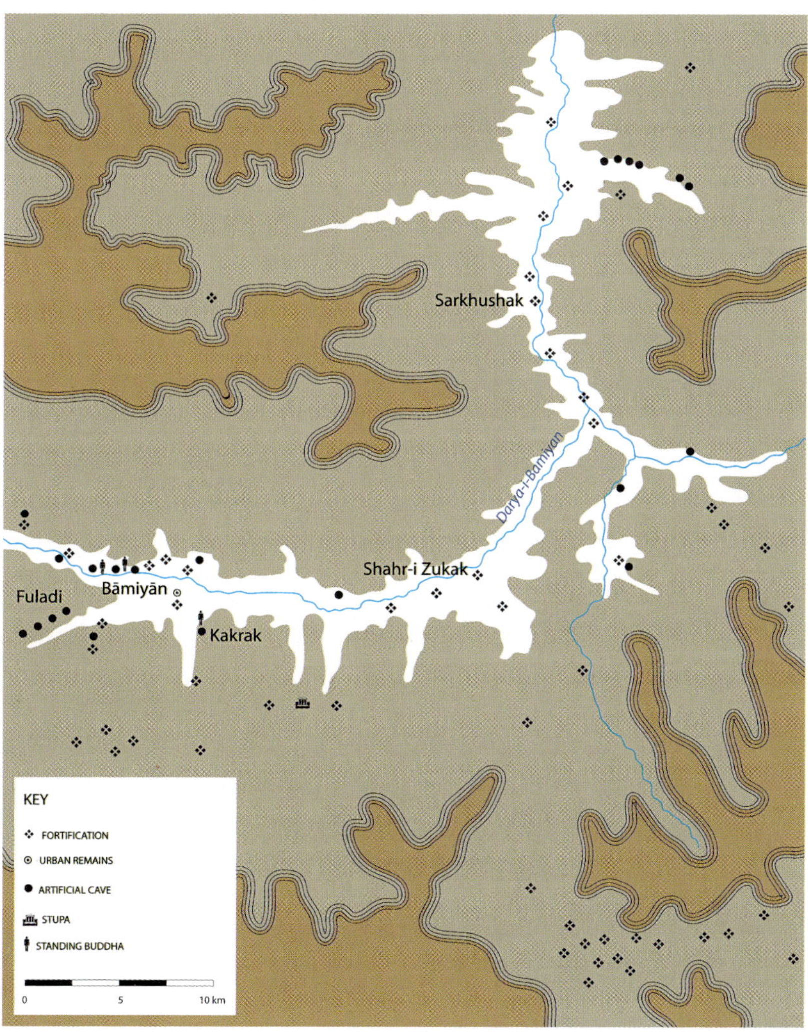

104 The Bamiyan region showing the extent of fortifications and artificial caves.

by the Turk ruler Toba Dao to combine secular and religious authority in the person of the ruler and translate this into massive, visible architectural statements is a precedent that surely would not have been lost on the later Buddhist Turk rulers of Bamiyan.

The connections are tenuous, of course. Can the construction of the giant Buddhas be attributed to Ishtemi or Tong Yabgu – or any of the other kagans? It is impossible at the moment to say. Can the Western Turks have kept alive a tradition – little more than a memory – of dynasticism and giganticism begun by their (very) distant cousins, the Tuoba Turks of the Northern Wei, thousands of miles away and centuries before? Whether or not this is true, Buddhist architecture reached a peak at Bamiyan. The caves cut out of the mountainside housed thousands of devotees; the colossal statues were the ultimate embodiment of the Buddha image, while the painting and sculpture combined Hellenistic, Iranian and Indian elements that influenced

105 The fortress of Shahr-i Zuhak guarding the eastern entrance to the Bamiyan Valley.

106 The fortress of Chehel Burj guarding the western approach to the Bamiyan Valley.

subsequent Chinese and Islamic art. As a sheer statement of both political and religious self-confidence Bamiyan ranked among the greatest works of mankind.

Beyond Bamiyan

Above all, Bamiyan was not the only 'principality' to benefit from this last great flowering of Gandharan art under the religiously tolerant rule of the Turk kagans. The numerous minor principalities that emerged in eastern Afghanistan during the seventh century AD were often little more than city states ruled by Hephthalite or Turk lords who enjoyed considerable independence and frequently encouraged the religious arts. Even though the empire of the Western Turks was little in the way of a centralized unifying power, Buddhism imposed a cultural unity throughout. At Funduqistan the monastery contains a courtyard with niches that were elaborately decorated with exquisite clay sculptures and paintings (illus. 96, 97). Near Ghazna (probably the site of a minor principality), excavations revealed a stupa and monastery complex at Tepe Sardar that was almost 'Baroque' in the richness of its sculptural decoration.[32] The main stupa, the largest in Afghanistan, was surrounded by many votive stupas and chapels, richly decorated in clay reliefs. The remains in the sanctuary include clay fragments of several colossal Buddha statues. Significantly, there is also a Brahman shrine in the Tepe Sardar complex, where a statue of the Hindu goddess Durga Mahishuramardini was found.

A site that has only recently become apparent in this late upsurge in Buddhism and Gandharan art is Kabul itself.[33] This largely became apparent from the Afghan excavations between 2004 and 2012 of a very large Buddhist monastic complex at Tepe Narenj overlooking the old city of Kabul, comprising one large stupa and five small stupas.[34] It consists of five groups of buildings on a series of nine artificial terraces, possibly the main Buddhist centre for the Kabul region for the Hun and Turk periods that remained active until the Muslim conquest in the ninth century. The terracing recalls both Kanishka's dynastic shrine at Surkh Kotal and the large-scale terraced Parthian fire temple complex of Sna Qal'a in Seistan mentioned in Chapter Five. The associated chapels contained many votive stupas and large numbers of Buddhist sculptures. Just 400 metres (1,310 ft) to the north and probably associated with it is a smaller monastery, Qol-i Tut, excavated at the same time. It comprises a main stupa and eighteen chapels on ten terraces containing painted bodhisattvas and a monumental seated Buddha. It was constructed in the sixth century and remained in use as late as the end of the eleventh century, confirming the continuing practice of Buddhism until well into the Islamic period. On another hill overlooking the old city is a site similar to Tepe Narenj at Khwaja Safa which also continued in active use into the ninth century. Clearly Kabul was another major Buddhist centre that enjoyed patronage under the Turk Kaganate, but was to enjoy a new lease of life after its collapse under two new dynasties.

The Kabul Shahs

The collapse of the Turk Kaganate brings about the end of the beginning of the Turks in world history, but already their achievement was impressive. The wealth of the 'neo-Gandharan' revival in the Hindu Kush and the Sogdian renaissance north of the Oxus are more than ample testament to their already significant legacy. Even this great achievement was simply a curtain-raiser of greater to come.

But the fall of the Turk Kaganate did not see the end of Gandharan art and its derivatives: there was a brief Indian summer under the two last dynasties of kings that witnessed a final flourishing of the style.[35] One of the petty rulers who survived the kaganate collapse was able to rally Turk forces around Kabul to create a new dynasty known as the Turk Shahs of Kabul. Not only did the Turk Shahs and their successors, the Hindu Shahs, create an island of stability in the ashes of kaganate collapse, but they resisted the first Muslim incursions and encouraged the last creative upsurge of the Gandharan style. The dynasty was founded by Barhatigin, who seized Kabul in about 666 after an Arab raid from Seistan. It was certainly the Muslim Arab invasions that forced Barhatigin to found his dynasty and defend both the region and its rich cultural identity from the new religion – with some success, as he routed an Arab army in 683 and again in 698–9. By a series of skilful negotiations backed up by military force the Turk Shahs of Kabul were able to safeguard their mountain stronghold and stave off the invading Arabs, as often as not by drawing them into their territory only to cut off their rear by blocking the passes.

One of the Turk rulers of Kabul between 738 and 745 was known as Frum Kesar, a name that means, literally, 'Caesar of Rome'. He was recognized as far away as China, where Tang annals mention the ruler Fulin Kiso of Kabul, which is identified with Frum Kesar. At the time his kingdom extended little further than the region around Kabul, extending north to the Hindu Kush, south to the Ghazni region and east to Swat and the region around Peshawar.[36] How and why he adopted the title is uncertain; one recalls that 'caesar' was one of the titles

107 The Manar-i Chakri.

adopted by the Kushans. Can the giant terraced shrine of Tepe Narenj in Kabul be a conscious emulation of Kanishka's terraced dynastic shrine at Surkh Kotal, with the adoption of the title of 'caesar' a memory kept alive for four centuries?

The last Turk Shah of Kabul was Lagartuman, who was forced in the end to buy off the Arabs of Seistan with tribute. It might have been this climb-down that prompted his chief minister, the Brahman Kallas, to overthrow Lagartuman in about 843, bringing about the end of the Turk dynasty and starting his own, the Hindu Shahs. This very vigorous dynasty of Hindu kings in Kabul was able to stave off the Arab advance a while longer and even initiate some monumental building programmes. These include the Bala Hisar fortress of Kabul and some extraordinary towers on the hills around Kabul, such as the Manar-i

Chakri and other stone towers on the mountains overlooking the Kabul Valley (illus. 107).[37] These stone towers may have been related to the ancient Indian tradition of victory towers – most famously, for example, the fourth-century BC victory columns of Emperor Ashoka – and as a building type were to assume a new lease of life under Islam (discussed in Chapter Eight).

There was also an important Hindu temple built at Khair Khana on the outskirts of Kabul, where finds included a marble statue of Surya (illus. 108), and excavations at Tepe Skandar further north revealed another Hindu shrine that included a statue of Uma Maheshvara.[38] But the Muslim advance was ultimately unstoppable (although Islam did not reach remoter parts of Afghanistan until the 1880s), with Kabul coming under the rule of the Muslim Saffarid dynasty of Seistan in the mid-tenth century. The Hindu Shahi dynasty lived on until 1026 at their subsequent capital at Hund on the Indus in Pakistan, but no longer formed a part of Afghanistan. Although ruling only a relatively brief time in Afghanistan, it was an important episode. They were Hindu rather than Buddhist, but represented the last of a long line of cultural influence from India that stretched all the way back to Mauryan rule in eastern Afghanistan, fusing both Indian and Greek cultural forms (and one recalls that even in the Bronze Age the Indus Civilization had an outpost in Afghanistan at Shortughai). After them the culture of Afghanistan was to change dramatically. The Hindu Shahs thus mark the end of one epoch and the beginning of another – but Hindu communities remain an important minority in Kabul to this day.

108 Statue of Surya from Khair Khana.

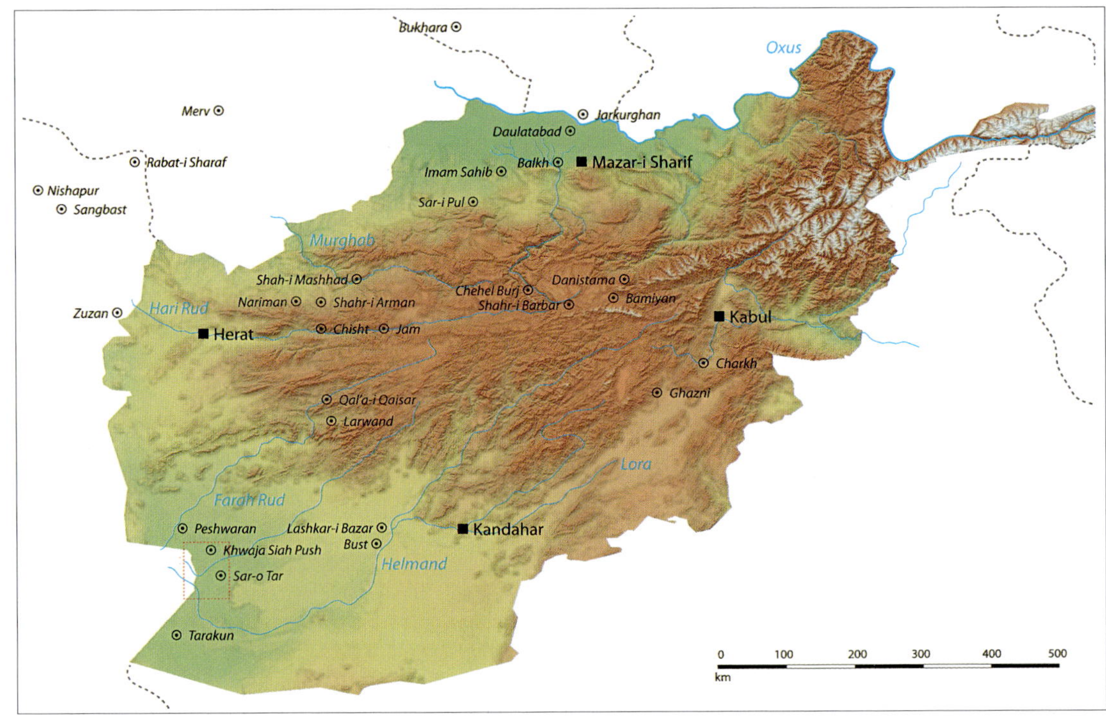

109 The main early Islamic sites under discussion.

8

A New Imperial Era: The Ghaznavid and Ghurid Empires

At about the same time as the collapse of the Turk Kaganate – indeed, perhaps one of its causes – a new power from the west extinguished Sasanian Iran and extended into Central Asia. In 622 the Prophet Muhammad proclaimed a new religion in Arabia and, less than a century later, these desert Arabs with their revolutionary new message ruled an empire that stretched from the borders of China to the Atlantic, an empire far greater than Cyrus or Shapur, Caesar or Alexander could ever have conceived. The age of Islam had arrived, ruled by the Umayyad dynasty of caliphs from their capital at Damascus.

Byzantium was the first to fall to this new power (although it survived), and Iran soon followed in 642. Like the equally spectacular advances of Alexander nearly a thousand years earlier, a brilliant empire vanished overnight. Our last glimpse of a Sasanian ruler was of Yazdagird III fleeing the Arab advances. Like Darius III's similar flight, Yazdagird escaped towards Central Asia, that traditional power base that Iran had previously turned to when challenged from the west. Yazdagird III was eventually killed on the Merv River near the present Afghan border, but it was a movement originating in the Afghan borderlands that was to fundamentally change Islam. This was the revolt in the 740s led by Abu Muslim from the region of western Afghanistan and Central Asia against the Umayyads of Damascus. This united the many disaffected religious and ethnic elements in the eastern Caliphate, especially the non-Arab descendants of the new converts to Islam who resented the discrimination shown to converts by the Arab elite.[1]

The revolt, known as the Abbasid Revolution of 750, was successful and had far-reaching results. It saw the establishment of the Abbasid dynasty and the move of the Caliphate from the essentially Hellenized and westward-looking climate of Damascus to Baghdad. With the move of the Arab court to Baghdad, the Arabs and Islam came increasingly under the influence of the far older civilizations to the east. This was brought about particularly with the rise of some extremely powerful families of Iranian and Central Asian viziers at the Arab court. The first of these families was the Barmakids, a family originally of hereditary priests from the great Buddhist temple of Nau Bahar at Balkh (see Chapter Five), who wielded enormous power through the Abbasid Caliphate.

The move to Baghdad turned Islam's back on the West. It also internationalized Islam. Hitherto, Islam was associated almost entirely with – or at least dominated by – the Arabs. But the Abbasid Revolution originated in the borderlands of Afghanistan, which meant that Islam was no longer dominated by the Arabs and the western Islamic lands: Islam became more universal. More importantly with regard to Afghanistan and Central Asia, it increasingly became implanted upon the native populations. This would have immense ramifications for the Middle East and for Islam generally. It was to be a reinvigorated Islam in the hands of a people from Central Asia who had no common cultural experience with the Arabs who were to transform the Middle East, Islam and eventually much of Europe and the Mediterranean, when the Turks came out of Central Asia some centuries later. The revival of Iran under Islam, when it did come, was in the eastern Iranian world of Afghanistan and Central Asia, not the western Iranian world from the direction of Islam itself. This was under the dynasties of the Tahirids, the Saffarids and, above all, the Samanids and Ghaznavids. This was largely due to the strength of the pre-Islamic east, of the Kushans, the Kushano-Sasanians, and the various Hun, Turk and Hindu polities that we have reviewed in the previous chapters.

The First Muslim Dynasties

The Turk Kaganate had already patronized a renaissance of the native Sogdians of northern Central Asia – mainly around Bukhara, Samarkand and Tashkent – and the subsequent establishment of Islam would result in a new upsurge of Central Asian civilization. By the ninth century, Abbasid rule began to weaken and some of the eastern provinces in and bordering Afghanistan began to go their own way, at first the Tahirids of Khurasan and soon after the Saffarids, who ruled Seistan and much of the adjacent parts of Iran and Afghanistan from 861 to 1003. Humble in origin, the Saffarid dynasty was founded by a coppersmith (*saffar*, hence the name of the dynasty), Ya'qub Ibn Layth, who broke away from central Abbasid rule in Baghdad (as well as, presumably, from coppersmithing) at the end of the ninth century. Ya'qub and his brother and successor, 'Amr Ibn Layth, were instrumental in extending Islam into Afghanistan at the expense of the Turk princes. After conquering the Tahirids of Khurasan, for a brief time the Saffarids were able to extend their rule over most of Iran, all of Afghanistan and even parts of Central Asia. They were eventually pushed back by the Abbasids in the west and by the upcoming power of the Samanids of Bukhara, but the family remained in Seistan for another six centuries, albeit as local rulers. They also, for the first time since the Muslim conquests, encouraged the revival of Persian as a literary language at court.

It was a family from Bukhara who brought about a renaissance – as opposed to just a revival – of Central Asian arts and the Persian language. This was the Samanid dynasty, who, under their founder Isma'il, established a brilliant court at their capital, Bukhara. Isma'il ruled from 892 to 907. The Samanid family itself were native Central Asian Iranians who had converted to Islam after the Arab conquest. In origin they were probably a family of Buddhist priests (the name *saman* is a root word that means 'priest' (our word 'shaman' comes from the same root, as does the town of Samangan in northern Afghanistan), and the transition from priests to rulers is a frequent theme of Iranian history. Indeed, the name 'Bukhara' itself may be derived from the root *vihara*, which means 'Buddhist monastery', so it is tempting to see pre-Islamic Bukhara as a Buddhist religious centre ruled by a dynasty of priest-kings, just as medieval Bukhara became the main Muslim religious centre for Central Asia.

Isma'il established the rule of his family at Bukhara, nominally under the Caliph in Baghdad but in practice ruling independently. All of present-day northeastern Iran came under Samanid rule, as well as most of present-day Uzbekistan and Afghanistan. More important, Isma'il made a point of using Persian as the court language rather than Arabic, which had hitherto enjoyed virtual monopoly throughout the Islamic world, in both Arab and non-Arab courts. Indeed, the word used for the Persian language in Afghanistan today is *Dari*, which means 'language of the court', rather than *Farsi*, which means 'language of Fars' (that is, Persia in southern Iran). This was the birth of modern Persian, now written in the Arabic script, soon to spread westwards back into the area of modern Iran. As well as a revival of Persian literature, this made Bukhara one of the great centres of learning in the Islamic world. One cannot stress the importance of Isma'il's patronage of Persian too strongly. Before, Persian as a literary language was in danger of dying out, replaced by Arabic. Instead, the following century would see an immense upsurge in Persian literature, dominated most of all by the epic poet Firdawsi (*c*. 935–1020): the age of classical Persian literature had arrived, and it is important to remember that modern Persian owes its origin to Central Asia rather than to Persia itself.[2]

It was the ruler of another principality on the eastern fringes of the Abbasid Caliphate who first brought Islam to the Turks and the Turks into the Middle East. Abdullah Ibn Talha (r. 828–45) was the head of the Tahirid dynasty of provincial governors – again, in practice independent – who ruled the area of Khurasan straddling northeastern Iran and the western parts of Afghanistan and the south of Central Asia. The Turk tribes who had migrated westwards with the former kaganate by then occupied the steppe land corresponding roughly to modern Kazakhstan. Abdullah raided deep into the Turkish steppe country, bringing back some 2,000 Turkish slaves. The Samanids of Bukhara were quick to realize the potential of the Turkish slave trade too, and the trade became a major commercial enterprise between the Central Asian Muslim kingdoms and the Arab Caliphate during the course of the ninth and tenth centuries. It is important, however, to recognize the different place that 'slaves' had in early Muslim society, as many could rise to senior administrative positions. In the case of the Turkish 'slaves', many were incorporated into the army as mercenary units – indeed, later Islamic history would see entire dynasties of Turkish 'slaves' becoming rulers (such as Mamluk – which means 'slave' – dynasties of both Egypt and India).

By the early tenth century many of the Turks in the steppe were in any case converting to Islam. These conversions seem to have been mainly pacific through contact with Muslim merchants and settlers in the Turk lands (contradicting the fallacy that Islam was largely spread by the sword). The situation was probably similar to that of the Germanic tribes on the borders of the Roman Empire in late antiquity: for the Turks, Islam represented the lure of prosperity and civilization.[3]

The Ghaznavid and Ghurid Empires

The Samanids had been relying increasingly upon Turkish mercenaries in their army, so that by the mid-tenth century the predominately Turkish guard in the Samanid army held real power while the reigning Samanid prince was little more than a puppet. On the death of the ruler in Bukhara, Abd al-Malik, in 961, the Turkish head of the Samanid army, Alptegin, attempted a coup. It failed, but the following year Alptegin fled southwards to Ghazni in Afghanistan to establish his own power base. A Turkish slave of Alptegin, Sebuktegin, established Ghazni as a separate kingdom after 977; his son, Sultan Mahmud of Ghazna, expanded it to a great empire after 997.[4] It was in Afghanistan that the first Turkish Muslim empire had come into being, and the Muslim world would never be the same.

The establishment of the Islamic Ghaznavid state marked both a new departure from and continuity with the past. It was new because it marked a religious break from the Hindu and Buddhist past. But otherwise it was business as usual. The Turk newcomers from the Samanid state – a military elite, not a mass migration – would have merged seamlessly with the older Turk elites, well established at Ghazni for centuries, as we saw in the previous chapter. Indeed, the long-established Turk presence in eastern Afghanistan was probably one of the factors in Alptegin and his successors coming there in the first place, and much of the Ghaznavid elite would have been the Islamized local former Buddhist families of Ghazni. Ghazni, now a Muslim capital, had long been a religious centre for Turk princes. And, like the Turk princes in the past, the long tradition of patronage of the arts was continued by the newcomers. It was certainly a characteristic of the Ghaznavid and Seljuk Turks, and the Ghaznavids found a ready-made vigorous tradition of cultural patronage by Turk princes when they arrived in the Hindu Kush. Thus it is important to emphasize, first, that non-Muslim rule in Ghazni overlapped with Muslim rule, and, second, that the arrival of Alptegin marked ethnic Turk continuity at Ghazni, not a break. The court of Ghazni only makes full sense against this background.

The birth of the first Turkish Muslim empire in history alone makes the Ghaznavids one of the more important empires of the Middle Ages.[5] There are other reasons. The Ghaznavids, particularly under their greatest ruler, Mahmud, were the first to bring Islam down onto the plains of India on a substantial scale when their empire was extended as far as Lahore and southwards to the Arabian Sea. Thus an additional overlay to the already rich multilayered nature of Indian civilization was added, probably the most important single event for India since the movement of Indo-Aryan peoples nearly 3,000 years previously in the way that it permanently affected the nature of Indian civilization. The Ghaznavids were more than just invaders, however. True to the legacy of the pre-Islamic Turk princes who ruled the petty states of the Hindu Kush under the kaganate, the Ghaznavid kings became great patrons as well. Just as their forebears had ushered in a renaissance of Gandharan civilization, their Ghaznavid successors patronized a new upsurge in civilization in the areas they ruled. Mahmud of Ghazni attracted poets, artists, scientists, mathematicians and men of learning generally to his court. There are too many to list here, but two must be singled out. The Persian epic poet Firdawsi was probably the greatest poet of the Persian language, whose work the *Shahnameh* or *Book of Kings*, is often regarded as single-handedly saving the Persian language from the onslaught of Arabic. It is written in a pure form of literary Persian and recounts the heroes of the pre-Islamic past and their exploits that took place in the Iranian–Afghan–Central Asian borderlands. Hence Firdawsi occupies a place in the hearts of Iranians as Homer does for the Greeks and Shakespeare for the English. He wrote it at the court of Ghazni and dedicated it to Mahmud. Another was one of the greatest polymaths of the Middle Ages – or indeed of any age – the universal scientist al-Biruni. Originally from Khwarazm on the lower Oxus, he practised mainly under the patronage of the Ghaznavid court. Armed with a knowledge of Persian and Arabic as well as Greek, Hebrew and Sanskrit, his scholarship was formidable and his curiosity insatiable, resulting in works as diverse as a history of India and accurately measuring the radius of the Earth.

The term 'renaissance' is chosen carefully here: not until the popes of Rome and the merchant houses of Florence would the world again see patronage on such a scale. Mahmud of Ghazna became the greatest potentate of the Islamic world, and his achievements outshone even the contemporary caliphs of Baghdad. For this he was awarded a title that henceforward would be associated with Turkish sovereigns above all: he was the first Muslim ruler to assume the title 'sultan'.

In the meantime, the Samanid state in Bukhara was crumbling fast under the ineffective rule of Nuh II (976–97). The Karakhanid prince Harun Bughra Khan (also Turkish) marched on Bukhara in 992, and on 23 October 999 his successor Nasr Ilig took Bukhara and ended the rule of the Samanid dynasty, thus bringing about an end to several thousand years of Iranian rule in Central Asia. There would not be another independent Persian-speaking state in that part of Central Asia until the establishment of Tajikistan in 1990.

The Oxus then formed the boundary between two rival Turkish states: the Ghaznavids to the south and the Karakhanids to the north. But a third and greater Turkish power was rising in the region east of the Caspian Sea that was soon to challenge both – and to take the Turkish peoples westwards to the Mediterranean and ultimately into Europe: the Seljuks. In 1063, Alp Arslan, leader of the Seljuks, led an invasion of Iran and the lands to the west. The Seljuks were to have a great subsequent history and a profound effect upon Iran and countries further west, but are peripheral to Afghanistan. For it was not the Seljuks who brought about an end to the Ghaznavid Empire but an indigenous dynasty from the remote mountain fastness of Ghur in western Afghanistan.

The Shansabanid dynasty – usually known as the Ghurids, after their homeland – traced their origin back to the mythical Iranian heroes of the *Shahnama*, but this may well have been an invented ancestry after they rose to prominence, as their origins are obscure. They may not even originally have been a Persian-speaking people but belonged to an eastern Iranian group whose origins are now lost (although the present Firuzkuhi tribes of western Afghanistan claim descent). The family were known to be petty rulers of the mountainous areas of Ghur during the Ghaznavid period, but they were never absorbed successfully into the empire by Mahmud, due mainly to the inaccessibility of the terrain. During the course of the twelfth century, the Shansabani princes of the remote mountain principality of Firuzkuh on the upper Herat River unified the rival mountain valleys of Ghur and began to threaten the position of the Ghaznavids by raids out of their mountain strongholds. Then in 1150–51 the greatest of the Ghurid sultans, 'Ala'-ud-Din, sacked Ghazni. For this 'Ala'-ud-Din acquired the epithet *jahan-suz*, or 'world-burner'. Their brief rule in Afghanistan, however, is marked largely by continuity from the Ghaznavid period, continuing the Ghaznavid tradition of building projects. They also extended their rule further east as far as Delhi. Their own capital, Firuzkuh (modern Jam), deep in the mountains, is marked by one of the most magnificent – and largest – minarets in the Islamic world, and they built an even larger one at Delhi (the Qutb Minar – the highest in the world), as well as some exquisitely decorated lesser buildings in their empire, often in remote places. The real end came at the hands of a conqueror compared to whom even 'Ala'-ud-Din the World Burner paled into insignificance when the Mongols invaded.[6]

The Architectural Tradition: Iranian or Afghan?

Before examining individual remains it might be worth making some general observations. The early Islamic architecture of Afghanistan – mainly Ghaznavid and Ghurid – is generally included within the overall subject of Persian Islamic architecture.[7] But there are important differences. Apart from regional variations – and these are important – of the approximately forty mosques prior to about 1500 recorded in the *Archaeological Gazetteer of Afghanistan*, there is not a *single* complete mosque still in use from the pre-Mongol period (and precious few after), only ruins.[8] This is in stark contrast to neighbouring Iran, which has a large corpus of extant Seljuk (and pre-Seljuk) mosques. Entirely absent too are tomb towers, so characteristic of the architecture of Iran in our period, particularly of eastern Iran. Indeed, there is little funerary architecture generally in contrast to either Iran or the very rich tradition in neighbouring Pakistan and India.

Why might this be so? The area of Afghanistan, corresponding approximately to the early Islamic divisions of Khurasan and Seistan, was not significantly less urbanized than Iran. Sources describe the regions of Balkh, Herat and Seistan in particular in terms of wealth, population and urbanization,[9] and later accounts of Mongol devastations speak of populations sometimes exceeding a million.[10] Even if such figures are exaggerated, they are nonetheless evidence of urbanization – and, with it, monumental building – as great as any part of the eastern Islamic world.

Perhaps this is one of the reasons why there are so few extant remains: the regions of Central Asia and Afghanistan were singled out for particular destruction by Genghis Khan, hence the Mongol devastations were more thorough. Furthermore, Seistan, where archaeological remains are some of the densest in Afghanistan in the early Islamic period, was further devastated by Tamerlane.[11] The region of western Afghanistan around Herat also suffered in the sixteenth and seventeenth centuries when it became a battleground between Safavid and Uzbek forces. Any generalizations on the Islamic architecture of Afghanistan therefore must come with a strong caveat: they are based on a limited number of examples.

There is another important difference. Attention was drawn in Chapter Seven to the fact that the first three centuries of Islam saw a sudden and massive increase in Buddhist art and architecture in Afghanistan, in particular at the Buddhist centres of Bamiyan, Kabul and Ghazni, part of a complex Buddhist communications network in eastern Afghanistan between the seventh and tenth centuries. The Buddhist religious complexes in Kabul remained active probably as one of the main centres of Buddhism in Afghanistan still in use until the end of the eleventh century, well into the period of the Ghaznavids. The major Buddhist complex of Tepe Sardar at Ghazni also remained active until the ninth century or later, and this was to have important ramifications, as we shall see. 'Pre-Islamic' art and architecture therefore remained longer in Afghanistan than in neighbouring Iran.

Mosques, Palaces and Forts

Despite the paucity of surviving early mosques in Afghanistan noted above, Afghanistan does boast the remains of one of the earliest of the eastern Islamic world (illus. 109). This is the remarkable Mosque of Nau Gunbad at Balkh (illus. 110, 111).[12] As its name implies – *nau gunbad* means 'nine domes' – it consists of a central dome surrounded by three domes on each side to form a square. A recent study has dated it to the end of the eighth century and related it to the building activity of Fazl b. Yahya the Barmakid, the Abbasid governor of Balkh between 792 and 803; it was deliberately built within the sacred landscape of the great Buddhist monastery of Naw Bahar, of which the Barmakids were hereditary priests.[13] It is particularly noted for its extremely fine stucco decoration. The linking of the Mosque of Nau Gunbad with the Buddhist monastery of Naw Bahar and the Barmakids assumes further significance, as several studies have highlighted the family for pre-Islamic – specifically Buddhist – survivals within Islam, further confirming the continuity of Buddhist traditions into early Islamic Afghanistan.

110 The Mosque of Nau Gunbad at Balkh.

111 Detail of the stucco decoration of the Mosque of Nau Gunbad.

Afghanistan also boasts the remains of some of the most outstanding palatial complexes of early Islam. In that windswept desert area of Seistan where so many ancient and medieval buildings have been preserved are the remains of the ninth-century Saffarid city of Taq, now the immense ruined urban site of Shahr-i Ghulghula, one of the largest sites in Seistan, swamped by sand dunes in the middle of the desert area known as Sar-o Tar (illus. 113).[14] The fortified area is more than a kilometre square and is surrounded by ramparts and a ditch that encloses the lower town. There is an inner circular city, also surrounded by ramparts, and an innermost citadel surrounded by two further lines of ramparts in the centre dominated by the palace off centre. The Saffarid upper palace in the citadel still survived two storeys in height with traces of a third when it was studied in the 1970s. In plan, its exterior walls are undulating on all four sides, which must have presented an extraordinary 'rippled facade', a feature entirely unique in Islamic architecture (illus. 112). The interior is a series of courtyards culminating in an audience hall. A second lower palace was built in the Ghaznavid period in the inner circular enclosure. It is a four-*iwan* courtyard plan similar to the South Palace at Lashkari Bazar (discussed

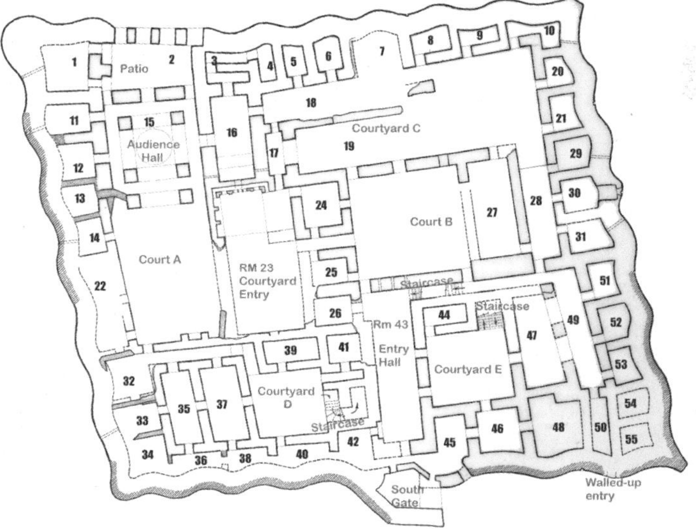

112 Plan of the Saffarid palace at Shahr-i Ghulghula.

113 The entrance to the inner circular city of Shahr-i Ghulghula (Seistan) with the citadel on the right.

below), but has a southern extension in the form of an octagonal courtyard with rooms opening off all eight sides: this too has no counterpart in Islamic architecture. Also in the circular enclosure are the remains of a large Friday mosque with adjacent caravanserai and a mint.[15] Outlying settlements extend for several kilometres beyond the walls, many of them large elaborate houses, probably mansions or estate houses, decorated with repeated blind arches, probably dating from the Saffarid period.[16]

The desert sands of Seistan in fact are one of the greatest repositories of ancient remains in Asia, where buildings from simple houses

114 The larger square buttressed fort at Chehel Burj.

and forts to temples and entire cities such as Nishk, Nad-i Ali, Shahr-i Ghulghula and others have been preserved. Such a high density of settlements and monuments must appear odd in the extremely arid conditions of today. However, a study of Seistan and the desert region by satellite imagery has revealed an astonishing quantity of pre-modern remains under the sands, far more than hitherto thought, much of them hydrological installations,[17] and in Chapter Two we drew attention to the sophisticated system of irrigation canals as far back as the Iron Age. Most of the standing remains are Islamic; there are too many to discuss here, but a good example is the vast area of ruined towers and eroded fortifications known collectively as Chehel Burj.[18] The main standing

115 One of the minarets at Ghazni.

remains are Ghaznavid, comprising an immense fortress 170 square metres (1,830 sq. ft) and an adjacent circular fortification 85 metres (280 ft) in diameter. The name Chehel Burj means 'forty towers', referring to the repeated alternative triangular and semicircular projecting buttresses or towers on the exterior of both fortresses (illus. 114; in fact 87 were counted on the large fortress). Such an unusual style – essentially decorative rather than structural – is also found on some of the early minarets in Afghanistan, such as the alternating rounded and triangular buttresses on the minarets of Khwaja Siah Push and Nad-i Ali.[19] It is also found in Seistan, as well as the 'stellate' plans of the Ghazni minarets. Those towers on the square fortress at Chehel Burj are entered from galleries on all four sides at second-floor level.[20] This distinctive style of essentially decorative projecting buttress seems more characteristic of the so-called *kushks*, palaces or mansions of the early Islamic period, in the Merv oasis in Turkmenistan. However, the style has a long history in Afghanistan as far back as the Bronze Age buildings at Dashli in the north and Mundigak in the south (illus. 18, 25). Such 'stellate' plans of the minarets at least, it is suggested, were inspired by the plans of votive stupas in Buddhist monasteries.[21]

The capital of the Ghaznavid Empire was Ghazni itself, but there is little to see today, due as much to 'Ala' ud-Din's destruction as to Genghis Khan's a short time later.[22] The most conspicuous remains are minaret of Masud III, interpreted as victory towers, covered in elaborate brick and terracotta decoration, built by Masud III (1099–1114) and Bahram Shah (1118–52; illus. 115). The palace, excavated by an Italian team, is a complex of buildings surrounding a central, marble paved courtyard. The most significant find was a long frieze decorated with repeated multi-lobed blind arches (illus. 116) with an inscription in Persian, 250 metres (820 ft) long. Other finds include objects of glass, ceramic and bronze; decorative stuccos; paintings; marbles; and tilework.

Rather more of an impression of Ghaznavid palatial magnificence can be seen at their winter capital, Lashkari Bazar ('Soldiers' Bazaar'), to the southwest of Kandahar.[23] Here, the remains of huge palace complexes line the banks of the Helmand River for a distance of over 7 kilometres (4 mi.), far exceeding in size any European palace, either contemporary or later (illus. 117–119). It was made the winter capital of the Ghaznavid Empire by Sultan Mahmud in the early eleventh century and it rapidly expanded northwards along the river. The site comprises a vast area of gigantic mud ruins of palatial residences, public buildings and fortifications, together with mounds, scattered building debris and sherds. Together with the extramural suburb of Kusrutabad on the right bank, the city covers some 20 square kilometres (215 sq. ft), although many more remains lie scattered in the surrounding region, making this figure a conservative estimate of the total area of occupation. The northern part of the site consists of the remains of three enormous palatial complexes built at the height of the Ghaznavid period on a bluff overlooking the river, each

116 Decorative panel from the palace at Ghazni.

surrounded by immense walled enclosures which were ornamental gardens and hunting parks. The largest and most elaborate palace is the southernmost one, which incorporated a magnificent audience hall originally decorated in paintings and carved stucco, with a small private mosque adjacent completely covered in carved stucco. This was removed and reconstructed in the National Museum in Kabul. The architecture of all three palaces incorporates many Central Asian influences.

The site of Bust forms the southern end of the Lashkari Bazar complex, dominated by an immense citadel on a mound of uncertain

117 Entrance to the Central Palace at Lashkari Bazar.

date surrounded by a high enclosure wall. On top of the citadel are the remains of many structures, in both mud-brick and baked brick, most notable of which is a seven-storey galleried 'well' or shaft constructed down through the centre of the mound. At the foot of the citadel is a free-standing archway of the Ghurid period covered in very elaborate brick and stucco decoration (illus. 120, 121). Both of these monuments have almost no counterparts in Islamic architecture. Outside the enclosure the most notable remains are those of another mud-brick Ghaznavid palatial complex. The Ghurid sultans inherited this Ghaznavid taste for opulence and were not entirely destroyers, the

118 The South Palace at Lashkari Bazar.

119 A palace facade at Bust, part of the Lashkari Bazar ensemble.

sack of Ghazna itself notwithstanding. It remained a royal residence during the Ghurid period, being eventually destroyed by the Mongol conquests in the thirteenth century.

Although the Lashkari Bazar palaces remained in use under the Ghurids, the sultans ruled from their capital of Firuzkuh ('turquoise mountain') on the Herat River in the remote mountain fastness of Ghur in western Afghanistan.[24] Their administrative centre was probably at Herat, but the only surviving remains from that period are a decorated portal in the Friday mosque.[25] However, Firuzkuh – modern Jam – boasts one of the most spectacular monuments in the Islamic world, its stupendous decorated minaret, the second-highest of such pre-modern structures in the world (illus. 122–4). It stands 65 metres (213 ft) high and has a diameter of 9 metres (29½ ft) at its base. It is made up of four tapering cylindrical shafts on an octagonal base, with a double spiral staircase inside. The outside is completely covered in elaborate decorative brickwork, except for one band of blue tile inscription near the top. Curiously, the distinctive criss-crossing vertical inscriptions are the verses of the Virgin Mary from the Qur'an. The date inscription has been read as either 1174–5 or 1193–4, the former

120 Detail of the arch at Bust.
121 The arch at Bust.

corresponding to the capture of Ghazni by the Ghurids, the latter the capture of Delhi. Immediately to the east of the minaret the remains of a large courtyard, presumed to be the mosque associated with the minaret, have been partially uncovered, and fragments of the town of Firuzkuh were traced on either side of the valley. Nearby, numerous Hebrew funerary inscriptions have been recorded, evidence of a Jewish community at Firuzkuh.

On the hills overlooking the site on either side of the river are mud-brick watchtowers forming a fortification line. More interestingly, the mountain passes to the south of Jam are honeycombed with an elaborate and extensive network of fortifications ranging from just

122 The Minaret of Jam.
123 Alternate view of the Minaret of Jam. Note horse and rider at the foot for scale.

single towers to immense fortresses such as the castle of Qal'a-i Qaysar guarding one of the main passes leading towards Firuzkuh. Many have elaborate plaster decoration. Together they form one of the most extensive fortification networks of the medieval Islamic world, a Ghurid 'Maginot Line'.[26]

124 Detail of the inscription of Mary on the Minaret of Jam.

This fortification network recalls the one defending the Bamiyan Valley. Although dating from the period of the Western Turk Empire these fortifications were reoccupied and perhaps extended during the Ghurid period when Bamiyan formed an important principality led by a branch of the Shansabani family who ruled Ghur.[27] The huge fortified palatial complex of Sarkhushak on a bluff overlooking the Bamiyan River to the east of Bamiyan was probably the seat of the Shansabani princes.[28] The complex includes a mosque and a tomb, and much of the architecture recalls pre-Islamic styles.

Another important Ghurid or Ghaznavid monument in the Bamiyan region also recalling pre-Islamic styles is the small *madrasa* or Qur'anic school at Danestama.[29] The excavators initially assumed that it was a Buddhist monastery because its style was so close to Buddhist models, but the building contained no traces of a stupa or Buddhist statuary and it was firmly dated no earlier than the Ghaznavid period in the eleventh century. Its interpretation as a madrasa therefore is a convincing one. Although only a modest building, what makes it important is that the madrasa did not exist in the

125 The two dome chambers at Chisht.
126 Brickwork detail at Chisht.

first few centuries of Islam, but was introduced by the Seljuks from Central Asia as a means to counter Shi'a heresy in the Near East (although the madrasa was eventually to become a feature as much of Shi'a architecture as of Sunni). It has been suggested that the Central Asian Buddhist *vihara* or monastery inspired the madrasa, both as an institution for religious teaching and architecturally as a building type. Central Asia was the original homeland of the Seljuks, so the suggestion is plausible. In eastern Afghanistan there would have been many Buddhist monastery complexes still extant at the time of the arrival of the Ghaznavid Turks – monastery complexes, furthermore, firmly rooted in existing Turk traditions of architectural patronage. In this context, the excavated building at Danestama in the central Hindu Kush might be viewed as a link.[30]

Given the probable origins of the madrasa building form in the Buddhist monastery, it comes as no surprise therefore that the main surviving religious buildings from the early Islamic period in Afghanistan are madrasas, albeit very ruinous (and extremely remote). At Chisht on the Herat River east of Herat is one of the few surviving Ghurid monuments comprising two adjacent monumental mausolea built of baked brick, both probably once forming a part of a single complex, presumed to have been a madrasa. One has a dated inscription, 1167, and the other is dated stylistically to the same period (illus. 125).[31] At Shah-i Mashhad in the remote mountainous district of northwestern Afghanistan are ruins of an elaborately decorated baked-brick madrasa. Only parts of the northern and eastern sides are still standing. Both monuments contain exquisite brick and stucco decoration.[32] Another very ruined – but again brick-decorated – building at Peshwaran in Seistan has also been interpreted as a madrasa.[33] Many more Ghurid monuments are found in Pakistan and India, such as the magnificent Adhai Din Ka Jhompra Mosque in Ajmer, beyond the scope of this volume.

Continuity from Buddhism

The new religion, therefore, ushered in important new building forms and styles that at first would seem to be completely at odds with the older ones. But alongside the new forms, old forms quickly reasserted themselves, or merely continued uninterrupted under new guise. How did this cultural continuity manifest itself? It is apparent mainly in the fields of architecture and ornament, and a number of elements may be examined in turn.

Surprisingly persistent was an import from Indian architecture. Under Islam many of the minarets, both those attached to mosques and those completely isolated, were built as victory towers commemorating specific victories. The most famous is the Ghurid Minaret of Jam (illus. 122), built to commemorate Sultan Ghiyath al-Din's conquests, but the earlier Ghaznavid towers of Mas'ud III and Bahram at Ghazni (illus. 115) have also been interpreted as victory towers. In India such commemorative towers have a very ancient tradition going back to the victory columns of the Mauryan Empire. Both the early Islamic victory towers/minarets and the ancient Roman victory columns have been traced back to this tradition.[34] A possible link in Afghanistan was the Manar-i Chakri and other stone towers of the Kabul region from the time of the Hindu shahs (illus. 107).

Another pre-Islamic element to continue was the *iwan* or monumental portal, which had its origins in Central Asia. Under Islam it survived as the four-*iwan* mosque, where a mosque courtyard has four *iwans* or portals on each of its sides. This type of mosque began with the Seljuk mosques of Iran, but soon became almost a universal feature of the mosque architecture of the eastern Islamic world. The *iwan* might also form a monumental entrance in secular as well as religious architecture. We have already seen this develop as the monumental portals in pre-Islamic palace architecture, such as at Ai Khanoum. In Parthian and Sasanian palace architecture the four-*iwan* plan became a major feature, such as at Parthian Ashhur and Sasanian Ctesiphon (both in Iraq). In Afghanistan the monumental portal became the dominant feature of the pre-fifteenth-century architecture of Seistan, where both entrances and courtyards would have one or more *iwans*, as well as at the twelfth-century Ghaznavid palaces at Lashkari Bazar.

At first sight, the decoration of Ghaznavid and Ghurid architecture appears to mark a complete break with the Graeco-Buddhist architectural decoration of the past: Islamic architecture with its emphasis on abstract patterns and calligraphy, the Buddhist with its emphasis on figurative art – the Buddha image in particular – and its derived Classical elements such as Classical entablatures and 'Indo-Corinthian' capitals. But were the two styles so far apart? Common to both was a *horror vacui*, the compulsion to cover – almost to swamp – every available space of a wall surface with decoration. Ghaznavid and Ghurid buildings are particularly noted for their surface decoration, 'whose ornateness consistently exceeds anything known in the rest of Iran in the Saljuq period . . . architectural decoration to a pitch of technical mastery never to be exceeded'.[35] Compare the richness of the decoration of Ghurid buildings with the comparatively plainer Seljuk buildings of the same period in Iran.

The architectural decoration of the Ghaznavid and Ghurid periods comprised brick patterns: bricks arranged in an infinite variety of ways to decorate entire wall surfaces and form inscriptions. The technique follows the Seljuk brick decoration of Iran, and in Afghanistan is seen at its finest on the minarets, mainly the two at Ghazni and the great Ghurid minaret at Jam (illus. 124), as well as on minor monuments at Shah-i Mashhad and Chisht (illus. 126). The Minaret of Jam, in addition to its brick patterns, has a band of blue-glazed brick decoration around near the tip. This marks the beginning of a new form of architectural decoration that in subsequent centuries was to replace virtually all others. It is tempting to view the abstract patterns of the built landscapes of Afghanistan that we described in the Introduction (illus. 6–9) as subconscious inspiration behind such decoration in the formal architecture.

It must be remembered that the newly arrived Ghaznavid patrons would have employed craftsmen – or at least a craft tradition – who were used to decorating Buddhist buildings. Such craftsmen could not, of course, cover the new buildings with human images, but they would have found decorating wall surfaces to be not only natural, but irresistible. Such richness applies only to the general spirit of decoration. But there are specific decorative elements in Ghaznavid buildings that can be traced back to Buddhist architecture. This can be seen mostly in Ghaznavid palace architecture at Ghazni and Lashkari Bazar. Common elements throughout Buddhist architecture are various forms of scroll patterns, vegetal motifs and garlanding: compare, for example, the many stucco examples from Tepe Sardar and elsewhere in Buddhist Afghanistan; such motifs are repeated on the marble friezes from the walls of the Palace of Mas'ud at Ghazni or the painted and stucco decorative friezes from Lashkari Bazar (illus. 127, 128). Such decorative elements, of course, are common elsewhere in Islamic architecture, and can ultimately be traced back to Classical forms, as can the same elements in Buddhist architecture. But it is difficult to imagine craftsmen working on the palace at Ghazni using second-hand copybooks while ignoring first-hand examples right on their doorstep at Tepe Sardar.

Attention has been drawn to Indian elements in Ghaznavid and Ghurid stone carving.[36] In particular are the multi-lobed blind arches, either singly or in series, that appear in relief carvings from Bust and especially at Ghazni, both the marble orthostats on which the monumental inscription is written and the many individual fragments on gravestones and other pieces (illus. 116). These are ascribed to the influence of craftsmen from northwestern India who may have arrived in the wake of Ghaznavid and Ghurid military incursions. Doubtless this did happen – and a wealthy court such as Ghazni would have attracted craftsmen from far and wide. But as an origin much closer to Ghazni for this motif are the multi-lobed blind arches that typically frame seated Buddha images and are an almost universal feature of Buddhist architecture (illus. 101, 103), particularly at Tepe Sardar,[37]

127, 128 Buddhist scroll work from Shotorak (*top*) and Islamic scroll work from Ghazni (*bottom*).

but its occurrence in the Buddhist monuments so close to Ghazni could hardly have gone unnoticed by the builders of Ghazni's palace. Tepe Sardar had the largest Buddhist stupa in Afghanistan; it was also one of the most elaborately decorated and one of the latest, remaining in use as late as the ninth century. In other words, much of it would still have been visible when construction of the Ghaznavid capital nearby commenced, and a monument of this size and richness would not have gone unobserved by craftsmen.

Repeated blind arches are perhaps the most distinctive features of all in the palaces of Lashkari Bazar and in the early Islamic architecture of Seistan, in the form of either repeated keyhole blind arches, horseshoe arches or simple pointed arches. Such a basic motif need not have any single origin, but its use in Buddhist architecture must surely be relevant. Here, it took two forms: either the repeated multi-lobed arches framing seated Buddha images discussed in Chapter Six (illus. 93), or repeated arches framing scenes of Buddhist iconography separated by Indo-Corinthian or Persepolitan columns (illus. 75, 78). In finding the motif used almost continuously in Afghanistan from Buddhist through to Islamic architecture it is difficult to escape the conclusion that the one has evolved from the other.

Very little survives of Ghaznavid painting, the lines of 'courtiers' in the royal audience hall of the South Palace at Lashkari Bazar being almost the sole complete examples. These have been convincingly related to the late Buddhist art of Afghanistan and the seventh-century Buddhist cave paintings at Kucha and Qizil in Xinjiang, particularly those that depict donors at the latter.[38] The Central Asian Sogdian paintings of Afrasiab, Panjikent, Ajina Tepe and Varakhsha are a part of this tradition, although the Xinjiang examples appear closer to the Lashkari Bazar paintings.[39]

Ceramic studies reveal a conscious archaizing movement in some of the pottery traditions of the tenth to twelfth centuries in western Afghanistan. This took the form of deliberately copying pre-Islamic motifs, mainly prehistoric – Chalcolithic and Bronze Age – that could only have survived into the early Islamic period in archaeological contexts. But it also included copying styles and decoration closer in time, such as Sasanian and Kushan. For many years this curious phenomenon misled some of the most discerning archaeologists, but is now placed convincingly in the early Islamic period.[40] Again, it demonstrates how craftsmen in Afghanistan looked to the past for inspiration. It also underlines a theme that runs throughout this book: that of continuity.

Conclusion

That the architecture of the Ghaznavid and Ghurid periods has elements of its own distinct from the broader eastern early Islamic world has long been recognized. These distinctive elements, when examined from within their own geographical, cultural and historical context, can be explained by their pre-Islamic past. This is not to deny elements from elsewhere in the Islamic world as well, or that they were somehow non-Islamic. But the survival of Buddhist architecture into the Islamic period and the establishment of Turk dynasties in eastern Afghanistan from the fifth century through to the Mongol conquest, with princes who furthermore patronized both the Buddhist and the Islamic arts, must be regarded as a continuum, and not as two separate histories.

The invasion of Genghis Khan in the early thirteenth century brought an end to these developments. The Mongol invasions were, without doubt, probably the most devastating in all history, especially for the region of Central Asia and Afghanistan. It is, therefore, perhaps appropriate to draw our account to a close here, except to emphasize that even then there was revival in Afghanistan and even great new resurgences of cultural achievement under the Timurids who came afterwards and moved their capital from Samarkand to Herat.

It is perhaps too simplistic to characterize Afghanistan's history as one of being invaded by one group of bastards after another. It is true that from the supposed Indo-Aryan invasions at the end of the Bronze Age, through the subsequent invasions by Persians, Macedonians, Scythians, Kushans, Huns, Turks and Arabs, Afghanistan has witnessed a grim catalogue of invasions still to this day. But such 'invasions' have as often as not been movements of peoples rather than cataclysmic single events. More importantly, Afghanistan has consistently shown a resilience that takes captive its invaders. After Alexander's invasion, for example, there was a reassertion of the indigenous cultures in Afghanistan out of which emerged Buddhism in its Indo-Hellenistic guise. Further 'invasions' by the Scythians and Kushans transformed Buddhism into the major world religion that it is today.

Accounts of ancient civilizations in the Middle East conventionally end with the arrival of Islam: the 'end of antiquity', as it is often termed. But the pre-Islamic/Islamic 'divide' in Afghanistan was not the break that it is often viewed as. It is appropriate to conclude, therefore, in this chapter which saw one major religion, Buddhism, coexisting for several centuries with another, Islam. While Islam eventually did replace Buddhism, its arrival in at the beginning of the eighth century was not the break that many perceive, but, like so much of Afghanistan's history, was one of cultural transition and continuity.

REFERENCES

Bibliographical references to archaeological sites are mainly limited to Warwick Ball, *Archaeological Gazetteer of Afghanistan*, for the sake of brevity, as each site entry contains a full list of bibliographical references, which the reader can then follow up. Also for brevity, the references are to *Gazetteer* followed by the site numbers rather than page numbers in order to be valid for the earlier 1982 edition as well as the 2019 edition.

Introduction: Elusive Definitions

1 Thomas Barfield, *Afghanistan: A Cultural and Political History* (Princeton, NJ, 2023), p. 274.
2 Ibid., pp. 55–6.
3 Gregory L. Possehl, 'The Middle Asian Interaction Sphere', *Expedition*, XLIX/1 (2007), pp. 40–42.
4 A refreshing exception is Richard E. Payne and Rhyne King, eds, *The Limits of Empire in Ancient Afghanistan: Rule and Resistance in the Hindu Kush, circa 600 BCE–600 CE* (Wiesbaden, 2020): 'Above all, the volume makes plain the interest and utility in placing Afghanistan at the center, rather than the periphery, of the history of ancient empires in West Asia', according to the editors' words on the rear cover.
5 In fact there is now a diaspora of 3–4 million Afghans living worldwide.
6 Raymond Allchin, Warwick Ball and Norman Hammond, eds, *The Archaeology of Afghanistan from the Earliest Times to the Timurid Period: New Edition* (Edinburgh, 2019), pp. 344–459.
7 Barfield, *Afghanistan*, pp. 47–9, 384–5.
8 The term first coined by Henri-Paul Francfort, 'The Early Periods of Shortughaï (Harappan) and the Western Bactrian Culture of Dashly', in *South Asian Archaeology, 1981*, ed. B. Allchin (Cambridge, 1984), pp. 170–75.
9 Probably the best geographical, cultural and ethnic background is Louis Dupree, *Afghanistan* (Princeton, NJ, 1980). See also Edgar Knobloch, *The Archaeology and Architecture of Afghanistan* (Stroud, 2002, although based on an earlier book he published in 1972 so now very out of date); Willem Vogelsang, *The Afghans* (Oxford, 2002); St John Simpson, *Afghanistan: A Cultural History* (London, 2012); and Barfield, *Afghanistan*.
10 Warwick Ball, *The Eurasian Steppe: People, Movement, Ideas* (Edinburgh, 2021).
11 Mountstuart Elphinstone, *An Account of the Kingdom of Caubul*, 2 vols (London, 1815), vol. I, p. 127.
12 David C. Thomas and Fiona J. Kidd, 'On the Margins: Enduring Pre-Modern Water Management Strategies in and around the

Registan Desert, Afghanistan', *Journal of Field Archaeology*, XLII/1 (2017), pp. 29–42.

13 For example, Elizabeth Errington and Joe Cribb, eds, *The Crossroads of Asia: Transformation in Image and Symbol in the Art of Ancient Afghanistan and Pakistan*, exh. cat., Fitzwilliam Museum (Cambridge, 1992).

14 See M. Jamil Hanifi, '"Afghan" in Afghanistan: Idols in the Land of Idols', *Afghanistan*, VI/2 (2023), pp. 151–77.

15 The second-largest group of Hazara numbering over 40,000 are now found in Australia, mainly Melbourne.

16 To paraphrase the title of Rory Stewart, *The Places in Between* (London, 2004).

1 Afghanistan and the Outside World

1 Frantz Grenet, 'An Archaeologist's Approach to Avestan Geography', in *Birth of the Persian Empire*, ed. Vesta Sarkhosh Curtis and Sarah Stewart (London, 2005), pp. 29–51.

2 M. T. Fisher and M. W. Stolper, 'Achaemenid Elamite Administrative Tablets. 3. Fragments from Old Kandahar', ARTA, I/1 (2015), p. 26.

3 Herodotus, *The Histories*, trans. Aubrey de Selincourt (London, 1954), 3.103.

4 Raymond Allchin, Warwick Ball and Norman Hammond, eds, *The Archaeology of Afghanistan from the Earliest Times to the Timurid Period: New Edition* (Edinburgh, 2019), p. 325.

5 Philostratus, *Life of Apollonius of Tyana*, trans. F. C. Conybeare (London, 1912), Book II.

6 This and the discussion of other Chinese travellers below is mainly drawn from Jeannette Mirsky, *The Great Chinese Travelers* (Chicago, IL, 1964).

7 Samuel Beal, *Buddhist Records of the Western World* (London, 1884), pp. 50–51.

8 These accounts are superbly summarized by G. Le Strange, *Lands of the Eastern Caliphate* (London, 1905).

9 Ibn Battuta, *Travels in Asia and Africa*, trans. H.A.R. Gibb (London, 1929), p. 590.

10 Warwick Ball, 'The Seven Qandahars: The Name Q.ND.HAR. in the Islamic Sources', *South Asian Studies*, IV/1 (1988), pp. 123–4.

11 Marco Polo, *The Travels of Marco Polo*, introduced by John Masefield (London, 1908), p. xi.

12 Ibid., pp. 78–9.

13 And still do today: see Frances Wood, *Did Marco Polo Go to China?* (London, 1995).

14 Charles Masson, *Narrative of Various Journeys in Balochistan, Afghanistan and the Panjab*, 3 vols (London, 1842), vol. II, p. 276. See also William Trousdale, '"A Person of Desperate Fortunes": On the Evaluation of Historical Sources', *Bulletin of the Asia Institute*, I (1987), pp. 139–43.

15 For the Europeans at Ranjit Singh's court see C. Grey, *European Adventurers of Northern India 1785 to 1849*, ed. H.L.O. Garrett (Lahore, 1929). The film *The Man Who Would Be King* was directed by John Huston and released in 1975. For Gardner see John Keay, *The Tartan Turban: In Search of Alexander Gardner* (London, 2017). According to Ben Macintyre, *Josiah the Great: The True Story of the Man Who Would Be King* (London, 2004), the model for Kipling's hero was the American Josiah Harlan rather than Alexander Gardner. Both are admirably fictionalized in George MacDonald Fraser's *Flashman and the Mountain of Light* (London, 1990).

16 Gérard Fussman, 'Kushan Power and the Expansion of Buddhism beyond the Soleiman Mountains', in *Kushan Histories*, ed. Harry Falk (Bremen, 2015), pp. 153–202 (p. 155).

17 Elizabeth Errington, *Charles Masson and the Buddhist Sites of Afghanistan: Explorations, Excavations, Collections 1832–1835* (London, 2017); Elizabeth Errington, *The Charles Masson Archive: British Library, British Museum and Other Documents Relating to the 1832–1838 Masson Collection from Afghanistan* (London, 2017). See also Gordon Whitteridge, *Charles Masson of Afghanistan: Explorer, Archaeologist, Numismatist and Intelligence Agent* (Warminster, 1986).

18 See Alexander Burnes, *Travels into Bukhara*, 3 vols (London, 1834); Alexander Burnes, *Cabool: A Personal Narrative of a Journey to, and Residence in That City* (London, 1841); Mohan Lal, *Travels in the Punjab, Afghanistan and Turkistan to Balk, Bokhara and Herat* (London, 1846); James Lunt, *Bokhara Burnes* (New York, 1969); Craig Murray, *Sikunder Burnes: Master of the Great Game* (Edinburgh, 2016).

19 The bulk of the results were published as secret documents by P. J. Maitland, W. Peacocke and J. West Ridgeway, *Records of the Intelligence Party, Afghan Boundary Commission*, 5 vols (Simla, 1887–91). Many of the boundary commission officers further published their own independent accounts, and the works by Thomas H. Holdich, *The Gates of India* (London, 1910); G. P. Tate, *Seistan: A Memoir on the History, Topography, Ruins and People of the Country* (Calcutta, 1910); and many others still remain major source books on Afghanistan.

20 Kerr Fraser-Tytler, *Afghanistan: A Study of Political Developments in Central Asia* (London, 1953), p. 139 (emphasis added). Also emphasized by J. L. Lee, *The 'Ancient Supremacy': Bukhara, Afghanistan and the Battle for Balkh, 1731–1901* (Leiden, 1996), p. 76.

21 Lee, *'Ancient Supremacy'*, pp. 74–8. See also Holdich, *The Gates of India*.

22 Anthony McNicoll and Warwick Ball et al., *Excavations at Kandahar 1974 and 1975* (Oxford, 1996), p. 9. See also Masson, *Narrative*; Aurel Stein, *On Alexander's Track to the Indus* (London, 1928); Warwick Ball, 'Some Talk of Alexander', in *The Alexander Romance in Persia and the East*, ed. Richard Stoneman, Kyle Erickson and Ian Netton (Groningen, 2012), pp. 127–58; Errington, *Charles Masson*.

23 Olaf Caroe, *The Pathans: 550 BC–AD 1957* (London, 1958), p. 44.

24 Michael Wood, *In the Footsteps of Alexander the Great: A Journey from Greece to Asia* (London, 1997), p. 8.

25 Ball, 'Some Talk'.

26 Wilfred Thesiger, *Desert, Marsh and Mountain: The World of a Nomad* (London, 1979), pp. 231–2.

27 Dervla Murphy, *Full Tilt* (London, 1965), pp. 56, 58, 69 (emphasis added).

28 Matthew Leeming, 'To Afghanistan, in Alexander's Footsteps', *The Times* (21 June 2003), p. 6.

29 Alex Spillius's review of Rory Stewart, *The Places in Between* (London, 2004), in the *Daily Telegraph Travel* (31 July 2004), despite Stewart himself never making such a preposterous claim (and the 'French explorer in 1957' presumably refers to André Maricq, who was Belgian, not French). The article also contained a colour photograph of 'the destroyed palace of former Afghan King Mohammad Zahir Shah' encountered by Stewart – again, the photograph is not in Stewart's book and is not of Zahir Shah's or anyone else's palace, destroyed or otherwise.

30 Leeming, 'To Afghanistan', for example, imagined the Khyber Pass to be in Afghanistan.

31 Nick Danziger, *Danziger's Travels: Beyond Forbidden Frontiers* (London, 1987); Sandy Gall, *Behind Russian Lines: An Afghan Journal* (London, 1983); Stewart, *Places in Between*.

32 Warwick Ball, *Archaeological Gazetteer of Afghanistan*, revd edn (Oxford, 2019).

33 Françoise Olivier-Utard, *Politique et archéologie: Histoire de la Délégation archéologique française en Afghanistan (1922–1982)* (Paris, 2003).

34 Ball, *Gazetteer*.

35 Nicholas Sims-Williams, *Bactrian Documents from Northern Afghanistan*, 3 vols (Oxford, 1991–2012).

36 Joseph Naveh and Shaul Shaked, *Aramaic Documents from Ancient Bactria (Fourth Century B.C.E.) from the Khalili Collections* (London, 2012).

37 Both the journal and book series were co-founded by Warwick Ball and published by Edinburgh University Press.

38 Jolyon Leslie, 'Conservation of Buddhist Heritage in Afghanistan, 2016–2022', *Afghanistan*, VII/1 (2024), pp. 1–21.

39 The title of Stewart's 2004 book.

2 A Land of Two Rivers: The Oxus and Helmand Civilizations of the Bronze Age

1 Kenneth Clark, *Civilisation* (London, 1969), p. 1.
2 Felipe Fernández-Armesto, *Civilizations* (London, 2000).
3 *Gazetteer*, Site 266.
4 *Gazetteer*, Site 46.
5 Richard Davis in Raymond Allchin, Warwick Ball and Norman Hammond, eds, *The Archaeology of Afghanistan from the Earliest Times to the Timurid Period: New Edition* (Edinburgh, 2019), p. 65.
6 *Gazetteer*, Map 2; Allchin, Ball and Hammond, eds, *The Archaeology of Afghanistan*, Chapter Two.
7 *Gazetteer*, Site 743.
8 See Allchin, Ball and Hammond, eds, *The Archaeology of Afghanistan*, Chapter Three; Bertille Lyonnet and Nadezhda A. Dubova, eds, *The World of the Oxus Civilization* (London, 2021).
9 *Gazetteer*, Map 3.
10 Pierre Gentelle, *Prospections archéologiques en Bactriane orientale (1974–1978). Sous la direction de Jean-Claude Gardin*, vol. I: *Données paléogéographiques et fondements de l'irrigation* (Paris, 1989); Eric Fouache et al., 'Palaeochannels of the Balkh River (Northern Afghanistan) and Human Occupation since the Bronze Age Period', *Journal of Archaeological Science*, XXXIX/11 (2012), pp. 3415–27.
11 *Gazetteer*, Sites 256–9.
12 *Gazetteer*, Site 1089.
13 Francfort in Allchin, Ball and Hammond, eds, *The Archaeology of Afghanistan*, p. 155.
14 See Allchin, Ball and Hammond, eds, *The Archaeology of Afghanistan*, Chapter Four.
15 *Gazetteer*, Sites 229, 335, 383. See also William B. Trousdale and Mitchell Allen, *The Archaeology of Southwest Afghanistan* (Edinburgh, 2022), pp. 331–45.
16 *Gazetteer*, Site 743.
17 By the 1970s the building had completely eroded away.
18 *Gazetteer*, Site 752; Allchin, Ball and Hammond, eds, *The Archaeology of Afghanistan*, pp. 243–4.
19 Trousdale and Allen, *The Archaeology of Southwest Afghanistan*, pp. 433–49.
20 Warwick Ball, *The Eurasian Steppe: People, Movement, Ideas* (Edinburgh, 2021), Chapter Two.
21 Andrew Robinson, *The Indus* (London, 2015).

3 Iron Age Changes: Indo-Iranian Languages and the Rise of the Persian Empire

1 Warwick Ball, *The Eurasian Steppe: People, Movement, Ideas* (Edinburgh, 2021), p. 63.
2 The best overview is J. P. Mallory, *In Search of the Indo-Europeans: Language, Archaeology and Myth* (London, 1989).
3 Mary Boyce, *Zoroastrians: Their Religious Beliefs and Practices* (London, 1997), p. 1.
4 For Zoroastrianism generally, see ibid. See also Vesta Sarkhosh Curtis, *Persian Myths* (London, 1993); Frantz Grenet, 'An Archaeologist's Approach to Avestan Geography', in *Birth of the Persian Empire*, ed. Vesta Sarkhosh Curtis and Sarah Stewart (London, 2005), pp. 29–51.
5 Victor Sarianidi, *Margiana and Protozoroastrianism* (Athens, 1998); D. Stronach and M. Roaf, *Nush-i Jan 1: The Major Buildings of the Median Settlement* (Leuven, 2007).
6 Thomas Barfield, *Afghanistan: A Cultural and Political History* (Princeton, NJ, 2023), pp. 47–9, 384–5.
7 *Gazetteer*, Site 99.
8 Jean-Claude Gardin, *Céramiques de Bactres* (Paris, 1957), p. 93; Paul Bernard, Roland Besenval and Philippe Marquis, 'Du "mirage bactrien" aux réalités archéologiques: Nouvelles fouilles de la Délégation archéologique française en Afghanistan (DAFA) à Bactres. 2004–2005', *Comptes-rendus de l'Academie des inscription et belles-lettres*, CL/2 (2006), pp. 1175–248.

9 *Gazetteer*, Site 186; Bernard, Besenval and Marquis, 'Du "mirage bactrien"'; Raymond Allchin, Warwick Ball and Norman Hammond, eds, *The Archaeology of Afghanistan from the Earliest Times to the Timurid Period: New Edition* (Edinburgh, 2019), pp. 275–6. According to Claude Rapin, 'On the Way to Roxane 2: Satraps and Hyparchs between Bactra and Zariaspa-Maracanda', in *A Millennium of History*, ed. Johanna Lhuillier and Nikolaus Boroffka (Berlin, 2018), pp. 257–98, Zariaspa is identified with Samarkand.

10 *Gazetteer*, Sites 37, 38, 295, 666.

11 *Gazetteer*, Site 522; Allchin, Ball and Hammond, eds, *The Archaeology of Afghanistan*, pp. 279–83; Anthony McNicoll and Warwick Ball, *Excavations at Kandahar 1974 and 1975* (Oxford, 1996); Svend W. Helms, *Excavations at Old Kandahar in Afghanistan, 1976–1978* (Oxford, 1997).

12 F. T. Hiebert and C. C. Lamberg-Karlovsky, 'Central Asia and the Indo-Iranian Borderlands', *Iran*, XXX/1 (1992), pp. 1–16.

13 M. T. Fisher and M. W. Stolper, 'Achaemenid Elamite Administrative Tablets. 3: Fragments from Old Kandahar', ARTA, I/1 (2015), p. 26.

14 McNicoll and Ball, *Excavations at Kandahar*, pp. 392–3.

15 W. J. Vogelsang, *The Rise and Organisation of the Achaemenid Empire: The Eastern Iranian Evidence* (Leiden, 1992), pp. 227–9.

16 Mitchell Allen and William B. Trousdale, 'Early Iron Age Culture of Sistan, Afghanistan', *Afghanistan*, II/1 (2019), pp. 29–69; William B. Trousdale and Mitchell Allen, *The Archaeology of Southwest Afghanistan* (Edinburgh, 2022).

17 Allchin, Ball and Hammond, eds, *The Archaeology of Afghanistan*, pp. 276–7.

18 Ute Franke and Thomas Urban, *Ancient Herat: Research Reports of the German–Afghan Archaeological Mission to Herat, Afghanistan*, vol. II: *Excavations and Explorations in Herat City* (Berlin, 2017).

19 W. Barthold, *An Historical Geography of Iran* (Princeton, NJ, 1984), pp. 6–11; M. A. Dandamayev, 'Media and Achaemenid Iran', in *History of Civilizations of Central Asia*, vol. II: *The Development of Sedentary and Nomadic Civilizations: 700 BC to AD 250*, ed. János Harmatta (Paris, 1994), pp. 40–42.

20 *Gazetteer*, Site 1192. I am grateful to Henri-Paul Francfort for this added note on Iron Age Tillya Tepe.

21 Pierre Gentelle, *Prospections archéologiques en Bactriane orientale (1974–1978): Sous la direction de Jean-Claude Gardin*, vol. I: *Données paléogéographiques et fondements de l'irrigation* (Paris, 1989); Eric Fouache et al., 'Palaeochannels of the Balkh River (Northern Afghanistan) and Human Occupation since the Bronze Age Period', *Journal of Archaeological Science*, XXXIX/11 (2012), pp. 3415–27; Trousdale and Allen, *The Archaeology of Southwest Afghanistan*, pp. 14–15.

22 See Warwick Ball, *Towards One World: Ancient Persia and the West* (London, 2010), Chapter Three, for alternative interpretations of the Persian Wars.

23 Wu Xin, 'Enemies of Empire: A Historical Reconstruction of Political Conflicts between Central Asians and the Persian Empire', in *The World of Achaemenid Persia*, ed. John Curtis and St John Simpson (London, 2020), p. 560.

24 Wouter F. M. Henkelman, 'Bactrians in Persepolis – Persians in Bactria', in *A Millennium of History: The Iron Age in Southern Central Asia (2nd and 1st Millennia BC)*, ed. Johanna Lhuillier and Nikolaus Boroffka (Berlin, 2018), pp. 223–56; Wu Xin, 'Exploiting the Virgin Land: Kyzyltepa and the Effects of the Achaemenid Persian Empire on Its Central Asian Frontier Bactria', in *A Millennium of History*, ed. Lhuillier and Boroffka, pp. 189–216.

25 For this interesting theory see D. T. Potts, 'Cyrus the Great and the Kingdom of Anshan', in *Birth of the Persian Empire*, ed. Curtis and Stewart, pp. 7–28. For the exact opposite view – that Cyrus was a Persian and Darius the Elamite – see Wouter F. M. Henkelman, 'Cyrus the Persian

and Darius the Elamite: A Case of Mistaken Identity', in *Herodotus and the Persian Empire*, ed. R. Rollinger, B. Truschnegg and R. Bichler (Wiesbaden, 2011), pp. 577–634.

26 Vogelsang, *The Rise and Organisation of the Achaemenid Empire.*

27 Fouache et al., 'Palaeochannels'.

28 *Gazetteer*, Sites 594, 631.

29 Gentelle, *Prospections*; B. Lyonnet, *Prospections archéologiques en Bactriane orientale (1974–1978)*, vol. II: *Céramique et peuplement du chalcolithique à la conquête arabe* (Paris, 1997); J.-C. Gardin, *Prospections archéologiques en Bactriane orientale (1974–1978)*, vol. III: *Description des sites et notes de synthèse* (Paris, 1998). Achaemenid pottery has also been observed on the citadel of Ai Khanoum itself (Philippe Marquis, personal communication).

30 O. M. Dalton, *The Treasure of the Oxus with Other Objects from Ancient Persia and India* (London, 1964); John Curtis, *The Oxus Treasure* (London, 2012).

31 *Gazetteer*, Sites 522, 698, 752.

32 *Gazetteer*, Sites 38, 209, 288, 631, 666, 931, 936.

33 *Gazetteer*, Site 2013.

34 I am grateful to Anthony Lauricella for this observation.

35 I am grateful to the late Donald Whitcomb for this observation.

4 Hellenism Transformed: Macedonian Invasion to Greek Kingdoms

1 The member of the dig team who posed the question, the late Lady Margaret Wheeler, was the estranged wife of the archaeologist Sir Mortimer Wheeler, who originally proposed the British excavations for the stated reason of looking for remains of Alexander following a visit they both made to the site when he was director general of the Archaeological Survey of India in 1946. See also Chapter One.

2 P. M. Fraser, *Cities of Alexander the Great* (Oxford, 1996).

3 John D. Grainger, *Alexander the Great Failure* (London, 2007). See also Warwick Ball, *Towards One World: Ancient Persia and the West* (London, 2010), Chapter Four, 'an excellent account of Alexander which I find easy to accept', according to John Boardman, *The Greeks in Asia* (London, 2015), p. 223, n.75.

4 Boardman, *Greeks in Asia.*

5 Peter Green, *Alexander the Great* (Berkeley, CA, 1991), pp. 6, 40.

6 See A. B. Bosworth, *Alexander and the East: The Tragedy of Triumph* (Oxford, 1996), for Alexander's eastern shambles. Of the many general accounts of Alexander, Green, *Alexander*, is probably one of the more readable and balanced.

7 Mary Boyce and Frantz Grenet, *A History of Zoroastrianism*, vol. III: *Zoroastrianism under Macedonian and Roman Rule* (Leiden, 1991), p. 361.

8 Green, *Alexander*, and Boardman, *Greeks in Asia*, give good accounts of this relationship and the ensuing events. See also Ball, *One World*, Chapter Four.

9 Josef Wiesehöfer, 'Greek Exiles in the Achaemenid Empire: A Case of Divided Loyalties?', in *The Persian World and Beyond*, ed. Mark B. Garrison and Wouter F. M. Henkelman (Münster, 2023), pp. 382–3.

10 See Claude Rapin, 'On the Way to Roxane 2: Satraps and Hyparchs between Bactra and Zariaspa-Maracanda', in *A Millennium of History*, ed. Johanna Lhuillier and Nikolaus Boroffka (Berlin, 2018), pp. 257–98, for a very careful reconstruction of these events.

11 Rachel Mairs, *The Hellenistic Far East: Archaeology, Language, and Identity in Greek Central Asia* (Oakland, CA, 2014), pp. 238–43.

12 Located to the south of Samarkand according to Rapin, 'On the Way to Roxane'.

13 On a visit to the Ferghana Valley in 2004 I was both intrigued and gratified to observe in book stalls a brightly illustrated children's book in Uzbek, *Spitamen* by Maqsud Qoriyev (Tashkent,

2001). On enquiring about it I was informed that 'Spitamenes is a great hero around here; Alexander is not' – an important corrective. On another visit to the region in 2007, I was further surprised – and gratified – to visit a small town between Istaravshan and Khojend in Tajikistan that had been renamed, appropriately, 'Spitamen'.

14 Frank L. Holt, *Into the Land of Bones: Alexander the Great in Afghanistan* (Berkeley, CA, 2005), reconstructs a graphic and very savage account of Alexander's reign of terror in this campaign (although his parallel with the U.S.-led invasion of Afghanistan is rather flimsy, especially since this part of Alexander's campaign was almost entirely outside the present borders of Afghanistan to the north).

15 Rapin, 'On the Way to Roxane', p. 281.

16 This argument was notably proposed by A. K. Narain, *The Indo-Greeks* [1957] (Oxford, 2003).

17 Warwick Ball, *The Eurasian Steppe: People, Movement, Ideas* (Edinburgh, 2021), Chapter Four.

18 It is glossed over in ancient and modern accounts as a 'marriage between east and west' (something that the Persian Empire that Alexander destroyed had previously achieved) in desperate attempts to cast Alexander's systematic brutality in a positive light. But it was a standard practice by ancient conquerors – a practice that distressingly still occurs – to hand the captive women over to the troops; I see no reason to believe that Alexander's treatment in Susa was in any way different.

19 The classic accounts of Greek Bactria and India are W. W. Tarn, *The Greeks in Bactria and India* (Oxford, 1948); and Narain, *Indo-Greeks*. More recent are several books by Frank L. Holt, *Alexander the Great and Bactria* (Leiden, 1995); *Thundering Zeus: The Making of Hellenistic Bactria* (Berkeley, CA, 1999); and *Lost World of the Golden King: In Search of Ancient Afghanistan* (Berkeley, CA, 2012), all three mainly numismatic. See also Mairs, *The Hellenistic Far East*; Boardman, *Greeks in Asia*; and Rachel Mairs, ed., *The Graeco-Bactrian and Indo-Greek World* (Abingdon, 2021), the last a detailed multi-authored series of studies on the subject aimed mainly at the specialist.

20 Holt, *Thundering Zeus*, pp. 178–84. Holt, *Lost World*, pp. 132–4, also has a good summary of the classical sources for Graeco-Bactria.

21 Strabo 15.1.3.

22 This numismatic evidence was originally pieced together in a masterly, although now outdated, study by Tarn, *The Greeks in Bactria and India*. The most recent overview is Simon Glenn, *Money and Power in Hellenistic Bactria* (Turnhout, 2020); see also his chapter in Mairs, ed., *The Graeco-Bactrian and Indo-Greek World*; and the works by Holt (note 18 above).

23 Such as the Kushan coin hoard found at Debre Damo in Ethiopia. See Stuart Munro-Hay, *Ethiopia, the Unknown Land: A Cultural and Historical Guide* (London, 2002), p. 336.

24 Holt, *Lost World*, Chapter Three.

25 *Gazetteer*, Site 99; Eric Fouache et al., 'Palaeochannels of the Balkh River (Northern Afghanistan) and Human Occupation since the Bronze Age Period', *Journal of Archaeological Science*, XXXIX/11 (2012), pp. 3415–27.

26 There is a huge bibliography, mainly in French, listed in the *Gazetteer*, Site 18. See also Henri-Paul Francfort et al., *Il y a 50 ans... la découverte d'Aï Khanoum. 1964–1978, fouilles de la Délégation archéologique française en Afghanistan* (Paris, 2014); Laurianne Martinez-Sève, 'Ai Khanoum and Greek Domination in Central Asia', *Electrum*, XXII (2015), pp. 17–46; and Raymond Allchin, Warwick Ball and Norman Hammond, eds, *The Archaeology of Afghanistan from the Earliest Times to the Timurid Period: New Edition* (Edinburgh, 2019), pp. 291–310, 324–6, for brief accounts.

27 Holt, *Lost World*, p. 187.

28 J.-C. Gardin, *Prospections archéologiques en Bactriane orientale (1974–1978)*, vol. III: *Description des sites et notes de synthèse* (Paris, 1998), p. 91, no. 506; *Gazetteer*, Site 495.

29 *Gazetteer*, Sites 294, 314, 475, 776.
30 See Mairs, *The Hellenistic Far East*, pp. 25–6, for a summary and bibliography of these two sites.
31 *Gazetteer*, Sites 122, 100.
32 *Gazetteer*, Site 522. See also Allchin, Ball and Hammond, eds, *The Archaeology of Afghanistan*, pp. 288–91, 320–22.
33 The whereabouts of this intriguing inscription remains unknown. See Mairs, *The Hellenistic Far East*, Chapter Three; and Ball, 'Arachosia, Drangiana and Areia', in *The Graeco-Bactrian and Indo-Greek World*, ed. Mairs, pp. 357–85, for discussions of this inscription and the Kandahar remains.
34 William B. Trousdale and Mitchell Allen, *The Archaeology of Southwest Afghanistan* (Edinburgh, 2022), pp. 346–9, 400–449. Although belonging to the Parthian or Indo-Parthian period (Chapter Six), they are included here because of their Hellenistic style.
35 Ute Franke and Thomas Urban, *Ancient Herat: Research Reports of the German–Afghan Archaeological Mission to Herat, Afghanistan*, vol. II: *Excavations and Explorations in Herat City* (Berlin, 2017); *Gazetteer*, Site 428.
36 Sir John Marshall, *A Guide to Taxila* (Cambridge, 1960).
37 C. P. Cavafy, *Collected Poems*, trans. by Edmund Keeley and Philip Sherrard (London, 1998), p. 114.
38 Mairs, *The Hellenistic Far East*, p. 144.
39 Nicholas Sims-Williams, ed., *Indo-Iranian Languages and Peoples* (Oxford, 2002), p. 229, notes the very few words in modern Pashtu that derive from Greek.

5 A Forgotten Empire: From Hunted Nomad Chiefs to Kushan Emperors

1 B. Ja. Staviskij, *La Bactriane sous les Kushans: Problèmes d'histoire et de culture* (Paris, 1986); and John M. Rosenfield, *The Dynastic Arts of the Kushans* (Berkeley, CA, 1967) are about the only single volumes. An Internet search came up with B. N. Mukherjee, *The Rise and Fall of the Kusāna Empire* (Calcutta, 1988), but I have been unable to obtain this. At the time of writing Joe Cribb, Robert Bracey and Lauren Morris were editing a multi-authored book on the world of the Kushans to be published by Routledge.
2 John M. Rosenfield, 'Prologue: Some Debating Points on Gandhāran Buddhism and Kuṣāṇa History', in *Gandhāran Buddhism*, ed. Pia Brancaccio and Kurt Behrendt (Vancouver, 2006), pp. 9–37 (p. 10).
3 Henri-Paul Francfort, personal communication.
4 Unlike one book with that title edited by John Curtis and Nigel Tallis, *Forgotten Empire: The World of Ancient Persia* (London, 2005), just about the best-known empire of antiquity.
5 The title of Chapter Nine in Laszlo Torday, *Mounted Archers: The Beginnings of Central Asian History* (Edinburgh, Cambridge and Durham, 1997).
6 See Nicola Di Cosmo, 'State Formation and Periodization in Inner Asian History', *Journal of World History*, X/1 (1999), pp. 1–40 (pp. 3–4).
7 Torday, *Mounted Archers*; Joe Cribb and Georgina Herrmann, eds, *After Alexander: Central Asia before Islam* (Oxford, 2007), Chapters Two and Three; Warwick Ball, *The Eurasian Steppe: People, Movement, Ideas* (Edinburgh, 2021), Chapters One to Four.
8 For example, Christopher I. Beckwith, *The Scythian Empire: Central Eurasia and the Birth of the Classical Age from Persia to China* (Princeton, NJ, 2023); or Kenneth W. Harl, *Empires of the Steppes: The Nomadic Tribes Who Shaped Civilisation* (London, 2023).
9 Rachel Mairs, *The Hellenistic Far East: Archaeology, Language, and Identity in Greek Central Asia* (Oakland, CA, 2014), Chapter Four.
10 Frank L. Holt, *Lost World of the Golden King: In Search of Ancient Afghanistan* (Berkeley, CA, 2012), pp. 200, 119–20.
11 J. Cribb, 'The Greek Kingdom of Bactria, Its Coinage and Its Collapse', in *Afghanistan, ancien carrefour entre l'est et l'ouest*, ed. O. Bopearachchi and M.-F. Boussac (Paris, 2005), pp. 207–25;

Jeffrey D. Lerner, 'A Reappraisal of the Economic Inscriptions and Coin Finds from Aï Khanoum', *Anabasis: Studia Classica et Orientalis*, II (2011), pp. 103–47.

12 *Gazetteer*, Site 728; Raymond Allchin, Warwick Ball and Norman Hammond, eds, *The Archaeology of Afghanistan from the Earliest Times to the Timurid Period: New Edition* (Edinburgh, 2019), pp. 257–8.

13 John R. Payne, 'Pamir Languages', in *Compendium Linguarum Iranicarum*, ed. R. Schmitt (Wiesbaden, 1989), pp. 417–44; Willem Vogelsang, *The Afghans* (Oxford, 2002), p. 30.

14 Warwick Ball, 'Kandahar, the Saka and India', in *South Asian Archaeology, 1995: Proceedings of the 13th International Conference of the European Association of South Asian Archaeologists*, ed. Raymond Allchin and Bridget Allchin (New Delhi, 1997), pp. 439–50; Allchin, Ball and Hammond, eds, *The Archaeology of Afghanistan*, pp. 265–6, 342–3.

15 Torday, *Mounted Archers*; Thomas Barfield, *Shadow Empires: An Alternative Imperial History* (Princeton, NJ, 2023), Chapter Three.

16 There has been a huge amount of confusion, misunderstanding, myth-making and general overblown statements about the Tocharoi/Tocharians, often conflated with the so-called mummies of Xinjiang: for example, Jeannine Davis-Kimball, *Warrior Women: An Archaeologist's Search for History's Hidden Heroines* (New York, 2002), Chapters Eight and Nine; and Harl, *Empires*. Ball, *The Eurasian Steppe*, pp. 73–6, is an attempt to straighten some of this out.

17 Xinru Liu, 'The Kushan Empire', *Oxford Research Encyclopaedia, Asian History* (2020), at https://doi.org/10.1093/acrefore/9780190277727.013.227.

18 Svenja Bonmann et al., 'A Partial Decipherment of the Unknown Kushan Script', *Transactions of the Philological Society*, CXXI/2 (2023), pp. 293–329; Harry Falk, 'Wema Takhtu, the Graveyard Near Almosi, and the End of an "Unknown" Script', *Annual Report of the International Research Institute for Advanced Buddhology at Soka University*, CXXI/2 (2023), pp. 253–64; Joe Cribb, 'Kushan Royal Inscription among the Almosi Rock Inscriptions Recently Discovered in Tajikistan', *Journal of the Royal Asiatic Society*, XXXIV/2 (2024), pp. 1–15.

19 *Gazetteer*, Site 122.

20 In fact one branch of the Yuezhi – known in Chinese sources as the Lesser Yuezhi – stayed behind in Gansu and may have founded the Northern Liang dynasty of China at the end of the fourth century.

21 Bonmann et al., 'A Partial Decipherment'.

22 See Michael Alram and Deborah E. Klimburg-Salter, eds, *Coins, Art and Chronology: Essays on the Pre-Islamic History of the Indo-Iranian Borderlands* (Vienna, 1999); and Michael Alram, Deborah Klimburg-Salter, Minoru Inaba and Matthias Pfisterer, eds, *Art and Chronology II: The First Millennium CE in the Indo-Iranian Borderlands* (Vienna, 2010) for discussions of these issues. See also N. Sims-Williams and H. Falk, 'Kushan Dynasty II: Inscriptions of the Kushans', *Encyclopædia Iranica*, www.iranicaonline.org, accessed 8 December 2014.

23 Stuart Munro-Hay, *Ethiopia, the Unknown Land: A Cultural and Historical Guide* (London, 2002), pp. 336–7.

24 Warwick Ball, 'The Sasanian Empire and the East: A Summary of the Evidence', in *Sasanian Persia: Between Rome and the Steppes of Eurasia*, ed. Eberhard W. Sauer (Edinburgh, 2017), pp. 151–78.

25 They also survived in the Armenian royal family, with the Armenian evangelist St Gregory the Illuminator also claiming descent.

26 *Gazetteer*, Sites 190, 824, 849, 962, 988.

27 *Gazetteer*, Sites 522, 752, 1006; William B. Trousdale and Mitchell Allen, *The Archaeology of Southwest Afghanistan* (Edinburgh, 2022).

28 *Gazetteer*, Site 1107; Trousdale and Allen, *The Archaeology of Southwest Afghanistan*, pp. 315–23.

29 Gherardo Gnoli, *Zoroaster's Time and Homeland* (Naples, 1980).

30 Trousdale and Allen, *The Archaeology of Southwest Afghanistan*, pp, 150, 313–23, 478–509.

31 *Gazetteer*, Sites 554, 595; Trousdale and Allen, *The Archaeology of Southwest Afghanistan*, pp. 245–6, 388–99.

32 E. Sachau, *Alberuni's India*, 2 vols (London, 1888), vol. ii, p. 21.

33 Warwick Ball, 'Some Rock-Cut Monuments in Southern Iran', *Iran*, xxiv (1984), pp. 95–115; Mostafa Vaziri, *Buddhism in Iran* (New York, 2012).

34 The name of the site in the local Uzbek Turk language should actually be transcribed as Tilla Tapa, 'Gold Mound'. This arrived into English as the slightly distorted 'Tillya' when 'Tilla' was transcribed into Russian as 'Тилля' by the excavators because of the final Russian '-я' or '-ya'. *Gazetteer*, Site 1192; V. I. Sarianidi, *Bactrian Gold: From the Excavations of the Tillya-Tepe Necropolis in Northern Afghanistan* (Leningrad, 1985).

35 Pierre Cambon and Jean-François Jarrige, eds, *Afghanistan, les trésors retrouvés: Collections du Musée national de Kaboul* (Paris, 2006); Fredrik Hiebert and Pierre Cambon, eds, *Afghanistan: Hidden Treasures from the National Museum, Kabul* (Washington, dc, 2008). See also the essays in Joan Aruz and Elisabetta Valtz Fino, eds, *Afghanistan: Forging Civilizations along the Silk Road* (New York, 2012), associated with the New York exhibition.

36 Kevin van Bladel, 'The Bactrian Background of the Barmakids', in *Islam and Tibet: Interactions along the Musk Routes*, ed. Anna Akasoy, Charles Burnet and Ronet Yoeli-Tlalim (Farnham, 2011), pp. 43–88.

37 Arezou Azad, *Sacred Landscape in Medieval Afghanistan* (Oxford, 2013), pp. 69–110.

38 Étienne de la Vaissière, Philippe Marquis and Julio Bendezu Sarmiento, 'A Kushan Military Camp near Bactra', in *Kushan Histories*, ed. Harry Falk (Bremen, 2015), pp. 241–54; *Gazetteer*, Sites 8, 1245.

39 Marquis, de la Vaissière and Bendezu-Sarmiento, 'Kushan Military Camp'; *Gazetteer*, Sites 520, 1198.

40 Eberhard W. Sauer, Jebrael Nokandeh and Hamid Omrani Rekavandi, *Ancient Arms Race: Antiquity's Largest Fortresses and Sasanian Military Networks of Northern Iran*, 2 vols (Oxford, 2022).

41 *Gazetteer*, Site 892; J.-C. Gardin, *Prospections archéologiques en Bactriane orientale (1974–1978)*, vol. iii: *Description des sites et notes de synthèse* (Paris, 1998), p. vi, no. 503.

42 *Gazetteer*, Site 122.

43 *Gazetteer*, Site 1088.

44 *Gazetteer*, Site 404.

45 David Jongeward et al., *Gandharan Buddhist Reliquaries* (Seattle, wa, and London, 2012).

46 *Gazetteer*, Site 127.

47 *Gazetteer*, Sites 1237, 519, 1087, 1036, 389.

48 *Gazetteer*, Site 19.

49 Rosenfield, *Dynastic Arts*; G. J. Wightman, *Sacred Spaces: Religious Architecture in the Ancient World* (Leuven, 2007), pp. 688–92; *Gazetteer*, Sites 944, 1223.

50 Gérard Fussman, 'Kushan Power and the Expansion of Buddhism beyond the Suleiman Mountains', in *Kushan Histories*, ed. Falk, pp. 183–4.

51 N. Sims-Williams and H. Falk, 'Kushan Dynasty ii. Inscriptions of the Kushans', *Encyclopædia Iranica*, at www.iranicaonline.org, accessed 8 December 2014; *Gazetteer*, Site 944.

52 Frantz Grenet et al., 'The Sasanian Relief at Rag-i Bibi (Northern Afghanistan)', in *After Alexander*, ed. Cribb and Herrmann, pp. 243–68; *Gazetteer*, Site 2227.

53 Nicholas Sims-Williams and François de Blois, *Studies in the Chronology of the Bactrian Documents from Northern Afghanistan* (Vienna, 2018), pp. 49–51. See also Allchin, Ball and Hammond, eds, *The Archaeology of Afghanistan*, pp. 379–84.

54 Claude Rapin, 'Nomads and the Shaping of Central Asia: From the Early Iron Age to the Kushan Period', in *After Alexander*, ed. Cribb and Herrmann, pp. 29–72; Kazim Abdullaev, 'Nomad Migration in Central Asia', in *After Alexander*,

pp. 73–98; Frantz Grenet, 'The Nomadic Element in the Kushan Empire (1st–3rd Century AD)', *Journal of Central Asian Studies*, III (2012), pp. 1–22; D. T. Potts, *Nomadism in Iran from Antiquity to the Modern Era* (Oxford, 2014), pp. 124–33.

55 Thomas J. Barfield, 'Supersize Me: Political Aspects of Monumental Tomb Building in Early Steppe Empires', in *Masters of the Steppe*, ed. Svetlana V. Pankova and St John Simpson (Oxford, 2020), pp. 30–42; Ball, *The Eurasian Steppe*, Chapter Four.

6 Buddhist Art: Greek, Roman and Indian Styles Merge in Afghanistan

1 Peter Stewart, *Gandharan Art and the Classical World: A Short Introduction* (Oxford, 2024), p. 39.

2 Ibid., p. 50.

3 S. Kuwayama, *Across the Hindukush of the First Millennium: A Selection of the Papers* (Kyoto, 2002), pp. 12–19, 44–68.

4 There is a huge literature on the subject. Lolita Nehru, *Origins of the Gandhāran Style: A Study of Contributory Influences* (Delhi, 1989); John Boardman, *The Diffusion of Classical Art in Antiquity* (London, 1994); John Boardman, *The Greeks in Asia* (London, 2015); Pia Brancaccio and Kurt Behrendt, eds, *Gandhāran Buddhism* (Vancouver, 2006); and Stewart, *Gandharan Art* are just some I have consulted. In addition, a series of 'Gandhāra Connections' workshops held in Oxford between 2017 and 2021 did much to resolve the many issues surrounding Gandharan art, published as Wannaporn Rienjang and Peter Stewart, eds, *Problems of Chronology in Gandhāran Art* (Oxford, 2018); Wannaporn Rienjang and Peter Stewart, eds, *The Geography of Gandhāran Art* (Oxford, 2019); Wannaporn Rienjang and Peter Stewart, eds, *The Global Connections of Gandhāran Art* (Oxford, 2020); and Wannaporn Rienjang and Peter Stewart, eds, *The Rediscovery and Reception of Gandhāran Art* (Oxford, 2022).

5 *Gazetteer*, Site 127; W. Zwalf, *A Catalogue of the Gandhāra Sculpture in the British Museum*, 2 vols (London, 1996), vol. I, pp. 348–50; Martha L. Carter, 'A Reappraisal of the Bīmarān Reliquary', in *Gandharan Art in Context: East–West Exchanges at the Crossroads of Asia*, ed. Raymond Allchin et al. (Delhi, 1997), pp. 71–94; J. Cribb, 'Dating the Bimaran Casket: Its Conflicted Role in the Chronology of Gandharan Art', *Gandhāran Studies*, X (2017) pp. 57–91.

6 Robert L. Brown, 'The Walking Tilya Tepe Buddha: A Lost Prototype', *Bulletin of the Asia Institute*, XIV (2000), pp. 77–87.

7 Joe Cribb, 'The Origin of the Buddha Image: The Numismatic Evidence', in *South Asian Archaeology, 1981*, ed. B. Allchin (Cambridge, 1984), pp. 231–4; Joe Cribb, 'Kanishka I's Buddha Image Coins Revisited', *Silk Road Art and Archaeology Archaeology*, VI (1999–2000), pp. 151–89.

8 Pia Brancaccio and Luca Maria Olivieri, 'Regional Workshops and Small Stūpas in the Swat Valley', in *The Geography of Gandhāran Art*, ed. Rienjang and Stewart, pp. 121–42.

9 Zwalf, *A Catalogue of the Gandhāra Sculpture*, vol. II, pp. 233–4.

10 Elizabeth Errington and Joe Cribb, eds, *The Crossroads of Asia: Transformation in Image and Symbol in the Art of Ancient Afghanistan and Pakistan*, exh. cat., Fitzwilliam Museum (Cambridge, 1992), pp. 118–35; Boardman, *The Diffusion of Classical Art in Antiquity*, pp. 125–45, with the 'Trojan horse' relief on p. 136; Zwalf, *A Catalogue of the Gandhāra Sculpture*, vol. II, pls 92, 98, 157, 340, 355–77, 470–71.

11 Boardman, *The Diffusion of Classical Art in Antiquity*, p. 143.

12 B. Rowland, *The Art and Architecture of India: Buddhist. Hindu. Jain* (London, 1977), pp. 167–70.

13 See Boardman, *The Diffusion of Classical Art in Antiquity*, pp. 122–3; and Zwalf, *A Catalogue of the Gandhāra Sculpture*, vol. I, pp. 67–9, for summaries of the controversy.

14 A. Foucher, *L'art gréco-bouddhique de Gandhara*, 2 vols (Paris, 1905–51); Errington and Cribb, eds, *The Crossroads of Asia*, pp. 36–7; Boardman, *The Diffusion of Classical Art in Antiquity*, pp. 122–3.
15 H.-P. Francfort, *Les palettes du Gandhara* (Paris, 1979); Boardman, *The Diffusion of Classical Art in Antiquity*, pp. 116–17; John Boardman, *The Greeks in Asia* (London, 2015), pp. 142–53.
16 R.E.M. Wheeler, 'Romano-Buddhist Art: An Old Problem Restated', *Antiquity*, XXIII/89 (1949), pp. 4–19; R.E.M. Wheeler, *Flames over Persepolis* (London, 1968), pp. 149–71; Rowland, *The Art and Architecture of India*, Part 3; D. Whitehouse, 'Begram, the *Periplus* and Gandharan Art', *Journal of Roman Archaeology*, II (1989), pp. 93–100.
17 Brancaccio and Olivieri, 'Regional Workshops and Small Stūpas in the Swat Valley', p. 134.
18 See A. C. Soper, 'The Roman Style in Gandhara', *American Journal of Archaeology*, LV/5 (1951), pp. 301–19.
19 Whitehouse, 'Begram, the *Periplus* and Gandharan Art', pp. 94–5; Boardman, *The Diffusion of Classical Art in Antiquity*, p. 119.
20 Whitehouse, 'Begram, the *Periplus* and Gandharan Art'; L. Nehru, 'A Fresh Look at the Bone and Ivory Carvings from Begram', *Silk Road Art and Archaeology*, X (2004), pp. 97–150; St John Simpson, *The Begram Hoard: Ivories from Afghanistan* (London, 2011), pp. 24–5.
21 Lauren Morris, 'Revised Dates for the Deposition of the Begram Hoard and Occupation of the New Royal City', *Parthika*, XIX (2017), pp. 75–104.
22 Boardman, *The Diffusion of Classical Art in Antiquity*, pp. 99–108.
23 Rowland, *The Art and Architecture of India*, p. 134.
24 John M. Rosenfield, 'Prologue: Some Debating Points on Gandhāran Buddhism and Kuṣāṇa History', in *Gandhāran Buddhism*, ed. Brancaccio and Behrendt, p. 25.
25 Errington and Cribb, eds, *The Crossroads of Asia*, pp. 46–8.
26 Strabo 15.1.4, 15.1.73; Dio 54. 9.
27 See Boardman, *Greeks in Asia*, p. 167, who quotes these precise lines I originally wrote in Warwick Ball, *Rome in the East* (London, 2000), p. 148; (2nd edn, 2016), p. 167.
28 For example, Errington and Cribb, eds, *The Crossroads of Asia*, p. 205.
29 M. Lyttelton, *Baroque Architecture in Classical Antiquity* (London, 1974).
30 Ball, *Rome in the East*, 2nd edn, pp. 433–45.
31 Boardman, *The Diffusion of Classical Art in Antiquity*, p. 108. See also the remarks on the essential unity of this region by John Curtis, 'Keynote Speech: British Near Eastern Archaeology and Museology on the Eve of the Millennium', BANEA *Newsletter*, XI–XII (1998–9), pp. 9–10.

7 The Great Buddhas of Bamiyan and Beyond: Huns, Turks and Hindus

1 Alka Patel, 'Objects and Material Cultures in Afghanistan, *c.* 100–1500 CE', *Oxford Research Encyclopedias, Asian History* (2023), p. 15, at https://doi.org/10.1093/acrefore/9780190277728.013.227.
2 Warwick Ball, *The Eurasian Steppe: People, Movement, Ideas* (Edinburgh, 2021), Chapter Eight.
3 Thomas Barfield, *Shadow Empires: An Alternative Imperial History* (Princeton, NJ, 2023).
4 Edward Gibbon, *The Decline and Fall of the Roman Empire*, 7 vols (London, 1897–1900), vol. III, p. 416.
5 Khodadad Rezakhani, *ReOrienting the Sasanians: East Iran in Late Antiquity* (Edinburgh, 2017); Christoph Baumer, *The History of Central Asia*, vol. II: *The Age of the Silk Roads* (London, 2014), pp. 94–101; Raymond Allchin, Warwick Ball and Norman Hammond, eds, *The Archaeology of Afghanistan from the Earliest Times to the Timurid Period: New Edition* (Edinburgh, 2019), Chapter Six; Robert

Haug, *The Eastern Frontier: Limits of Empire in Late Antique and Early Medieval Central Asia* (London, 2019), Chapter Two; Cameron Petrie, *Resistance at the Edge of Empires: The Archaeology and History of the Bannu Basin from 1000 BC to AD 1200* (Oxford, 2021), pp. 52–61.

6 Especially for me.

7 Eberhard W. Sauer, Jebrael Nokandeh and Hamid Omrani Rekavandi, *Ancient Arms Race: Antiquity's Largest Fortresses and Sasanian Military Networks of Northern Iran*, 2 vols (Oxford, 2022).

8 William B. Trousdale and Mitchell Allen, *The Archaeology of Southwest Afghanistan* (Edinburgh, 2022), pp. 137–95.

9 *Gazetteer*, Sites 1173, 332.

10 Willem Vogelsang, *The Afghans* (Oxford, 2002), pp. 186–8. This Hun origin of the Khalji is doubted by Nicholas Sims-Williams, ed., *Indo-Iranian Languages and Peoples* (Oxford, 2002), pp. 234–5.

11 Ball, *The Eurasian Steppe*, Chapter Eight.

12 Joy Lidu Yi, *Yungang: Art, History, Archaeology, Liturgy* (London, 2018); Warwick Ball, 'Giganticism and Bamiyan: Türk, Iranian, and Chinese Traditions of Dynasticism', in *Persian Cultures of Power and the Entanglement of the Afro-Eurasian World*, ed. Matthew P. Canepa (Los Angeles, CA, 2024), pp. 109–35.

13 Ball, *The Eurasian Steppe*, Chapter Eight; Petrie, *Resistance*, pp. 61–6.

14 Deborah Klimburg-Salter, 'Buddhist Painting in the Hindu Kush ca. VIth to Xth Centuries', in *L'Islamisation de l'Asie centrale: Processus locaux d'acculturation du VIe au XIe siécle*, ed. Étienne de la Vaissière (Leuven, 2008), pp. 131–59, 357–8; and Deborah Klimburg-Salter, 'Corridors of Communication across Afghanistan 7th to 10th Centuries', in *Paysages du centre de l'Afghanistan: Paysages naturels, paysages culturels*, ed. Véra Marigo et al. (Paris, 2010), pp. 167–86.

15 *Gazetteer*, Site 100; Deborah Klimburg-Salter, *The Kingdom of Bāmiyān: Buddhist Art and Culture of the Hindu Kush* (Naples and Rome, 1989); Llewelyn Morgan, *The Buddhas of Bamiyan* (London, 2012).

16 *Gazetteer*, Site 330.

17 *Gazetteer*, Site 1042.

18 *Gazetteer*, Sites 330, 508.

19 *Gazetteer*, Site 305.

20 *Gazetteer*, Sites 2141, 2261.

21 *Gazetteer*, Site 332.

22 Ball, 'Giganticism and Bamiyan'.

23 Marc Le Berre, *Monuments pré-islamiques de l'Hindukush centrale* (Paris, 1987).

24 *Gazetteer*, Sites 1052, 1004.

25 *Gazetteer*, Sites 1039, 189.

26 *Gazetteer*, Site 1139.

27 Ball, 'Giganticism and Bamiyan'.

28 Akashi Shoten, *Radiocarbon Dating of the Bamiyan Mural Paintings* (Tokyo, 2006).

29 Klimburg-Salter, *Kingdom of Bāmiyān*, pp. 134–6.

30 Thomas J. Barfield, 'Supersize Me: Political Aspects of Monumental Tomb Building in Early Steppe Empires', in *Masters of the Steppe*, ed. Svetlana V. Pankova and St John Simpson (Oxford, 2020), pp. 30–42; Ball, *The Eurasian Steppe*, Chapter Four.

31 Lidu Yi, *Yungang*.

32 *Gazetteer*, Site 1180.

33 *Gazetteer*, Site 483; Allchin, Ball and Hammond, eds, *The Archaeology of Afghanistan*, pp. 369–75.

34 *Gazetteer*, Site 2268; Zafar Paiman and Michael Alram, *The Tepe Narenj Buddhist Monastery at Kabul: Buddhist Art during the First Muslim Raids against the Town* (Paris, 2013).

35 Abdur Rahman, *The Last Two Dynasties of the Shahis: An Analysis of Their History, Archaeology, Coinage, Palaeography* (Islamabad, 1979); Petrie, *Resistance*, pp. 68–82.

36 Frantz Grenet, 'A Historical Figure at the Origin of Gesar of Phrom: Frum Kēsar, *King of Kābul (737–745)*', in *The Many Faces of King Gesar: Tibetan and Central Asian Studies in Homage to Rolf A. Stein*, ed. Matthew T. Kapstein and Charles Ramble (Leiden, 2022), pp. 39–52.

37 *Gazetteer*, Site 718; Warwick Ball, 'The So-Called Minars of Kabul', *Studia Iranica*, XIII/1 (1984), pp. 117–27.

38 *Gazetteer*, Sites 586, 1185.

8 A New Imperial Era: The Ghaznavid and Ghurid Empires

1 Patricia Crone, *The Nativist Prophets of Early Islamic Iran: Rural Revolt and Local Zoroastrianism* (New York, 2012); Robert Haug, *The Eastern Frontier: Limits of Empire in Late Antique and Early Medieval Central Asia* (London, 2019), Chapter Six.

2 Richard N. Frye, *The Golden Age of Persia* (London, 1975), writes of the early Islamic history of Iran from this Central Asian perspective.

3 Warwick Ball, *Sultans of Rome: The Turkish World Expansion* (London, 2012), Chapter Four.

4 C. E. Bosworth, *The Ghaznavids: Their Empire in Afghanistan and Eastern India, 994–1040* (Edinburgh, 1977).

5 In fact the Karakhanid state, first established in Kashgar in Xinjiang in about 734, was the first Turkish state to convert to Islam.

6 David Thomas, *The Ebb and Flow of the Ghūrid Empire* (Sydney, 2018); Alka Patel, *Iran to India: The Shansabanis of Afghanistan c. 1145–1190 CE* (Edinburgh, 2022).

7 For example, in Robert Hillenbrand, ed., *Architecture of the Iranian World, 1000–1250* (Edinburgh, forthcoming).

8 *Gazetteer*, Subject Index.

9 Guy Le Strange, *The Lands of the Eastern Caliphate* (London, 1910), Chapters 24, 29, 30.

10 J. A. Boyle, 'The Mongol Invasion of Eastern Persia 1220–1223', *History Today*, XIII/2 (1965), pp. 614–23.

11 Raymond Allchin, Warwick Ball and Norman Hammond, eds, *The Archaeology of Afghanistan from the Earliest Times to the Timurid Period: New Edition* (Edinburgh, 2019), Chapter Seven; William B. Trousdale and Mitchell Allen, *The Archaeology of Southwest Afghanistan* (Edinburgh, 2022).

12 *Gazetteer*, Site 410.

13 Lisa Golombek et al., *The Nine Domes of the Universe: The Ancient Noh Gonbad Mosque. The Study and Conservation of an Early Islamic Monument at Balkh* (Bergamo, 2016).

14 *Gazetteer*, Site 1006; Trousdale and Allen, *The Archaeology of Southwest Afghanistan*, Chapter Nine.

15 Trousdale and Allen, *The Archaeology of Southwest Afghanistan*, pp. 511–651.

16 Ibid., pp. 83–9.

17 David C. Thomas and Fiona J. Kidd, 'On the Margins: Enduring Pre-Modern Water Management Strategies in and around the Registan Desert, Afghanistan', *Journal of Field Archaeology*, XLII/1 (2017), pp. 29–42.

18 *Gazetteer*, Site 190; Trousdale and Allen, *The Archaeology of Southwest Afghanistan*, pp. 55–60.

19 *Gazetteer*, Sites 607, 752.

20 *Gazetteer*, Site 190; Trousdale and Allen, *The Archaeology of Southwest Afghanistan*, pp. 55–60.

21 Warwick Ball, 'Buddhist Elements in the Architecture of Afghanistan 1000–1250', in *Architecture of the Iranian World*, ed. Hillenbrand, forthcoming.

22 *Gazetteer*, Site 358.

23 *Gazetteer*, Site 685; Daniel Schlumberger and Janine Sourdel-Thomine, *Lashkari Bazar: Une residence royale ghaznévide et ghuride. Planches* (Paris, 1978).

24 *Gazetteer*, Site 468.

25 *Gazetteer*, Site 428.

26 Warwick Ball, 'The Towers of Ghur: A Ghurid "Maginot Line"?', in *Cairo to Kabul: Afghan and Islamic Studies Presented to Ralph Pinder-Wilson*, ed. Warwick Ball and Leonard Harrow (London, 2002); Patel, *Iran to India*.

27 Patel, *Iran to India*, Chapter Three.

28 *Gazetteer*, Site 1004.

29 *Gazetteer*, Site 231.

30 Robert Hillenbrand, *Islamic Architecture: Style, Function, and Meaning* (Edinburgh, 1994), pp. 174–5.

31 *Gazetteer*, Site 212.

32 *Gazetteer*, Site 1023.

33 *Gazetteer*, Site 638.

34 Warwick Ball, *Rome in the East: The Transformation of an Empire*, 2nd edn (London, 2016), pp. 336–42.

35 Robert Hillenbrand, 'The Architecture of the Ghaznavids and Ghurids', in *Studies in Honour of Clifford Edmund Bosworth*, vol. II: *The Sultan's Turret: Studies in Persian and Turkish Culture*, ed. C. Hillenbrand (Leiden, 2000), p. 129.

36 Finbarr B. Flood, 'Masons and Mobility: Indic Elements in Twelfth-Century Afghan Stone-Carving', in *Fifty Years of Research in the Heart of Eurasia, Istituto Italiano per l'Africa et l'Oriente*, ed. Anna Filigenzi and Roberta Giunta (Rome, 2009), pp. 137–60; see also Hillenbrand, 'The Architecture of the Ghaznavids and Ghurids', pp. 162–5.

37 Indeed, the caption to one of the orthostats from the Palace of Mas'ud III now in the San Francisco Museum of Asian Art reads, 'A close study of tool marks on similar panels has revealed that the carving techniques are connected to ancient local stone-carving methods, like those on Gandhara sculpture.'

38 Schlumberger and Sourdel-Thomine, *Lashkari Bazar*, pp. 61–5. See also in general Mario Bussagli, *Central Asian Painting from Afghanistan to Sinkiang* (Geneva, 1978).

39 Bussagli, *Central Asian Painting*, Chapter Three; Guitty Azarpay, *Sogdian Painting: The Pictorial Epic in Oriental Art* (Berkeley, CA, 1981).

40 The best study of this is Ute Franke, 'Unglazed Painted Pottery from the 10th to the 13th Century: Magic Motifs', in *Ancient Herat: Research Reports of the German–Afghan Archaeological Mission to Herat, Afghanistan*, vol. III: *Herat through Time: The Collections of the Herat Museum and Archive*, ed. Ute Franke and Martina Müller-Wiener (Berlin, 2016), pp. 231–71.

SELECT BIBLIOGRAPHY

Allchin, Raymond, Bridget Allchin, Neil Kreitman and Elizabeth Errington, eds, *Gandharan Art in Context: East–West Exchanges at the Crossroads of Asia* (Delhi, 1997)

Allchin, Raymond, Warwick Ball and Norman Hammond, eds, *The Archaeology of Afghanistan from the Earliest Times to the Timurid Period: New Edition* (Edinburgh, 2019)

Alram, Michael, Minoru Inaba and Matthias Pfisterer, eds, *Art and Chronology*, vol. II: *The First Millennium CE in the Indo-Iranian Borderlands* (Vienna, 2010)

—, and Deborah E. Klimburg-Salter, eds, *Coins, Art and Chronology: Essays on the Pre-Islamic History of the Indo-Iranian Borderlands* (Vienna, 1999)

Aruz, Joan, and Elisabetta Valtz Fino, eds, *Afghanistan: Forging Civilizations along the Silk Road* (New York, 2012)

Ball, Warwick, *Archaeological Gazetteer of Afghanistan*, revised edn (Oxford, 2019)

—, *The Eurasian Steppe: People, Movement, Ideas* (Edinburgh, 2021)

—, *The Monuments of Afghanistan: History, Archaeology and Architecture* (London, 2008)

Barfield, Thomas, *Afghanistan: A Cultural and Political History* (Princeton, NJ, 2023)

—, *Shadow Empires: An Alternative Imperial History* (Princeton, NJ, 2023)

Baumer, Christoph, *The History of Central Asia*, vol. II: *The Age of the Silk Roads* (London, 2014)

Boardman, J., *The Diffusion of Classical Art in Antiquity* (London, 1994)

—, *The Greeks in Asia* (London, 2015)

Bosworth, A. B., *Alexander and the East: The Tragedy of Triumph* (Oxford, 1996)

Bosworth, C. E., *The Ghaznavids: Their Empire in Afghanistan and Eastern India, 994–1040* (Edinburgh, 1977)

Boyce, Mary, *Zoroastrians: Their Religious Beliefs and Practices* (London, 1997)

Brancaccio, Pia, and Kurt Behrendt, eds, *Gandhāran Buddhism* (Vancouver, 2006)

Caroe, Olaf, *The Pathans: 550 BC–AD 1957* (London, 1958)

Cribb, Joe, and Georgina Herrmann, eds, *After Alexander: Central Asia before Islam* (Oxford, 2007)

Curtis, Vesta Sarkhosh, *Persian Myths* (London, 1993)

Dupree, Louis, *Afghanistan* (Princeton, NJ, 1980)

Errington, Elizabeth, *Charles Masson and the Buddhist Sites of Afghanistan: Explorations, Excavations, Collections, 1832–1835* (London, 2017)

—, and Joe Cribb, eds, *The Crossroads of Asia: Transformation in Image and Symbol in the Art of Ancient Afghanistan and Pakistan*, exh. cat., Fitzwilliam Museum, Cambridge (Cambridge, 1992)

Franke, Ute, and Thomas Urban, *Ancient Herat: Research Reports of the German–Afghan Archaeological Mission to Herat, Afghanistan,* vol. II: *Excavations and Explorations in Herat City* (Berlin, 2017)

Fraser, P. M., *Cities of Alexander the Great* (Oxford, 1996)

Glenn, Simon, *Money and Power in Hellenistic Bactria* (Turnhout, 2020)

Green, Peter, *Alexander the Great* (Berkeley, CA, 1991)

Haug, Robert, *The Eastern Frontier: Limits of Empire in Late Antique and Early Medieval Central Asia* (London, 2019)

Hiebert, Fredrik, and Pierre Cambon, eds, *Afghanistan: Hidden Treasures from the National Museum, Kabul* (Washington, DC, 2008)

Holt, Frank L., *Lost World of the Golden King: In Search of Ancient Afghanistan* (Berkeley, CA, 2012)

—, *Thundering Zeus: The Making of Hellenistic Bactria* (Berkeley, CA, 1999)

Le Strange, G., *The Lands of the Eastern Caliphate* (London, 1910)

Lyonnet, Bertille, and Nadezhda A. Dubova, eds, *The World of the Oxus Civilization* (London, 2021)

Mairs, Rachel, ed., *The Graeco-Bactrian and Indo-Greek World* (Abingdon, 2021)

—, *The Hellenistic Far East: Archaeology, Language, and Identity in Greek Central Asia* (Oakland, CA, 2014)

Mallory, J. P., *In Search of the Indo-Europeans: Language, Archaeology and Myth* (London, 1989)

Morgan, Llewelyn, *The Buddhas of Bamiyan* (London, 2012)

Narain, A. K., *The Indo-Greeks* [1957] (Oxford, 2003)

Nehru, Lolita, *Origins of the Gandhāran Style: A Study of Contributory Influences* (Delhi, 1989)

Patel, Alka, *Iran to India: The Shansabanis of Afghanistan, c. 1145–1190 CE* (Edinburgh, 2022)

Payne, Richard E., and Rhyne King, eds, *The Limits of Empire in Ancient Afghanistan: Rule and Resistance in the Hindu Kush, circa 600 BCE–600 CE* (Wiesbaden, 2020)

Rezakhani, Khodadad, *ReOrienting the Sasanians: East Iran in Late Antiquity* (Edinburgh, 2017)

Rosenfield, John M., *The Dynastic Arts of the Kushans* (Berkeley, CA, 1967)

Sarianidi, V. I., *Bactrian Gold: From the Excavations of the Tillya-Tepe Necropolis in Northern Afghanistan* (Leningrad, 1985)

Simpson, St John, *Afghanistan: A Cultural History* (London, 2012)

Stewart, Peter, *Gandharan Art and the Classical World: A Short Introduction* (Oxford, 2024)

Stewart, Rory, *The Places in Between* (London, 2004)

Tarn, W. W., *The Greeks in Bactria and India* (Oxford, 1948)

Thomas, David, *The Ebb and Flow of the Ghūrid Empire* (Sydney, 2018)

Torday, Laszlo, *Mounted Archers: The Beginnings of Central Asian History* (Edinburgh, Cambridge and Durham, 1997)

Trousdale, William B., and Mitchell Allen, *The Archaeology of Southwest Afghanistan* (Edinburgh, 2022)

Vogelsang, Willem, *The Afghans* (Oxford, 2002)

Whitteridge, Gordon, *Charles Masson of Afghanistan: Explorer, Archaeologist, Numismatist and Intelligence Agent* (Warminster, 1986)

Zwalf, W., *A Catalogue of the Gandhāra Sculpture in the British Museum*, 2 vols (London, 1996)

ACKNOWLEDGEMENTS

I once asked a colleague why no single book has been written on the Kushan Empire, probably the single most important empire to emanate from Afghan soil. He replied that 'the Kushan empire is divided between indologists, iranologists, hellenists, sinologists, even turcologists, etc., in short, divided by the academic disciplines as they exist since the 18th century, dominated by linguistics, philology and history.' In other words, in order to write such a book one would need to combine all such disciplines, not to mention a reading knowledge of Bactrian, Prakrit, Greek, Latin, Chinese, Middle Persian, Arabic and old Turkish, in addition to the main European languages, as well as Russian and Japanese in recognition of the important modern studies on the Kushans by scholars in those countries. Needless to say, I belong to none of those disciplines (curiously, archaeologist was not included in his list of disciplines, even though my colleague was himself an archaeologist). Moreover, in writing not only about the Kushans but everything else from the Bronze Age to the early Islamic period, I am clearly attempting the near-impossible. I can only apologize for the bits I have left out and the bits I have included with a superficiality that would make a specialist cringe.

An apology all the more necessary in view of the many who have helped bring this book to fruition. Mitchell Allen, Wendy Ball, Joe Cribb, Norman Hammond, Jonathan Lee and Rachel Mairs kindly read parts or all of the manuscript. I owe particular thanks to Joe Cribb for guiding me gently through the minefield (to me!) of numismatics, and to Mitch Allen, who lent his huge experience as a professional scholarly editor and experienced archaeologist in reading the entire manuscript and commented extensively. All comments have proved invaluable, and I need hardly add that I am entirely responsible for comments ignored and errors that have occurred despite their scrutiny. I am also grateful to Mitch Allen, Paul Bucherer-Dietschi, Edinburgh University Press, Elizabeth Errington, Henri-Paul Francfort, the Khalili Family Trust, Jonathan Lee, Philippe Marquis and Lolita Nehru for kindly providing photographs. I am grateful too to Wendy Ball and Monica Barnes, who digitally enhanced many of my older photographs. I would also like to thank Ajmal Maiwandi of the Agha Khan Trust for Culture, who kindly made a generous grant available for additional colour reproduction in this book and to Michael Leaman of Reaktion Books for his patience.

The genesis of this book lies in a number of earlier books I have written on the archaeology of Afghanistan, in particular the *Archaeological Gazetteer of Afghanistan*, first published in Paris in 1982, with an extensively revised and updated edition published in Oxford in 2019. Too many have helped along the way with this and other books written since to list here, but I owe a particular debt to the late Jean-Claude Gardin. I would also like to thank Henri-Paul Francfort for his many words of wisdom going back some fifty years.

PHOTO ACKNOWLEDGEMENTS

The author and publishers wish to express their thanks to the sources listed below for illustrative material and/ or permission to reproduce it. Some locations of artworks are also given below, in the interest of brevity. All images are by the author unless otherwise stated.

Wendy Ball: 68; J.-M. Casal, Mission Archéologique de l'Indus: 24; Cleveland Museum of Art: 78 (www.clevelandart.org/art/1930.328); courtesy of Edinburgh University Press: 16, 26, 35, 43, 54, 61, 109; Elizabeth Errington: 77; Foundation Bibliotheca Afghanica/ Collection Klaus Fischer: 65, 83; J.-C. Gardin: 33; Khalili Collection of Aramaic Documents © The Khalili Family Trust: 36; plans by J. Knudstad © Helmand Sistan Project: 41, 50, 112; Jonathan L. Lee: 49, 53, 55, 106; © Archives Mission d'Aï Khanoum: 38; Archives of the Mission archéologique de Shortughaï, MAFAC/CNRS: 19; Lolita Nehru: 39, 46; V. Sarianidi: 51; photographs by R. K. Vincent Jr © Helmand Sistan Project: 113, 114; John Watson: 104; Wikimedia Commons: 37 (Gallica Digital Library/Public Domain), 45 (map created from DEMIS Mapserver/Public Domain).

INDEX

Illustration numbers are indicated by *italics*